EMERGING PRACTICES

Designing in Complexity

ited by
n Ma Yongqi Lou Yubei Gong

UNIVERSITY PRESS

Contents

1 Introduction: Emerging DesignX Practices
Jin Ma

Viewpoints

30 Globalization, and the "Effective Supply" of Design Education
Ping Xu

50 Design and the Economy of Choice
Patrick Whitney

66 The Expanding Scope and Paradigm Shift of Design
Yongqi Lou

80 Making Things Happen:
Design for Inclusivity, Diversity, and Humanity
Sooshin Choi

92 The Ethics of Ignoring Rashomon:
All Choices Involve Ethics—Simplification Is No Exception
Michael Lissack

110 Chicken Run:
Designing for Complex Food Systems
Clare Brass

128 Information Visualization:
Where Design Meets Engineering
Nan Cao

142 Design, Work, and Intelligence
Ling Fan

Cases

158 Embedding Designers in Government Innovation Teams: Insights from the Designmatters Fellowship Program at ArtCenter
Mariana Amatullo, Jennifer May

184 Policy Design to Improve the Delivery of Old Age Security in Canada for Vulnerable Seniors
Alexander Keith Eady, Ryan James Hum

204 *Inovando Juntos*: Design Research and Practice for the Public Good
Sabine Junginger

220 *Movable Feasts*: An Exploration of the Heritage, Flavors and Possible Futures for Shanghai Street Food
Francesca Valsecchi

232 Design for Human-Robot Acceptability: The Case of Edutainment Robotics for Children
Maria Luce Lupetti

254 DREAM Complexity: An Approach to Ambulance Design
José Augusto Rodrigues de Sousa Coelho, Vasco Afonso da Silva Branco

Figure 1 *Emerging Practices: Practices, Values, and Approaches in Design* (2014). Copyright ©2014 by Tongji University College of Design and Innovation.

Emerging DesignX Practices

Jin Ma

It's late September. The Emerging Practices Conference 2017 is just around the corner. I am writing this introduction in a small office, densely packed with all sorts of materials—stacks of colorful sample paper for printing program booklets, prototypes of exhibition installations, bottled water re-dressed in a belt tailor-made for this event, plus ribbons, plastic sheets, and pins waiting to be assembled into participant badges. The wall is half covered with posters of the conference that will be held in ten days, whose theme, "The Social World," vividly stands out. The rest of the wall is filled with printed proofs of the anthology that I am now writing about, consisting of essays and papers selected from the conference hosted by our school one year ago. The juxtaposition of the two conferences, with a year in between, allows me to think a bit beyond the 2016 conference per se.

Every autumn since 2012, the school where I work—the College of Design and Innovation, Tongji University—organizes a small design research and education conference titled "Emerging Practices." My colleagues and I like to call it "EPC." The themes that the EPC has focused on include "Values, Approaches, and Professions in Design" (2012), "Open Design" (2013), "Developing Community/Economic/Education/Research/Exploration" (2014), "Design Activism" (2015), and "Design in Complexity" (2016). This year, in about a week, we will embrace the sixth EPC, whose theme is "The Social World"—the first part of a duet that will be complemented by the seventh EPC in 2018 themed "The Technological World."

We have developed a peculiar pattern for the EPC. One year we call for papers; the next year we invite speeches. As a result, every two years an EPC anthology will be published around the time the next EPC kicks off. So far, we have published *Emerging Practices: Professions, Values, and Approaches* (China Architecture and Building Press, 2014)[1] and *Emerging Practices: Inquiry into the Developing* (Tongji University Press, 2015).[2] And, this anthology—*Emerging Practices: Designing in Complexity*—will be the latest in the series.

The College of Design and Innovation's enthusiasm for the EPC might be a myth to many people. It is rare to see a Chinese design school that devotes its efforts to organizing an international conference series as we have for the past five years. The size of the EPC audience—200 participants—is extremely tiny when compared with the most successful conferences in China organized by associations or institutions from such powerful industries as industrial design, user experience design, and service design. Why, then, do we need another conference? What is special about the EPC?

The answer is simple. The EPC witnesses the developing trajectory of

1. Jin Ma and Yongqi Lou, eds., *Emerging Practices: Practices, Values, and Approaches in Design* (Beijing: China Architecture & Buildings Press, 2014).

2. Jin Ma, Davide Fassi, and Yongqi Lou, eds., *Emerging Practices: Inquiry into the Developing* (Shanghai: Tongji University Press, 2015).

design as a discipline in a Chinese design school that is grounded in thinking and practice addressing local issues and is in the meanwhile actively connected globally.

EPC: Witnessing the Growth of Tongji's Design Discipline

Design education at Tongji University, Shanghai, dates back to the middle of 1940s, when its architecture program—steeped in the Bauhaus tradition—was established. The first industrial design program was launched in 1986. That program later became the Art and Design Department, part of the College of Architecture and Urban Planning. Not until 2009 was the College of Design and Innovation, Tongji University established. The transition from an Art and Design Department to an independent school named "Design and Innovation" attests to the university's vision to move design education and research beyond an artifact-centered crafts tradition and toward a design discipline that drives innovation at the intersection of business, technology, and the humanities.

The College of Design and Innovation, as young as it is, is taking a unique path. It seeks to link design with innovation in design education, research, and practice. Across numerous initiatives started by the college, the EPC is one of the best ways to trace that pathway, because it mirrors what this college has achieved, is considering, and will endeavor to accomplish at different points in its growing process. In addition to serving as a venue for reflection at the college, the EPC is also a stage that attracts leading thinkers, educators, practitioners, and researchers from different parts of the world and invites them to share their experiences and thinking. The topics raised by the College of Design and Innovation strike a chord with guests and participants alike—each is dealing with different matters, but facing challenges of the same kind. Our common challenges arise out of a need to reform design education, bridge design research and practice, design for social well-being, and target sustainability on a planet with limited resources.

It is inspiring to see that our drive to reform design education and research—and situate design within a shifting social, economic, and technological context—has attracted the attention and participation of a wider community. This attention enables the College of Design and Innovation to have its voice heard, meet its allies, and weave together people and communities that have a common appreciation for the challenges facing our time. The EPC annually brings together an archipelago of active nodes pursuing emerging practices in design.

To illustrate the pathway that our explorations have followed, let's take a quick look at the past five EPCs.

The College of Design and Innovation initiated the first Emerging Practices Conference in 2012. At the time, the burning issue at the college was restructuring its curriculum, and integrating the undergraduate, postgraduate, and doctoral programs within a coherent framework that would provide students with adequate capabilities to cope with present-day design and research. Based on the discussions at EPC 2012 around professions, values, and approaches in design, the College of Design and Innovation further developed a 3D T-shaped educational framework,[3] and contributions from the invited speakers mapped the changing landscape of design and design education, providing rich annotations to that framework.

3 Jin Ma and Yongqi Lou, "Restructuring Design Foundation Based on the Framework of Four Orders of Design," in *Emerging Practices: Inquiry into the Developing*, ed. Jin Ma, Yongqi Lou, and Davide Fassi (Shanghai: Tongji University Press, 2015), 175–89.

Shortly after EPC 2012, the College of Design and Innovation began to consider openness, sustainability, and human-centeredness as the three key values we would pursue through our practice. Compared with the other two, open design lacked significant approaches to support it. By opening up the design process to different forms of collaboration and input, open design challenges conventional understandings about the notion of "user," the design outcome as an embodied and stable deliverable, the designer's role, and the needs for organizational design capability. In particular, the College chose to focus on how design can contribute to two specific areas within the field of open design—social innovation toward sustainability, and industrial transformation. The timely discussions at the 2013 EPC conference explored the topic of "Open Design."

The theme of EPC 2014 was "Developing," and it was further contextualized across several areas that design had been increasingly involved in: communities, economies, research and openness, education, and exploration. The word developing can be used to frame a situation that is still in progress, one full of potential and energy, and at the same time a process in need of input, skills, and resources.

For each parallel sub-theme, we focused on various sets of issues. For communities, we looked into enabling and empowering, connectedness and relationality, and practices in modeling social awareness. For economies, topics varied from alternative economies and emerging business models, to best practices for transitions from product to service, and the global landscape of creative industries. The sub theme of developing research and openness aimed to explore emerging forms of academic publishing, managing the fuzziness that occurs in an open design process, and challenges and strategies to explore. Where design education with a shifting agenda was concerned, we encouraged serious responses and ideas for re-designing curriculum, challenges and lessons learned, and leadership and entrepreneurship. And, for explorations under way, we embraced thoughts and practices on topics ranging from critical reflection on alternative futures, to innovation inspired by nature, and new ways of making.

More interestingly, EPC 2014 culminated with the birth of an initiative called "DesignX." A small group of design scholars and educators,[4] who gathered at the EPC in 2014, announced their intention to explore how design can address the complex issues the world faces today. They called their agenda "DesignX," using "X" to refer to the turbulent, unknown future of design.

4 The initial DesignX Collaborative includes Don Norman, Pieter Jan Stappers, Ken Friedman, Yongqi Lou, Ena Voûte, and Patrick Whitney.

The initial *DesignX Manifesto*,[5] loaded with inquiries that have been triggered but have yet to be resolved, was published shortly after EPC 2014. As a follow-up, one year later, a two-day working conference on DesignX was held, right before EPC 2015. Around thirty scholars and practitioners from different disciplines and domains participated in the dialogue, in an effort to advance our understanding of how designers could play a role in designing for complex sociotechnical systems, using cases from healthcare, education, urban systems, and so on. EPC 2015 began with Don Norman's reflective conclusions on the ongoing DesignX dialogue. He emphasized that, although the problems that design aims to deal with are not new problems, we need to explore and provide new approaches at the implementation level, and such an endeavor is inherently interdisciplinary.[6] This observation nicely echoed the theme of EPC 2015—"Design Activism." How design can be proactively involved in and drive such interdisciplinary practices is a burning issue.

The DesignX initiative was successful in bringing together people from various disciplines to examine the design of complex sociotechnical systems. It sparked a genuine curiosity toward the meaning of complexity and complex systems. As a response, the College of Design and Innovation held the fifth Emerging Practices Conference in 2016 to explore the topic "Design in Complexity." From this very conference, we have selected essay and papers and complied them into the anthology you are currently holding in your hands.

5 Ken Friedman, Yongqi Lou, Don Norman, Pieter Jan Stappers, Ena Voûte, and Patrick Whitney, "DesignX: A Future Path for Design," *jnd.org*, last modified December 4, 2014, http://www.jnd.org/dn.mss/designx_a_future_pa.html.

6 Don Norman later developed his observations and thinking into an article. See Donald A. Norman and Pieter Jan Stappers, "DesignX: The Design of Complex Sociotechnical Systems," *She Ji: The Journal of Design, Economics, and Innovation* 1, no. 2 (2015): 83–94, DOI: https://doi.org/10.1016/j.sheji.2016.01.002.

Designing in Complexity: The Anthology

This anthology consists of two parts. The first comprises articles and essays developed by invited speakers, while the second is devoted to cases. These are viewpoints and practices related to designing within complexity—a preliminary attempt to explore DesignX.

Viewpoint Essays

This part includes eight contributions from the EPC 2016 guest speakers. They are based on the original EPC speeches but were further developed and enriched by the authors. Ping Xu, Patrick Whitney, Yongqi Lou, and Sooshin Choi all review the evolution of design from distinct perspectives and, in doing so, enrich the context surrounding the kinds of complexity that design confronts today. Michael Lissack demonstrates that even simplification involves complexity arising from ethical choices. Clare Brass shows a case of designing complex systems that are greater than what the conventional anthropocentric viewpoint could possibly accommodate. Na Cao and Ling Fan deal with technology, and ensuing opportunities and challenges toward design.

Ping Xu reflects on design education in China, while considering the economic notion of effective supply in the context of globalization.

Inspired by the central government's national strategy of supply-side structural reform, Xu asserts that design education in China must go through a similar transition, moving from the blind expansion of enrollment numbers toward an education that would adequately prepare the students with skills and expertise to cope with today's design challenges.

Patrick Whitney's essay "Design and the Economy of Choice" begins with a predicament that many enterprises are facing: finding certainty in an unpredictable world. The economic change requires inevitable changes in design. To do so, Whitney offers a holistic view and a set of useful tools.

In his essay "The Expanding Scope and Paradigm Shift of Design," Yongqi Lou examines the evolution of design—from design as form giving to design as innovation driver in the era of the knowledge economy. In this context, the development of a brand-new, evidence-based design culture—which addresses complex sociotechnical systems by means of rapid iteration—is becoming increasingly necessary and urgent when facing real-world change. This is Lou's addition to the DesignX dialogue.

Sooshin Choi looks into the social side of complex systems by seeing design as making things happen. He reviews the evolution of design, maintains that design has become a change agent in the industry and society, and introduces examples that illustrate how to design for inclusivity, diversity, and humanity.

Michael Lissack builds on the idea of complexity by examining simplification and its ethical challenges. In his essay "The Ethics of Ignoring Rashomon: All Choices Involve Ethics—Simplification is No Exception," Lissack looks into the process of choice making and observes that Simplification is NOT just a design choice. It is a series of ethical choices highly revelatory of the values and beliefs of the simplifying designer.

In her essay titled "Chicken Run: Designing for Complex Food Systems," Clare Brass introduces cases of food system design undertaken at the Royal College of Art, London. Brass reminds us that the food production sector is a domain where designers have rarely intervened. Food system issues are multifarious, complex, and interconnected, and innovative solutions may change the future of the human and natural world. She also provides a set of principles for designing for such complex systems.

Nan Cao presents an inspirational introduction to data visualization in the essay "Information Visualization: Where Design Meets Engineering." As a data scientist, Cao reviews the development of visualization techniques over the last few decades, introduces new challenges in the era of big data, and highlights its applications in the domain of information security from his recent studies.

The last piece from the speech collection comes from Ling Fan, the essay on "Design, Work, and Intelligence." As an entrepreneur as well as a design scholar, Fan uses his own startup Tezign.com to examine the problems with growing complexity that enterprises and organizations confront today. Data technology is used to help companies assign and manage creative work.

Cases

This part includes six cases in domains ranging from public sector design, policymaking, and design and culture to complex tangible systems design of robotics and ambulances.

Mariana Amatullo and Jennifer May contribute a case from the ArtCenter College of Design, Pasadena, which shows a promising approach by professional designers joining multi-disciplinary practices in city- and country-level "innovation" divisions of the government. Based on the theoretical framework of the design attitude construct, the authors analyze empirical data collected from a sample of designers and managers affiliated with the Designmatters Fellowship program. In addition, they provide the survey they used and full survey results as supplementary materials for the reader's reference. Many talk about what value designers can bring to the work of government innovation. This case offers new evidence.

Design for policymaking has become a popular topic in designing for complex systems. In their paper "Policy Design to Improve the Delivery of Old Age Security in Canada for Vulnerable Seniors," Alexander Keith Eady and Ryan James Hum report that a multi-disciplinary team triggered a cultural shift to human-centered perspectives in a specific division of the Public Service by applying design methods and processes to generate understanding, insights, and solutions. It is very interesting to note that there is a small but growing body of research on the evidence of design students' intervention as innovation catalysts as part of multi-disciplinary teams tha work for such complex organizations as government.[7]

7 See, for example, Cara Wrigley, "Design Innovation Catalysts: Education and Impact," *She Ji: The Journal of Design, Economics, and Innovation* 2, no. 2 (2016): 148–65, DOI: https://doi.org/10.1016/j.sheji.2016.10.001.

Sabine Junginger's paper "*Inovando Juntos*: Design Research and Prac tice for the Public Good" goes in concert with the above two, but takes the distinct perspective of management and organizational change. Junginger argues that "the ability to integrate product, process, and service systems with the needs, capabilities, powers, and values of people is of essence to policy makers and public managers." Through sharing the project funded by the EI-Brazil Sectorial Dialogues Program, she attempts to shed light to managing as a design practice and how design methods and process could possibly contribute to civil servants' practice to cope with complex problems.

Complexity also arises from the cultural issues. Francesca Valsecchi presents a case about how to preserve cultural diversity in the course of radical urbanization through a project called "Moveable Feasts." *Moveable Feasts* is an online platform aiming to honor and promote the city of Shanghai's culinary heritage, provide safe and nutritious snacks, and susta Shanghai's richly diverse street life and culture.

While the social factor contributes significantly to the complexity of all sorts of systems designers work to improve, technical systems based on tangible objects also merit attention. The expanding scope of design does not necessarily mean that tangible objects and systems—often wedd to technological advancements—should be forsaken. Creating aesthetic experiences of such objects and systems in the age of networked information involves a level of complexity that requires new design processes and methods. In this regard, Maria Luce Lupetti and José Augusto Rodrigues de Sousa Coelho contribute two interesting cases.

Even though robots are gaining in popularity in our everyday lives, robotics is entangled with moral issues, and social and economic impacts, especially when the people they serve are vulnerable users such as children. As a response to this concern, Maria Luce Lupetti considers the idea of acceptability and its role in human-robot interaction in the paper titled "Design for Human-Robot Acceptability: The Case of Edutainment Robotics for Children."

José Augusto Rodrigues de Sousa Coelho is an industrial designer who is researching the process of designing medical ambulances as an important touchpoint for the complex hospital healthcare system. Based on an in-depth understanding of the intangible system greater than the ambulance per se, Rodrigues de Sousa Coelho and Vasco Afonso da Silva Branco present a convincing ambulance design case in the paper titled "DREAM Complexity: An Approach to Ambulance Design."

The Future Imprint of DesignX on the EPC

As mentioned above, this anthology contains a preliminary attempt to explore DesignX. We have good reason to believe that the inquiry into DesignX is an ongoing endeavor at the College of Design and Innovation, and the future Emerging Practices Conferences will be one of the major arenas where the College and its allies communicate and reflect on these explorations.

As Don Norman rightly says, DesignX issues are issues of designing complex sociotechnical systems. If we do not wish to merely pay lip service to such issues, future DesignX inquiry must examine the nature of systems in general, and sociotechnical systems in particular. More and more designers have embarked on the journey into the social sphere of complex systems ever since the emergence of design for social innovation. Knowledge about the social sphere is crucial but not enough, on its own, for designers to competently make contributions to complex systems they target for intervention. To borrow Ezio Manizini's words, "every change that concerns [society] is, at the same time, social and technical. Therefore, referring to social innovation is a simplification in terms. To be more precise, in these cases we should talk about innovation in the sociotechnical system triggered by a social change."[8]

8 Ezio Manzini, *Design, When Everybody Designs* (Cambridge, MA: MIT Press, 2015), 16.

We are, thus, happy to announce that the following two Emerging Practices Conferences will focus on sociotechnical systems. The first, in 2017, considers complex sociotechnical systems from the perspective of society. The second, in 2018, will examine complex sociotechnical systems in the context of technology. To focus on "The Social World," EPC 2017 will cooperate with the DESIS Network.

We look forward to achieving new insights that will navigate the

Emerging Practices Conference in the direction where promising DesignX practices emerge. By opening up the discourse, the College of Design and Innovation invites schools, organizations, and individuals who are interested in emerging DesignX practices to contribute best practices and thinking. We are deeply grateful to our EPC participants, authors, reviewers, volunteers, and many others, for their contributions, support, and patience. It is their hard work and generous sharing that enrich possible futures of design with inspiring content and practical reflection.

第五届「新兴实践」
设计研究与教育会议
设计X复杂性
EMERGING PRACTICES
DESIGN RESEARCH AND
EDUCATION CONFERENCE
2016 — Design in Complexity
10.13-16
同济大学设计创意学院
College of Design and Innovation, Tongji University

where you want to be ∩

A
B
A B
① John Dewey
+
② Bertrand Russel
③ Confucius

Theme
Technologi
new

The MET

challenges
新挑战
同济设计周
Tongji Design Week
2016 10.12-10.30
PROCESS / TOOLS of D. RESEARCH
USERS
CONTEXT
complexity

Theme
Doing & Thinking

DEMY
challenges
new
新挑战

new

TheME

EPC 2016

Viewpoints

HD

REC
02:51:14:16
233分
HD
LPCM
CH1
CH2
25
-3dB

Globalization, and the "Effective Supply" of Design Education

Ping Xu

Central Academy of Fine Arts, China

The Chinese central government is determined to adjust the type of fast development that focuses on grandiosity at the expense of efficiency and the welfare of subsequent generations. For this reason, the central government is now supporting supply-side structural reform as a strategic objective, enabling it to impose the necessary constraints and norms on social and economic development as well as more stringent, rational requirements on various aspects of social and cultural development. Situated in this context, this essay argues that more efficient and effective supply should, therefore, be among the strategic considerations contributing to a radical reform of design education.

Ping Xu is Professor at the College of Design, China Central Academy of Fine Arts (CAFA). He is the Convenor of Academic Degrees Committee of the Chinese State Council for the subjects of design, head of the Institute of Design Culture and Policy Studies (CAFA), Vice Director of Industrial Design Council of the China Artists Association, and President of Beijing Design Association. His publications include, for example, *The Vast Land of Design* (2014), *Studies on Graphic Design of 20th Century* (2012), *Vision and Border* (2004), *Creation of the Gate* (1998). He completed various major projects including: A Study on the Application of Traditional Cultural Elements into Modern Art and Design (Key Project of Philosophy and Social Sciences Research, Ministry of Education, 2015), A Comparative Study on Chinese and Foreign Public Policy on Design and Art (Humanities and Social Sciences Project, Ministry of Education, 2010).

Thoughts on Supply-Side Reform, Triggered by a Caricature

Not long ago, at the exhibition titled "Social Encyclopedia: Qimei Wei's Caricatures" organized by the Art Museum of the Central Academy of Fine Arts, a caricature from 1986 caught my attention. This ordinary looking piece, titled "Multi-Shot Award," depicted a shooter happily holding a trophy, surrounded by fallen arrows, none of which had hit the bull's-eye. The middle of the bull's-eye contained the words "production needs." (Figure 1) The work is simple, but all of a sudden, it made me think of a trending phrase at the moment—Supply-Side Reform.[1]

Although Qimei Wei was a famous oil painter, few knew of his caricature works. They are rich with profound meanings. That thirty-year-old caricature demonstrates that he was considering what continues to be a timely issue even today—the supply side of public goods. Although the work is simple, it directly addresses the glorification of simple, crude-minded shooters, who are only concerned with actions and not effects. That criticism, from more than three decades ago, came entirely out of the goodwill and intuition of the artist's conscience, which reflected the sensitivity, penetration, and rationality of artistic thinking around daily life. The mindset that the work was grappling with is exactly the type of mentality that modern China still cannot get rid of, and it is a sharp, powerful reminder of the persistence of that reality. This shallow and ineffective multi-shot award mentality is still prevalent in today's economy. Promoting structural reform of this supply and demand relationship is directly linked with promoting efficient social production.

In fact, not only is this a problem of economic efficiency, it also touches China's underlying culture and a certain inertia in its mindset. The Chinese central government is determined to adjust the type of fast development that focuses on grandiosity at the expense of efficiency and the welfare of subsequent generations. For this reason, the central government

1 President and CCP General Secretary Xi Jinping first introduced the notion of "supply-side structural reform" at the 11th meeting of the Finance and Economics Leadership Small Group on November 10, 2015.

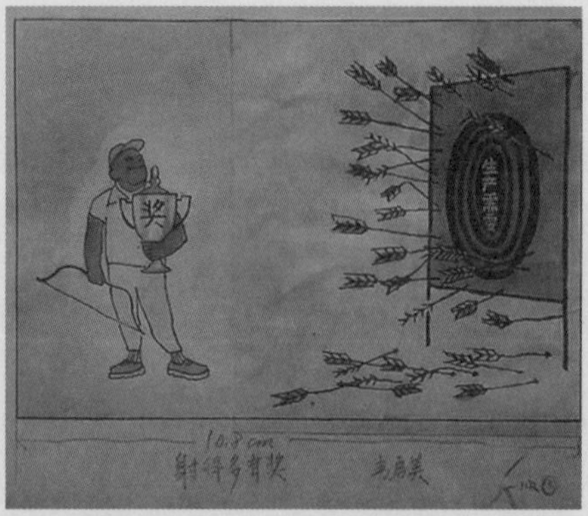

Figure 1 "Multi-Shot Award," caricature by Qimei Wei.

is now supporting supply-side structural reform as a strategic objective, enabling it to impose the necessary constraints and norms on social and economic development as well as more stringent, rational requirements on various aspects of social and cultural development. This is very important for the development of China. China is the world's second largest economy—the scale of our society means that the accuracy and scientific validity of this nation's basic principles is crucial. Supply-side reform does not simply imply a decrease in production capacity and overstocking, but, rather, a new understanding of the scientific, systematic, and symbiotic nature of development, that emphasizes the inherent quality of social production supply and the advancement of control mechanisms. More efficient and effective supply should, therefore, be among the strategic considerations contributing to a radical reform of design education.

Tertiary-Level Design Students in China: The Size of Two Million

According to an eight-year tracking survey from a design culture and policy study by the Central Academy of Fine Arts, by 2012 there were more than 1,900 higher institutions in China offering design and related majors; this number dipped slightly in 2013 to over 1,800. The annual enrollment of new design students rose from some 200,000 in 2006 to a peak of 570,000 in 2012. That number also declined slightly in 2013, to 550,000. Although the data from 2013 show some signs of a downturn, overall, the trend will likely continue to move upward.

According to rankings of over one hundred countries' design competitiveness by Cambridge University and the UK Design Council, among the top forty countries, the annual number of design graduates is included as an important statistic indicating design investment. Based on the number of design graduates entering the workforce, this index reflects the number of design professionals that these countries introduce into the market each year and the extent of demand. Out of the top ten countries known for the quality of their design education, in 2003 the United States produced more than thirty-eight thousand graduates, South Korea, produced in excess of thirty-six thousand, Japan produced over twenty-eight thousand, and the UK over sixteen thousand. How does this compare with China? Over five hundred thousand new design students have enrolled each year for the past four years.[2] This means that the annual number of design professionals entering the workforce is also nearly five hundred thousand strong. Moreover, because most college students spend four years in higher education, at least two million people are studying design in China in any given year. There are, of course, differences in the ways statistics on design professionals are gathered in different countries—the numbers may not be entirely accurate. However, a scale difference between tens of thousands and hundreds of thousands certainly exists. This is an enormous population of professionals that cannot be overlooked in any country. Whether it is the content and

2 James Moultrie and Finbarr Livesay, *International Design Scoreboard: Initial Indicators of International Design Capabilities* (Cambridge: University of Cambridge Institute for Manufacturing, 2009), also available at http://www.naylornetwork.com/IDC-nwl/assets/090406int_design_scoreboard.pdf.

impact of their school activities or the employment that society must provide after their graduation, these issues are not small problems for any country. What we are most worried about is whether these millions of students can receive effective higher education in design. The issue is not only the manner and extent to which these two million young graduates will be able to fulfill their professional duties in the future, but also whether their parents' investment in four years of higher education is worth the effort. In this manner, does not Qimei Wei's caricature also include us—we who are partly responsible for the expansion in design enrollment numbers? Should not every design institution contemplate whether the design education that we give to class after class of hopeful young people is truly an effective and high-quality education?

The Historical Mission of Design as a Discipline

Let us consider the *Design Harvests* social innovation project that Dean Yongqi Lou of College of Design and Innovation has been promoting over the years with creative design teams from Tongji University. *Design Harvests* is an imaginative, unique, and forward-looking teaching experiment. (Figures 2–6)

In 2016, I had the opportunity to travel with Dean Lou to Chongming Island, Shanghai, to learn about his vision for a new kind of agricultural ecology. Over the journey, we discussed the positioning and content of design education, among other issues. I was familiar with the *Design Harvests* project prior to the trip, but personally experiencing it touched me very much. We met a group of people enjoying the cultural service tour provided by the *Design Harvest* team in the field. Apart from the core managing team, student volunteers were also involved in maintaining facilities and cleaning rural hostages there.

This was a very imaginative educational experiment, with a unique aesthetic, detailed planning, and profound meaning for the future. It questions the developmental and cultural strategies behind the ways we enable cities and villages to coexist. The problem that the project tackles is common across the globe—given the ongoing waves of urbanization, how we should think of and design cities and villages so that they become connected communities that are truly interdependent, and interact, cooperate, and coexist with one another? There are many topics worthy of study here. Chongming Island is a small case, but one with a strategic vision and great imagination.

Design Harvests is an attempt at an innovative education mechanism that integrates three aspects. First, there is a cultivation of regional development ability—a practical process that gives villages opportunities for growth and new development they can search for on their own. Second, there is the formation of sustainable innovation markets. And thirdly, it is an experimental education project with vision ahead of its time—just as its name suggests it is a "harvesting" project. Not only does it help the students gain tangible rural experience and other benefits, it is also a new model that attempted

Figure 2 The Xianqiao base of *Design Harvests*, offering endless possibilities for design in the countryside. Courtesy of *Design Harvests*.

Figure 3 *Design Harvests* converted an agricultural greenhouse into a multi-functional place for various events happening on the farm, including dinner, party, movie, and local drama. Courtesy of *Design Harvests*.

Figure 4 Interior of the B&B named "Hua Mi" at *Design Harvests*. Courtesy of *Design Harvests*.

Figure 5 *Design Harvests* initiated a program for farm-based artists, who have introduced micro environmental renovations to Xianqiao Village. Courtesy of *Design Harvests*.

Figure 6 Student volunteers at *Design Harvests*. As the program grows, some of the volunteers participated more deeply in the day-to-day management of the farm and the services provide there. Courtesy of *Design Harvests*.

to break the boundaries delimiting conventional schools, creating a design education *experience* in real communities and, simultaneously, offering the communities a powerful incentive to transform the existing education system.

To date, the teaching materials, pedagogies, and content that most Chinese design schools use still follows the methods and procedures that European design education explored a century ago. The education currently delivered at China's two thousand plus institutions shows very little difference—which is a travesty. The two million students at these institutions undoubtedly have their own personalities and strengths and require different degrees and depths of education. Moreover, considering the vastly different levels of socioeconomic development and situations across our provinces, cities, and municipalities, do we not need exploration into new teaching content and pedagogies for ourselves? The *Design Harvests* project is valuable because it refocuses design education on the important issues that are converging in the wider development of Shanghai and surrounding regions. Additionally, similar issues are unavoidable for cities and villages across the country during the course of their inevitable development. This design institution in Shanghai has tested practices that now serve as an in-depth case for further reference and research on differentiated education. In another case from the Dalian Nationalities University in Northeast China, a leader of its design school relinquished the existing campus environment and moved the design faculty to the urban rural fringe, where he led the school to settle the accommodation and teaching facilities on its own. He redesigned pedagogies and procedures to support an innovative curriculum and turned a class of young students from the bottom end of the intake spectrum into enthusiastic, up-and-coming new designers. If only ten percent of the more than two thousand design institutions in China could achieve such differentiated pathways with high quality content, their design education would produce designers who impact the world. The effective supply of design education would no longer be merely an idea on paper, and the bizarre phenomenon of the multi-shot award would never appear again.

gure 7 Chinese and English editions of *esign, When Everybody Designs*. Courtesy of e Ji Publishing Platform, Tongji University ollege of Design and Innovation.

I was very happy that I received a copy of the Chinese edition of *Design, When Everybody Designs*, translated and published by the College of Design and Innovation of Tongji University. (Figure 7) Hot out of the oven, the book by Italian designer Ezio Manzini was a pleasant surprise. I was excited to receive it, as though meeting an old friend. The questions discussed in it from beginning to end are exactly what we contemplate when we think about design education in China. I jotted down some excerpts of some very well written parts, for instance,

> "For a century, designers have seen themselves and have been seen as sole incumbents and managers in the design field. Today they find themselves in a world where everybody designs and where, as we have seen, their task tends to be to use their own initiatives to help a variegated array of social actors to design better. This change in role

3 Ezio Manzini, introduction to *Design, When Everybody Designs* (Cambridge, MA: MIT Press, 2015), 1–2.

> calls them to become something different from what they have been until now. This means that in order to adapt to what is required of them, they must redesign themselves and their way of operating."[3]

This near-perfect visionary interpretation explains the effective supply problem of design. When pioneers in Germany began to create a modern design education, Bauhaus was only a vocational school—the curriculum was largely comprised of artists' creative experience and training in hands-on operation and craftsmanship. Naturally, some emerging scientific knowledge and methods—including Moholy-Nagy's experimental course—were also included. Granted, at the time, the sources of these experiences were limited, application was confined to a very small range, and it was very difficult for the general public to gain access to experimental contemporary design works. Presently, however, these contexts and circumstances have undergon tremendous changes. The majority of the factual teaching content can be obtained through public networks, and the position of schools as resources centers has changed. While there is a significant lack of relevant experience across society, the ways that schools are attempting to independently explore new forms, crafts, and effects have changed tremendously as well. At present, it is incredibly common for the general public to obtain basic desig knowledge and capabilities from various channels, and therefore, it is no exaggeration for Manzini to describe it as an era in which everybody design Under these circumstances, what professional design education should do has become a real problem.

Design as a Mature, Independent Discipline: Methodology, Values, and Academic Scope

Art was officially promoted to the rank of independent discipline after the Academic Degrees Committee of the Chinese State Council discussed and a proved the motion in 2010.[4] Design is now officially a first-level sub-catego under the discipline of art. The Committee has been discussing how this di cipline should position and develop itself, given that it must answer import ant, constructive academic questions that are commensurate with its status alongside one hundred and forty other independent disciplines. Indeed, my concern with the problem of the effective supply of design education starte here. Compared to other first-level sub-disciplines of mature domains, wha types of knowledge, ideas, and academic values must design education provide to support its existence as an independent discipline? If our discipline is limited to designing candy packaging, TV boxes, and renovation plans, then it does not need to be ranked as a first-level discipline or set up doctor studies—vocational schools can teach the skills such execution requires. A mature academic field in its own right, it must have a well-established scop a means of approaching and solving the problems within its scope, and the methodologies and values to construct a specialized system. We also need t

4 For more information, see http://old.moe.gov.cn//publicfiles/business/htmlfiles/moe/moe_820/201104/117375.html.

Figure 8 The *Design Harvests* team. Courtesy of *Design Harvests*.

establish a reference system and concrete pathways for talent training. More importantly, even though design in China is only beginning to explore, experience, and digest its learnings in the field, international design trends have changed dramatically—old ways no longer apply to new professional areas, and new challenges calling for new attitudes and new positions have appeared. Ezio Manzini's words reflected almost all of these ideas, which is why I felt that they came at the right time.

Presently, design is no longer the type of mysterious, individual, and isolated art form that it used to be. Information technology and network technology are ever changing. Mobile apps, for example, continue to grow in popularity and convenience. Our smart phones enable us to set the user interface according to our own preferences—is this not design? The reality is that we have entered an era when everybody designs—so what do we need professional designers for? How can educated design experts add specialist knowledge? What types of knowledge and expertise should they supplement to help people make better designs?

In the *Design Harvests* case study from Chongming Island, we saw our designers and elite research talents of the discipline step out of their ivory tower and come to rural Chongming to help the remote, then undeveloped village to foster its own market and sustainable production capacity.(Figure 8) We watched designers and researchers working with village people on strategies for rural development, and, in doing so, to enable a harmonious urban-rural interaction. Although we cannot say how mature this model is, the values that it encapsulates are clearly evident.

This is only one of the numerous emerging design practices presently occurring all over China. It shows that today's design may require a broader perspective of design problems and social innovation than ever before. As social innovation shifts more collective resources from pure business design and market-driven innovations toward an open social model, we will find that we must enter fields that we did not know—or care to know—anything about before, each of which presents a wide range of varied needs for design.

Two Cases of Social Innovation

Muhammad Yunus

The 2006 Nobel Peace Prize was awarded to Muhammad Yunus, the founder of Grameen Bank—in Bengali, Grameen means "Bank of the Villages"—in Bangladesh. His idea for and execution of a microcredit experiment is a case study deserving of designers' attention. Although a banker from an impoverished, developing country and not a designer, he designed a successful social innovation.

After completing his Ph.D. in economics in the United States, Yunus returned to Bangladesh in the 1970s, where he taught economics at Chittagong University. At the time, the economic situation in Bangladesh was bleak, with frequent disasters, withered industries, and destitute people. He found that the economic principles taught in classrooms did not match Bangladesh's economy at all—the so-called classical theories appeared pale and impotent in the face of reality.

Yunus took his students to rural Bangladesh to conduct field surveys. Once, in a village near his school, he encountered a poor peasant woman who made small stools with local bamboo and craft techniques. Despite having the necessary skills, she had no funds and had to borrow from usurers to buy raw materials. However, after the products were sold, eighty percent of the proceeds went to the usurers. Yunus learned that if the peasant woman had her own basic capital, then her income could increase six- to tenfold. A sociological survey conducted by his students found forty-two women of similar circumstance in the same village, and Yunus gave them the $27 he had on him to use as their capital. They agreed that the women would repay only the capital and no interest after selling their bamboo stools at the market. Without signing any contracts, the women all repaid Yunus within a few days. This outcome shocked him. He realized that among the poor, personal credibility was the only real asset—they cherished their reputations more than the rich did. Here was a resource from which value could be generated. The basic law of banking is that you have to have money to borrow money, and the more money you have, the more banks chase you to lend you money. By contrast, the less money you have, the lower the chances that banks will lend you anything. The mortgage that banks require becomes the greatest barrier to obtaining a loan for the poor.

The lack of loan funding for those in real need of financial assistance is the real reason that businesses, and even designers, who need support often do not receive real, effective loans at present. From here, Yunus began to create the world's first microcredit service for the poor—especially poor women. Since 1976, he has established over twelve hundred rural bank branches at more than forty thousand banks across Bangladesh. The Grameen Bank—lender to the poor—was officially recognized in 1983. The bank has granted loans to nearly seven million people in Bangladesh, and Yunus' small business has become a world-class loan business. This globally popular microfinance business started from a social innovation by an economist.

As a true social innovation expert, Yunus's aim was not only to solve the problem of poverty—it was also to find a fundamental solution for issues pertaining to rural women's survival and social dignity through an effective mutual aid mechanism. He even established a social development Constitution, known as the "Sixteen Decisions" among the depositors of the Grameen Bank.[5] The content of the Constitution is somewhat touching. For example, the first principle of the Constitution states, "we must comply with and promote the four principles of Grameen—discipline, unity, courage, and hard work—in all aspects of our lives."[6] It is obvious that Yunus's initiative had gone far beyond a bank loan business. He had become invested in reorganizing the lowest levels of society and stimulating their cultural self-esteem. Other examples include "we want to make our family prosperous," "we do not want to live in broken houses; we want to repair them and work hard to build new ones as soon as possible," "we want to grow vegetables all year round; we will eat more vegetables and sell the surplus," "we want to plant as many seedlings as possible in growing seasons," "we want to keep our children and the environment clean," "we want to build and use toilets," and "we want to drink the water from the wells that we drill," among others.[7] In this manner, he organized the entirety of Bangladesh's poor rural areas into a very competitive team of innovators and even developed the first modern communications business in Bangladesh. At that time, Bangladesh did not have a landline network, and his bank funded a new telecommunications company and a telephone operator business. The telephone company managed the talk time of the operator company and sold the call time to rural bank depositors—the "Grameen" women. Although there were no telephone networks in villages, there was demand for telephone communication. As soon as the women who ran these telephone businesses received a call, they would run with the mobile phone to the recipient's homes. In this manner, these women became the mobile communication infrastructure in rural Bangladesh. The government saved a considerable amount of money on infrastructure construction, the users had solved the problem of telephone communication, and the "Grameen" women increased their business income and became the drivers of telephone communications in Bangladeshi villages. This case study also attracted the attention of Stuart L. Hart, a world-renowned

5 "Sixteen Decisions," Grameen Bank, accessed November 20, 2017, http://www.grameen.com/16-decisions/.

6 Ibid.

7 Ibid.

strategist for sustainable development, who wrote about the case in his book *Capitalism at the Crossroads.*[8]

The inspiration from this case is that a great number of problems await solutions in today's world, and we need imaginative and innovative trailblazers to lead the exploration and design of reform programs.

8 Stuart L. Hart, *Capitalism at the Crossroads: The Unlimited Business Opportunities in Solving the World's Most Difficult Problems* (New Jersey: Pearson Education, 2005).

A Basement Transformation for One Million Underground Residents in Beijing

The *Digua* (*Sweet Potato*) *Community* is an ongoing social innovation project. A group of young people—including citizens, designers, artists, public and private entities—set about transforming dark bunkers in Beijing,[9] turning those poor living environments into more livable spaces. *Digua* has touched many hearts, and continues to involve many newcomers.(Figures 9–13) The lead designer, Zishu Zhou, is a young teacher from the Central Academy of Fine Arts with a master's degree in graphic design. Aiming to transform the living conditions of one million underground-dwelling residents in Beijing, Zhou wishes to enable them to achieve the dream of surviving in Beijing, and, at the same time, rebuild the social capital reforming the city. The project sounds like a sociological proposition, but it actually started with a design and was implemented by a designer. After graduating from graphic design studies in China, Zhou went to the Chinese Art Museum to do exhibition planning and design. Later, he studied at St. Martin's College in the UK, majoring in narrative space. This major is problem-oriented, and so he set the direction of his research accordingly—something one would be hard pressed to find in Chinese academia even today.

9 Just like big cities all over the world, Beijing is facing heavy migration, forcing many—especially migrants—to turn to unusual places to reside, including all sorts of underground spaces. Approximately one million people are living underground in former nuclear bomb shelters, despite the risk of being evicted by local authorities. See Annette M. Kim, "The Extreme Primacy of Location: Beijing's Underground Rental Housing Market," *Cities* 52 (March 2016): 148–58.

For his graduation project, he initially chose urban space and urban development as his subject matter. He saw that the urbanization process since the Industrial Revolution has led to a large influx of rural residents into cities, inevitably creating housing shortages and new poverty, both of which force people to use urban space creatively. From people living in cellars in Manchester in the Victorian era to the basement dwellers in contemporary New York, only underground spaces in large metropolises can provide a temporary habitat for new immigrants. In Beijing, a similar demographic feature exists, but because of the special circumstances in China, what would be secluded underground spaces in other countries exist semi-legally as underground civil defense fortifications in Beijing. When these civil defense works were built decades ago, the government invested a considerable amount of money into them, and today there is a need to find ways to make use of the sites. In the absence of other reasonable uses, these civil defense sites are outsourced to real estate contractors who sublet them over and over. Tenants sit at the end of a long chain of interests. In this intricate and entangled relationship of interests, the rent increases are manifold—from the original price of four or five Yuan per square meter to more than 30 Yuan, a highly unreasonable rate. Despite frequent attempts by government authorities to solve problems and risks associated with public health management and public safety presented by the project, government efforts have inevitable ended prematurely due to the overlapping and complex interests involved. At present, over one million temporary residents live underground in Beijing—a big headache for the municipal government.

Zishu Zhou's original design concept intended merely to bring some cultural elements into the difficult lives of underground dwellers. In the course of his work, however, he realized that superficial improvements would barely help them, and that in fact, his non-solution intervention would instead cover up the real need to address structural conflicts and would just create an illusion of social cohesion. He realized that what he was engaging with had a lot to do with building trust in the community. This was not a simple social problem that housing renovation could solve. It is not realistic to ask a designer to solve such a complex social problem, but the designer can push for a solution in his own manner. Zhou wanted to use design approach to rebuild and reconstruct social capital of this community that would allow future developments in the community.

Zhou and his team believed that the core obstacle was the tense relationship and conflicts that existed among the stakeholders of these underground spaces, and that removing this obstacle was the key to solving these problems. They also realized that a sound strategy and approach for sustainable development using a viable business model was lacking. This discovery opened up the horizon for the design team, who embarked on researching and developing a social innovation strategy to address these conflicts.

They targeted a lived-in civil defense work in Wangjing district, Beijing, and spent two years surveying the bunker tenants. The communication between the team and the underground residents opened up, and some residents even joined the team. In a series of actions they called the debug test—including an energy exchange program and a project called "designing a common prospect"—they attempted to rebuild a trusting relationship between the underground residents and those living aboveground. After some effort, people slowly found that they would be able to have dialogues and communicate. For example, the residents found the underground space complex, dark, and obscure—a place altogether uncomfortable to stay and hard to navigate through—feelings that represented a significant source of psychological harm to the underground residents.

Taking a different perspective, however, why couldn't they use the spatial arrangement of living aboveground as a metaphor to restructure the living space underground—there are floors upstairs, how about underground? The team redesigned the underground spaces with eye-catching colors and graphics to distinguish "the first floor" from "the second floor" and "the third floor"—only "the floors" expand horizontally. Each floor had a distinct color, creating a completely different, colorful environment unique to it.

One day, the team happily discovered that an underground

Figure 9 (L) The "White House" project—also known as *Digua*. Courtesy of Zishu Zhou.

Figure 10 (M) A basement room before renovation. Courtesy of Zishu Zhou.

Figure 11 (R) The community center hosting activities among the underground residents. Courtesy of Zishu Zhou.

Figure 12 (L) A transformed basement bunker, with a foldable bed, bench, and worktable, each of which effectively disappears into the wall thanks to an embedded design. Courtesy of Zishu Zhou.

Figure 13 (R) The Book Cave, where books can be read, borrowed, and bought, in the first basement at Anyuanbeili. Courtesy of Zishu Zhou.

household had taken away a leftover bucket of paint and used it to paint the interior of its own dwelling. This indicated that the underground residents were recognizing the design effort and that a heavily guarded mental barrier to communication was finally starting to dissolve. When the team subsequently began to design future prospects with the residents, the process became much smoother. For example, the team collected more than three hundred questionnaire responses from these households and gathered many ideas of changing the underground lifestyle—everything from a low profit model to a more reasonable, income-generating possibility. For example, one idea proposed to use the underground space as a theater where the income generated would be the equivalent to what a typical household made in six months. They found that the funding problem had a solution after all, and therefore, the project slowly thrived. Some households began to lease some of their space out as part of a multi-functional space to generate funds they could use to subsidize an eventual move aboveground. That is, the underground dwellers would have the chance to live aboveground, while the vacated underground space would be open for re-development that aboveground residents might be interested in. In this manner, the interests and profits of underground and aboveground residents were able to complement each other, and a community came into being in some sense. With a change in the uses of the underground space, the residents would also enjoy a positive change in their lifestyle.

This process confirmed the rationality and feasibility of the preliminary findings of the project, which turned into a social touchpoint. The government and real estate businesses sought to become partners of the project, and some communities expressed an interest in funding them to develop and manage the public spaces. This project, which has spanned over three years, was spontaneously organized and implemented by young designers, and it is still ongoing in its promotion and development. This case shows that our existing design education and our academic configuration have a considerable amount of content that we must adjust and re-position. The form and content of social innovation that the world needs right now far exceed our imagination. This is the purpose and the foundation from which we can consider how our design education ought to adapt to social needs and try new educational approaches.

Design for the People

The School of Design at the Central Academy of Fine Arts once had an informal but widely used teaching motto: "Design for the People." The motto sounds like a political slogan, but it reflects our basic positioning for future design education. Design should become an effective assistant to people's lives and the future of society. It should—it must—serve the people. Design has a broad context. A public-oriented cultural perspective is different from the elite education of yesterday; life-oriented innovation education is different from the previous formal education; reality-based social education is different from a conventional school education; professional education that aims to foster students' visions and capabilities is different from the previous technique-focused education. In short, designers are placed in a three-dimensional, reticular, and authentic network of social relations and become nodes that actively enhance quality, coordinate relations, and contribute values. They design and adjust people's behaviors in a professional and original way that has a real-world impact. The examples mentioned above illustrate the real-world, professional, future directions of designing for the people.

Our era is undergoing massive changes, and everyday life is a field that has played very important roles in both modern and postmodern cultures and philosophies. Human needs are a basic theme that enables lifestyle design to go beyond narrow, greedy, unscrupulous commercialist manipulations to challenge and to deconstruct the logic of false propositions that de-ethicize, devalue, and dehumanize. The rich content and profound meanings that it creates go to show that design's focus will be increasingly concerned with the lives of ordinary people. In addition, we must seek to emphasize the unity of "knowledge, action, and spiritual pursuit." Designers are the creators of future ways of living, and we hope that their beliefs and professional practices are consistent. Being a designer does not automatically mean that one is a moral being; designing nevertheless requires a corresponding moral standing. That stance means that designers must continue to enrich their knowledge, and remain aware of the natural and artificial world where everybody resides. They ought to actively think about how people may collectively address problems or even lead communities in their efforts. In particular, massive innovations in ecological, biological, energy, information, communication, artificial intelligence, deep-space, and deep-sea technologies continue to emerge, triggering new waves of scientific and technological breakthroughs. Today's advances of science and technology evolution bring along with them rapid changes, which rumble over our societies like thunder and lightning before a storm, rippling down through our modes of social productivity and production relations, and endowing innovation and economic activity with more complex humanity values. Before designers determine the form of their products, they must make value judgments, and "design, for what?" has become a more important and complex question than ever. We need persistent practice and thinking to create value, change lives, and positively impact the world. Only in this manner, can we formulate and implement valuable design education, and only then can our students become competent designers.

Since the end of 2015, the Central Committee of the Communist Party of China has attached great importance to and clearly proposed the major strategic goal of supply-side structural reform. In 2016, Chinese General Secretary Xi Jinping and Premier Li Keqiang repeatedly stressed the theoretical significance and practical value of the reform on many occasions, including in the National People's Congress, the learning meetings of the Central Political Bureau of the Central Committee, and during periodic field inspections. The meaning of this goal is profound, extensive, and creative. It is different from the supply side school that emerged in the 1970s in Western politics and economics, and not the same as the simple propositions calling for stricter conservation practices or tighter controls on wastage—such campaigns were implemented from an efficiency indicator perspective. Supply-side structural reform is a profound measure to comprehensively adjust the scientific methods, values, resource awareness, structural layout, and rational goals of sustainable development; it contributes to China's socioeconomic development in a way that includes continually adapting to the interconnection between market regulation and the supply structure. Design education must actively align with this strategic goal on two levels—first, we must carry out rational planning and precise adjustments for the effective use of educational resources and, second, place an emphasis on efficiency via precision design, precision service, and precision investment in terms of supplying the content of our design education.

Design and the Economy of Choice

Patrick Whitney

Institute of Design, Illinois Institute of Technology, USA

A dominant view of design for the last twenty years has been on "human-centered design." This emerged in response to runaway advances in technology enabling information and products that were useful, but seldom usable and never delightful. We have won this battle; it is now normal for designers to define the user experience at the inception of a project. But more user-friendly products mean little in a world that creates excess choice under the false assumption that this leads to greater happiness. The essay presents a model of how design can reframe how things are made, used and valued.

Patrick Whitney is Steelcase/Robert C. Pew Professor in the Institute of Design, Illinois Institute of Technology. He is also an IIT Distinguished Professor. He led the Institute of Design since 1988 until stepping down as Dean in 2016. Whitney has published and lectured throughout the world about ways of making technological innovations more humane, the link between design and business strategy, and methods of designing interactive communications and products. His writing has focused on new frameworks of design that responds to two transformations: the shift from mass-production to flexible production, and the shift from national markets to markets that are both global and "markets of one." He advises numerous companies and governments. He frequently speaks to audiences outside the design field, such as China Daily's CEO Summit, the Delhi Sustainable Development Summit, the 50th anniversary of the Aspen Institute, Harvard School of Public Health and TED. His research about design and learning, economic development, and organizational strategy has received support from MacArthur and Gates Foundations.

Introduction

Historians tell us the industrial revolution was the catalyst for design emerging as a field distinct from arts and crafts. Early indicators of this in 18th-century Europe had, by the early 20th century, evolved into the set of practices that, although still informal, could be recognized as the core of a new field—design.

Design is quite different from art and craft. Designers do not make final objects. In general, we create specifications and plans for manufacturers to make standardized products and information. Three of my favorite examples of the shift from making to specifying are a series of small constructivist paintings by Lazlo Moholy-Nagy at New York's Museum of Modern Art. They are *EM1*, *2* and *3*—also known as the "Telephone Paintings."[1] They are considered master works from the time Moholy-Nagy was at the Bauhaus. Rather than paint them himself, he specified the exact size, shape, position, and color of each rectangle, and telephoned a local sign painting shop to have them made. Why? Because one of the areas the Bauhaus focused on was the shift from hand production to mass production. It was one of many experiments exploring the future they saw coming but did not yet understand.

1 Patrick Whitney, "Design and the Economy of Choice," *She Ji: The Journal of Design, Economics, and Innovation* 1, no. 1 (2015): 63–64; for more information on "Telephone Paintings," see: https://www.moma.org/collection/works/78747.

The quest to bring cheaper products to an emerging middle class changed everything. Production processes became fixed, heavy, expensive, and long lasting. As a result, companies and their factories became larger. Consumers' lives changed too. The shift to industrial jobs gave them higher salaries to buy their first automobiles, washing machines, and TVs. At that time, production required product standardization, and consumers were hungry for what companies could make, so it was only moderately difficult to make predictions about what people would buy. Now, production is flexible, light, and agile, and consumers are overrun with choices, so it is much more difficult to predict demand—or even discern whom the competition is. Later, we will come back to this theme and consider the current shift to flexible production and what it means for design. But first let me tell you a short story about how new frameworks, methods of working, and even institutions had to be invented to cope with the economy of scale that went hand-in-hand with mass production.

Seeking Certainty in an Unpredictable World

Three decades ago, General Motors and Toyota each made a billion-dollar bet. Both had the same market research data saying that the largest SUV was the most popular vehicle. Both were well aware of growing environmental concerns among the public and scientists, but this was having no discernible influence on the US car industry. Toyota, without much formal data that would grant any degree of certainty, made the decision to invest in hybrid technology. The engineer chosen to be in charge of the venture viewed it as a career-ending assignment. No one knew how to make an engine that was four times as efficient and twice as clean as current engines. And even if the engineer could figure it out, there was no evidence that people wanted it.

GM decided to buy Hummer, which seemed like the correct choice—the data showed that buying the biggest, most powerful line of vehicles was the surest way to meet the market's demands. On the other hand, Toyota was looking at a wider set of indicators that gave them a more complete, albeit hazier picture of the future. Although these indicators did not say building a hybrid would lead to certain success, they raised doubts about the certainty that ever-larger SUVs would please the market. Toyota's logic was that energy would become more expensive and environmental concerns would continue to grow in the future—making the choice to pursue hybrid technology a sensible one. All this makes sense in hindsight—but, at the time, both paths were uncertain. How do executives make good decisions when the wider indicators seem more important and standard data seems less reliable? And why did it seem easier to make decisions with greater certainty a few decades ago than it does now?

Much further back in time, expensive processes tied to manual labor governed the economics of production. For most people, this meant making food, clothes, furniture, dwellings, and entertainment for themselves, or for others. Concepts like social progress and economic development were irrelevant in localized, static economies such as these. The industrial revolution changed this. Maker and user became separate. Instead of making things for their neighbors, designers conceived things to be manufactured by others for markets—first at a national level, then regional, and eventually global. This shift led to a drastic reduction in manufacturing costs, a massive increase in availability, and a drive towards standardization. People left the world of having a few things that had been made for them to having a large number of things that were the same as those owned by everyone else.

The rules of the economy of scale led inexorably to bigger factories, wider distribution systems, flexible supply chain strategies, and the kinds of global services that were needed to support companies and markets of unprecedented scale. Of equally unprecedented scale were the investments required to build these new production capabilities. Business leaders were faced with making bets that their investments would produce returns reliably within specific timeframes.

This incessant growth required new ways of working. These included frameworks, such as the middle class, consumer society, and market segments; institutions such as the public company, stock exchanges, and the public school system; and methods like demographic research, surveys, and prototyping. These kinds of organizations—for people, business operations, and societies—did not naturally occur. We invented it to help us contend with the massive increases in scale and speed.

In the 1920s, James McKinsey, a professor at the University of Chicago, formed the revolutionary idea that executives could use an organization's budget differently. At that time, budgets were used only to recall the performance of the previous year. He showed that describing the way an organization performed in the past could be used to predict and plan for the coming year. He wrote a book about it, called *Modern Budget Planning*.[2] His insight was so phenomenal that Marshall Field's (a major department store) offered him the job of the CEO. McKinsey turned the job down, and founded McKinsey & Company instead.

2 James O. McKinsey, *Budgetary Control* (New York: The Ronald Press Company, 1922).

A few decades later, Columbia University Professor Robert Merton realized that, maybe before adapting machinery to make a new product, manufacturers should make a model of the potential product, show it to people, and ask if they like it. He didn't use the name "focus group," but he did create the protocol for one of the most ubiquitous methods companies use to understand large groups of consumers. Even more than the frequent use of focus groups, Merton's work—along with that of others—led to a huge array of consumer research methods, and eventually the formation of market research companies such as AC Nielson, SRI, and Yankelovich, who harvest, compile, and sell consumer insights that guide company strategies. This new type of organization emerged out of the need to increase the accuracy of companies' ever-larger bets.

When GM and Toyota placed their bets on the future, the techniques for divining consumer desires were mature and treated like science. What led GM to choose the wrong horse? Part of the answer lies in their quest for certainty, causing them to focus on variables that had proven salient in the past and miss a major shift in consumers' perspectives. Only a short time before, companies were offering new household appliances, cars, TVs, and other products at prices that allowed many first-time buyers the chance to improve their comfort, safety, and status. There were only a small number of national brands in each category, and consumers had few real choices. By the time GM was betting on Hummer, consumers were inundated with choices, many from other countries. Their experiences with earlier offerings and the variety of choices available had made them more sophisticated. Consumers would learn about a distinguishing characteristic offered by a single company in one category and then wonder why it did not exist in other categories. Think of how the following examples were surprising when launched, but now help define their respective brands even though they have been copied: FedEx tracking, Nordstrom customer service, the Toyota hybrid, and Apple's overall brand identity. Each set a benchmark not only in their industry, but in many other industries. Innovations like these, which helped companies leap ahead of their competitors, are seldom inspired by consumer demand or market research. More often, such innovations occur thanks to a kind of luck—the luck of employing a person who has exceptional insight into people using the company's products.

Changing Economics—Changing Design

Why does consumer research not drive unusual ideas? Why don't people ask for what they really want? The brief answer to the first question is that companies think about consumers as buyers of products, not as people with aspirations and needs. Focusing on the product means missing the broader picture—people buying the products that suit their needs, goals, and desires. People do not ask for big changes in the products they use because they do not know what they want until they see it. They only care about a product to the extent it helps them live their lives, or live them better. And their loyalty to the product lasts only up to the second something comes along that does a better job.

This creates an impasse—neither the maker nor the users create ideas for major improvements. Up to now, companies have tended to respond to this dilemma in one of two ways.

The first was to add functions and features that they believe will make their offering more valuable. For example, before the advent of the iPhone, a VP at Motorola visited me to better understand mobile phone users. He said, "I've got this problem, I ask people about what they want on their next phone. Do you want fifty features or two hundred features? Eighty percent said they wanted two hundred features. I made the phone, and they said they hated it because it was too complicated." It turns out they didn't really want fifty features or two hundred features. We now know that each person wanted the five to twenty features they expected to use. But they did not ask for this, because it did not occur to them that any company would tailor a phone for a single person's needs. And because the engineers at Motorola did not find their phones too complicated—after all, they had made them—they did not ask about ease of use.

The second response was to use "human-centered design." This method uses longstanding principles of design, but it did not become a specific practice until the arrival of IT, networking, and the Internet, and the kinds of products and services these inventions fostered. The convergence of IT engineering, digital technology, products, and communications led to a dramatic increase in novel offerings, changes to infrastructures, and a bewildering variety of functions and features for everyday products. And, naturally, this led to a dramatic increase in user confusion and exclusion.

The IT revolution offered phenomenal promise to almost every industry. It was obvious there was potential for increased efficiency, speed, and functionality that would be a major influence on how companies work and how we live. The only problem was that at the beginning, IT-based products were virtually impossible to use. Obviously, asking consumers what they wanted in greater detail would not address this problem. How could they know? The answer was to observe small groups of people using the products, and allow them to reveal their experiences, and address these in the design.

Observing users as part of the design process began in the early 1980s with John Seely Brown, then head of the Cognitive Systems Group at Xerox's Palo Alto Research Center (PARC). Seely Brown realized that PARC and Xerox needed to learn about their products from watching people in their daily lives. He asked Lucy Suchman to lead an initiative that would use standard ethnographic methods used for anthropological research to match PARC's interest in the future of work. A key difference between Suchman's approach and the interviews conducted at a standard consumer research firm was that Suchman aimed to uncover patterns of use, not validate an existing concept. This approach was adopted by the Illinois Institute of Design (IIT) in the mid-1980s, resulting in the restructuring of their academic program into two closely related tracks of study: Human Centered Design and Strategic Design Planning. At the same time, strategic design planning firm Doblin adopted the methodology. The founding of E-Lab, a consulting firm focused solely on applied ethnography, soon followed. Within five years, almost every design school and design firm in the US was teaching or practicing some form of user research.

The value of this approach was obvious. It was a clear alternative to traditional consumer research that frequently produced precise answers to what were often the wrong questions. Ethnography as applied to design did not give precise answers—it was based on observing people's activities rather than asking them questions about a company product. This broader viewpoint helped design teams understand the context for users' aspirations and needs, which were the reasons behind their choice of products. This helped design teams overcome their assumptions *and* those of their clients. They found it more useful to be close(r) to right rather than precisely wrong about their choices.

Since its emergence as a distinct field at the beginning of the last century, design has evolved in response to changes in three areas: peoples' daily lives, our technological and organizational ability to create new offerings, and how companies decide which markets to enter and beat the competition they may find there. Human-centered design is one example of this. It created new frameworks to understand user experience, which guided the creation and adoption of new methods such as ethnography, and it linked user experience to work by economists in areas like the measurement of intangible value.

Many younger designers who entered the field after the emergence of human-centered design as a specialty may wonder what design's next set of methods could be, or indeed whether there will be a new specialty. After all—if you are not designing for humans, what are you designing for?

Other specialties have followed the same general pattern but used different details about the desires and needs of users, the strategic goals of companies, and the organizational and technological capabilities of the company. New specialties do not replace those that emerged before; rather, they add to the knowledge surrounding the practice of design and are fodder for the expansion and refinement of the frameworks and methods that constitute the body of design knowledge. Interaction design and corporate identity creation are two examples from the history of design.

Interaction design came about because integrated circuits were placed in physical products and media. This increased the functions of the products, but also made them more complicated and harder to use. Think of word processors, which some of you will remember as the combination of a computer and a typewriter. They offered a much faster way to produce a document—once you went to a class to learn how to use one. In the case of interaction design, we know who created the name and when he did it. Bill Moggridge was working on the grid laptop in 1984 when he realized the real design challenge was not the design of the physical product, which of course was a beautiful object. The difficulty was designing how people would interact with the physical controls and graphic elements on the screen. Naming the specialty made it easier for clients to identify their new challenges, and made it possible for schools like Carnegie Mellon, IIT Institute of Design and the Royal College of Art to create teaching and research programs around it.

Corporate identity creation was a hot specialty in the mid 1960s because of the unprecedented number of mergers and acquisitions. For financial reasons, there were four or five times the number of mergers and acquisitions happening each month than earlier in the decade. American Airlines was one of the iconic examples being a combination of over 50 small regional airlines. Massimo Vignelli brought them all together under the AA symbol and related identity system. Focusing on that high-level business challenge paved the way for subsequent work in branding and design management.

Interaction design, corporate identity, and human-centered design are three specialties among about twenty or thirty that have emerged in the past or are being formed now. All are in response to changing context defined by the three questions that help leaders of organizations decide what to make: Who is it for? Why should I invest in this given all the other options? How do we get it done, both organizationally and technically? While these specialties came as a response to the changing context of users and producers, they all draw from different parts of the body of knowledge that defines design. This knowledge is still in its early stages of formation, but there are signs of progress. As the field faces new challenges, designers reach into the body of knowledge as a base for their creation of new frameworks and methods, which builds the field we call design.

The Whole View

Today, we are again faced with changes in how companies address their strategic questions about what businesses they should be in, and operational and technical questions about how to bring ideas to reality. We are also faced with consumers buffeted by global markets, the maker movement, sustainability, and other forces. The underlying tectonic change, as covered earlier, is the shift from a producer-centered economy of scale to a consumer-centered economy of choice. Companies have unprecedented knowledge of business, operations, and technology. Consumers have an overwhelming number of choices when selecting an offering.

This gives rise to the ironic dilemma I call the *innovation gap*, in which companies have increasing knowledge of business models and operations, but decreasing knowledge of users, and therefore do not know what to make. Adding to their problem, as their uncertainty grows the pressure to reduce product, service, and platform development time increases. In response, they have created positions like "chief innovation officer" and departments with names like "innovation center." These are normally created to strengthen the early stages of conceiving of the right concepts that answer the question, "What to make?"

On the surface, this seems like a situation that needs design methods that are more pliant and broader than those normally used in companies. And because the challenge is caused by increased ambiguity about what users will buy, it seems the approach embodied in human-centered frameworks and methods would be perfect. This approach is represented by common statements like "start projects by discovering users' unmet needs," and "all projects should begin by studying users," or "design the total user experience and then develop the business model and operating plan." What is more, people use the term "design research" interchangeably with "user research" as if design does not have other research areas.

The problem is that great concepts for creating wonderful user experiences, while being loved by innovation teams using human centered design, seldom get through the development and commercialization stages that come after concept development. The better known, more formal frameworks and methods from engineering and business overwhelm the softer and less predictable approach from design. Inexorably, the innovative proposals that come out of the ideation phase are faced with the rigors of production and strategy and are normalized to the point of being essentiall the same as the current offering.

For innovation teams to succeed at getting strong ideas through the company that will have major benefits for users, they will have to adopt a *whole view* of innovation. By this I mean *applying design methods not only to users' needs, but to the early development of strategy and operations*. All three developmental dimensions—users, strategy, and operations—need to fit together. This means teams involved in early stage concept development need ways of doing early explorations of strategy and operations similar to the sketching of an early idea for a product. My contention is that designer need to do more to understand value creation and operation and produce a holistic view of an innovation for their work to survive development and move to commercialization.

There is a general sense that planning bold innovations is much more difficult than simply taking the step of creating a CIO or a center. Innovation suffers from not having an agreed upon definition. A very general statement like "something new that gets used"—distinguishing it from an invention that does not have to be used—is about as close as we come. But this leaves room for many conflicting opinions about working pace, profitability, acceptable failure rates, and more. Even more problematic than the fuzzy definition is that companies seldom recognize that different levels of ambition should use different processes and have different expectations. I find it useful to think of projects fitting one of three types, each type defined by how grounded it is in the company's knowledge and how ambitious the company's growth strategy is.

Step Change

Step change projects create a new feature, function, or form of an existing successful product. They are highly desirable, can be executed quickly, should have a high success rate, and should fit into the company's existing operations. Given that step changes are grounded on successful products, the company will already know a lot about who uses it, how to make it, and why it is a good business. However, others probably know this too, and there will be competitors that prevent step changes from being high growth opportunities.

Jump Change

Jump change projects are usually line extensions. They too start with an existing offering, but are trying to attain more ambitious growth where there is greater opportunity and less competition. Along with increased opportunity comes less certainty, when compared to step changes.

Leap Change

Leap change projects refer to what companies often call "moonshots"—transformations, and visionary or breakthrough innovations. These kinds of projects are what make Apple, Google, and Tesla famous. They do not use an existing offering as a starting point, but are driven by an idea that will change the market or create a new one. Because there is scant knowledge about sales and profits, uncertainty about the appropriate technology, and no firm evidence that people will use it, they have a high rate of failure. For example, when Roger Martin interviewed AG Lafley at the Institute of Design Strategy Conference, Lafley said he wanted to keep P&G's fifty percent failure rate for these type of projects—a lower failure rate he saw as a sign that the company was not being adventurous. To Lafley, exploring these unknown areas was a means for finding extraordinary growth. And, even when projects failed, P&G would learn things that could be applied to step and jump projects.

Of course, almost all companies, with the exception of start-ups, will want a mix of types, with most of their projects being step and jump types to sustain the current business, with a few leap projects as sources of future growth.

Let us look at the different points of view when approaching step projects and leap projects. The center of the following diagram (Figure 1) shows four main functions that businesses use to help them decide *why* to enter a business (strategy), *how* to make the offering (operations or supply chain managers), *who* it is for (marketing), and *what* should be made (brand manager). In the outer grey ring are standard questions managers ask about new projects. These questions work well when used with extensions of an existing offering. But consider what would happen if they were applied to a leap initiative like the first iPhone or Tesla auto. Demanding that leap project produce a solid answer to any one of these questions at the outset of a project would kill it before it starts.

Let's see what happens if you change the point of view from one that wants to be certain of the outcome before the outset to one that is more exploratory and based on design creation. The following diagram (Figure 2) starts with the four fundamental questions: What to make? Why make it? Who is it for? How to do it? The eight core capabilities of design are represented as circles in the second ring. These are an attempt to identify the design field's main areas of knowledge. They lead to a different set of questions that are more suitable when attempting leap projects. Suggestions for methods and frameworks that designers can use to answer these questions are in the outer ring of the diagram.

I call this the *Whole View* model.[3] It does not put the user alone at the center; rather, it puts the whole initiative in the center. It uses design to look at the whole problem. In a way, user insight becomes a source of disruption, helping a company reframe projects. I think this will help get valid but unusual ideas through the company, and increases the rate of success in serving people's aspirations and needs.

3 Whitney, "Design and the Economy of Choice," 72–77.

Running Forward While Looking Backward

It is almost impossible to predict the future of new and unusual technology uses and applications. There are many examples of visionaries being myopic about technology and business models; here are two from business leaders who were more often correct than wrong. Thomas Watson, CEO of IBM, reportedly said in 1943 that the world would not need more than five computers. Clearly he was limiting his view of the need base on the computations people were doing at that time by hand, most likely limited because there was not a machine to help them do them quickly. In 2007 Steve Jobs declared that there would never be a market for subscription music.[4] In these exceptions, near-sightedness gave the speakers a clear view of the capability—but a foggy view of future use. Looking at current behavior kept them from seeing how users would generate new demand.

4 Duncan Martell, "Jobs Says Apple Customers Not into Renting Music," *Reuters*, April 26, 2007, https://www.reuters.com/article/us-apple-jobs-idUSN2546496120070426.

Figure 1 Who and what to ask about step and leap projects. Copyright © 2015 Patrick Whitney.

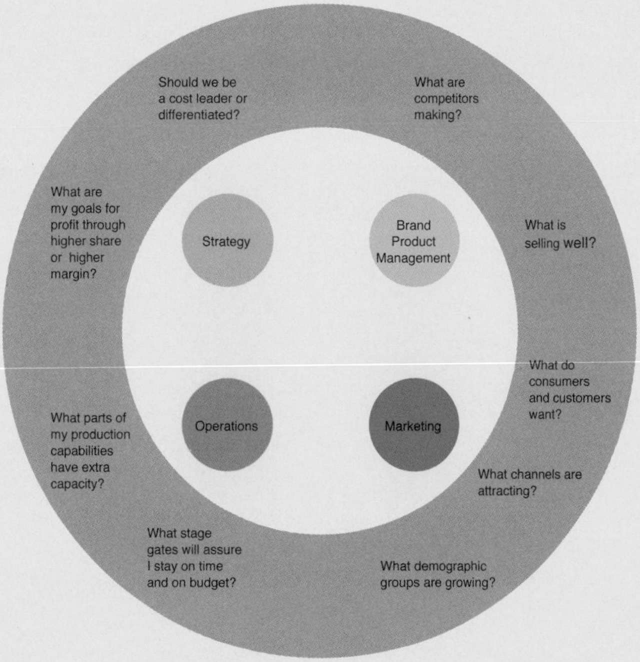

gure 2 Eight core capabilities form the undation for a range of questions relevant innovation capacity today. The methods nd frameworks in the outer circle can ork in concert to sketch options for novel usiness models, operations, use cases, d offerings. Copyright © 2017 Patrick hitney.

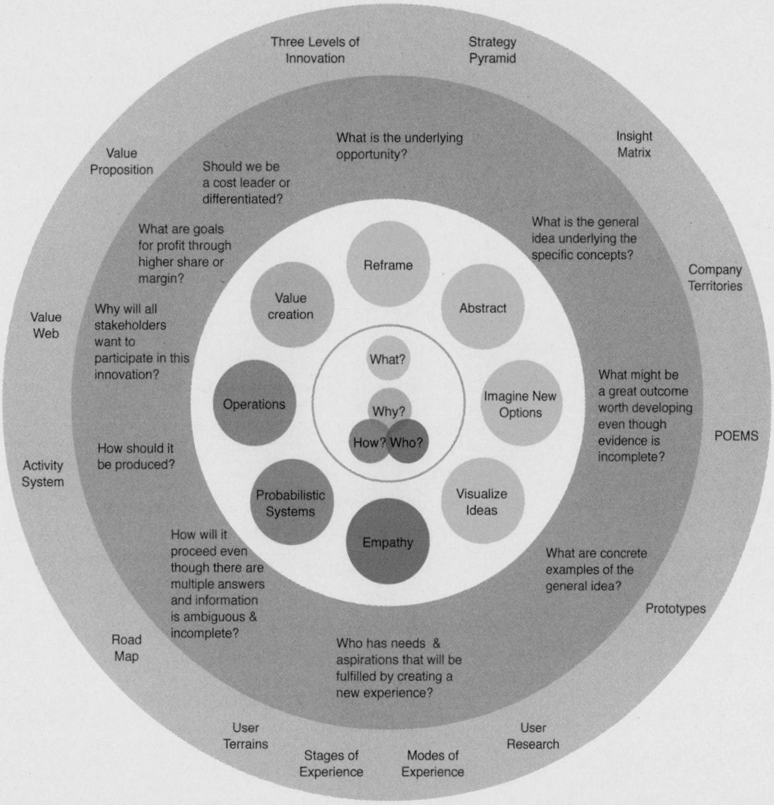

To help with planning, people involved in creating a new technology or new businesses often create a roadmap outlining a logical progression of the capability, expected market size, costs, expected revenue, and other factors. If done by technologists, a roadmap shows the path to offerings that are some combination of being more powerful, having more features, and being cheaper than current offerings. If planning a new way to create value, the roadmap will show how the current market can be served more efficiently or effectively, and how the current market can grow.[5] While they are moving forward in capability, and modeling value creation, they almost always look backwards at how it will be used. For example, imagine the roadmap for embedding cameras into smart phones. It would be safe to predict the progress for sensitivity to light, color accuracy, resolution, and (one could extrapolate) how soon they would put an end to film-based consumer cameras. Planners could predict their size and profitability. But the roadmap would miss the rise of Instagram, Snap Chat, and all the other start-ups creating new genres and applications for photography. It will be interesting to see if the same pattern is followed by big data and the confluence of AI and robotics, the two hot technologies of today. So far, the first part is holding true with all the predictions aimed at solving problems of today and yesterday.

5 Both approaches were evident in GM's decision to buy Toyota.

Design can help companies see change that, although already available, is invisible when viewed through the lenses of yesterday. Design enables this, not by asking consumers what they want or showing them prototypes to see if they like them, but by direct observation. Any one of several observation methods can be used, ranging from self-documentary photo diaries to co-design, to discover patterns of daily life. This can work at any scale—product or offering, system or platform, and even at the level of the organization.

By itself, observing user activities is a core part of human-centered design. The difference with the Whole View is that the concerns of operations and strategy are central, together with user concerns. The goal is to create fit among the three areas from the beginning, not after the project moves into development.

The defining elements of the twentieth century took decades to evolve to the present situation, where all the major elements underpinning society and business will be influenced by the core factors defining the economy of choice.

I will give one brief, concrete example of a project we did in Hong Kong over eight weeks during the summer of 2016. We worked with Hong Kong Polytechnic University to develop a plan for improving the lives of seniors in Hong Kong. The traditional family structure in China used to include a very close relationship between seniors and their adult children and grandchildren. Due to large-scale emigration and the forces of modern ization, now there are many elderly citizens who live lonely lives enduring social and health problems alone.

The original concept as defined by the funder was to develop elderly housing that would provide services that fit their needs, and enabled them to socialize with each other. The housing would be efficient, well designed, and most likely subsidized.

We adopted the Whole View model as our way of working and began the project with an understanding of the general framework of the situation. This included researching current options for elderly housing, understanding what agencies were supporting the elderly and how they were financed, hearing how these agencies operated, and observing the daily activities of the elderly and listening to their stories.

We rapidly discovered that the elderly did not want housing that was just for them. Many of them were working very hard to integrate into life in Hong Kong, and viewed specialized housing as a ghetto.

It became clear that new housing was not the solution. The observations caused us to reframe the challenge from providing "well-designed but standardized housing that would serve the general needs of the elderly" to a plan for "My Hong Kong," a "system of services and environments that would give each person the ability to construct the support they wanted." The focus had changed from standardized scale to providing seniors with choices. And, while we were generating ideas that would serve them better, we were also "sketching" business models by drawing value webs that showed the way the ideas might affect the value creation and expenditure. At the same time, we were sketching operating models, by diagraming activity systems that illustrated pathways to the ideas becoming a reality.

My Hong Kong came up with several unique offerings that supported the lives of the elderly. For example, we proposed a time bank, a service allowing them to "deposit" their volunteer hours for "withdrawal" in the future, when they wanted help but did not want charity. One of the surprising aspects of this idea is it will be of value to anyone—regardless of age—who volunteers their time and occasionally wants help. We applied the same principle to the housing we proposed. Considering the activities it needed to support, such as light meal service, help with shopping, and other conveniences, it became clear that the same facility and services could serve younger people (such as visiting students) or tourists. By expanding the types of people using the time bank, housing services, and the other ideas, opportunities for revenue were created that made the value web for *My Hong Kong* look much more viable than the value web for elderly housing alone. In eight weeks, the team had prevented the initiative from going in an undesirable direction, reframed it to meet the desires of the elderly related to housing, suggested a number of services beyond housing, and expanded the user group leading to new revenue sources and streams.

Designing support systems for the elderly is no easy challenge, yet it is just one of the wicked problems we face. How do we educate our kids in ways that do not treat them like material for one of Henry Ford's factories? How we reconnect the health care system to our everyday habits? What happens to the nature of work as we face the confluence of AI and robotics? How do we shift to a type of innovation that counts the real value of natural resources and the real expense of disposal?

The answers are not obvious. Nor are the questions, in fact. We need to go beyond the standard reductive processes invented for a more predictable world if we are going to succeed and indeed if our planet is going to survive. We need to see beyond symptoms to the underlying challenges. We need to discover unexpected patterns, reframe orthodoxies about what is valuable, recognize the aspirations and needs of all stakeholders, and understand the new flexibility available to organizations and technologies that changes how ideas are realized.

We are at a turning point in human history. We need a whole view of the context of the economy of choice. It will not only enable organizations to offer meaningful choices, it will also help us choose a sustainable future.

The Expanding Scope and Paradigm Shift of Design*

Yongqi Lou

College of Design and Innovation, Tongji University, China

This essay examines the evolution of design, its expanding scope, and the paradigm shift of the field of design from "form giving" to "innovation driving" during the era of the networked knowledge economy. On the one hand, design's role, tasks, tools, and methods continue to radically change, and the scope of design to broaden, to accommodate a variety of new subject matters ranging from relationalities, interactions, and services to systems, organizations, and mechanisms. On the other hand, design has grown from a mere link between industry and innovation chains into a contributor to the entire system and process of creating sustainable change. In this context, the development of a brand-new, evidence-based design culture—which addresses complex sociotechnical systems using rapid iteration—is becoming increasingly necessary and urgent when facing real-world change.

* The Chinese version of this article was published as: Yongqi Lou, "设计的疆域拓展与范式转型" [The Expanding Scope and Paradigm Shift of Design], 时代建筑 [Time+Architecture], no. 1 (2017): 11–15.

Yongqi Lou is Dean of the College of Design and Innovation at Tongji University in Shanghai. He is a full professor at Tongji, Visiting Professor at Aalto University in Finland and Politecnico di Milano in Italy. Lou is a leading figure in sustainable interdisciplinary design education, research, and practice. He is one of the first designers in China who connected social innovation and sustainable design thinking with rural development. Lou has been the pioneer in China for design-driven innovation education that combines design, business, and technology. He also furthers this agenda through international collaborations. Lou is the board director of World Design Organization (ICSID). He is Founding Executive Editor of *She Ji: The Journal of Design, Innovation, and Economics* published by Tongji University in cooperation with Elsevier. Lou is also the Editorial Board Member of the journal *Design Issues* (MIT Press) and *Journal of Visual Arts* (Taylor & Francis). He currently chairs the international advisory board of University of Applied Arts University Vienna, and he serves on the advisory boards of the Alta Scuola Politecnica in Italy, Kolding Design School in Denmark, and the DESIS Network. In 2014, the President of Finland honored Lou with the Order of the Lion of Finland as a Knight, First Class.

Technological Revolution and Design Evolution

The dawn of a new era is often heralded by an iconic event. On March 15, 2016, "AlphaGo" defeated Lee Sedol, the Korean ku-dan master player of Go, signifying the advent of the era of artificial intelligence (AI). In fact, the story of chess games between humans and machines began a long time ago. In 1950, six years before the Dartmouth Conference—the "first year of artificial intelligence," according to some—Claude Elwood Shannon published a related paper.[1] A milestone event occurred in 1997, when IBM's Deep Blue defeated Garry Kasparov, the international chess champion. From a historical perspective, in chess games that rely on algorithms, humans are ultimately no match for machines. If this man-machine mega-war has indeed opened an era, the era should be one in which the general public begins to discuss future man-machine relations together.

Computers were created only 70 years ago, and the Internet only 30 years ago, but the impact of each is unprecedented,[2] and the mark they have left on our world is indelible. This bits-based development of computers and the Internet has long passed the stage where only technology and infrastructure are at issue. Digitalization, informatization, and networking all contribute to the flux and development of the present era, redefining our social relations, economies, lives, production methods—and our design culture. This has always been the case, both from a disciplinary perspective and a practical perspective. New eras, new challenges, and new issues need new designs—and new roles, new missions, new objects, new methods, and new tools for design.

Issues tied to globalization—climate change, the population explosion, economic crises, and resource shortages, among others—have nations worldwide facing challenges of an unprecedented scope and magnitude. And yet, these issues have provided us with the opportunity to deconstruct many of the organizational and infrastructural principles of everyday life. The digitalized way of life, an increasingly flattened socio-economic structure, and various "2.0"s have also made our new global societies full of possibilities.[3]

Where there is a problem, there is a demand for design. Technological innovation, ways of social organization, methods of economic operation, and changes in people's ways of producing and living have expedited changes in design teaching, research, and practice. Modern design education has been developed for decades, but the design industry is ever changing—and changing fast. Design education, although increasingly complete still lags far behind the rapidly changing era. Design educators and institutions must address the critique that contemporary design education has not yet made any contribution to behavioral science, technology, commerce, scientific method, or the exploration and resolution of complex social and political issues by means of experimental method.[4] The best ways of identifying new insights, ideas, knowledge, and methods through innovation research has become a new topic at universities and in the industry as well

1 Claude E. Shannon, "Programming a Computer for Playing Chess," *Philosophical Magazine* 41, no. 314 (1950): 256–75.

2 For more information, see: https://en.wikipedia.org/wiki/ENIAC.

3 Yongqi Lou, "创新之道：创意、创新和城市" [On Innovation: Creativity, Innovation, and City], 时代建筑 [Time+Architecture], no. 6 (2010): 16–19.

4 Donald A. Norman, "Why Design Education Must Change," *Core 77*, November 26, 2010, http://www.core77.com/posts/17993/Why-Design-Education-Must-Change.

Figure 1 Time-space box of the definition of "design." Copyright ©2008 Yongqi Lou.

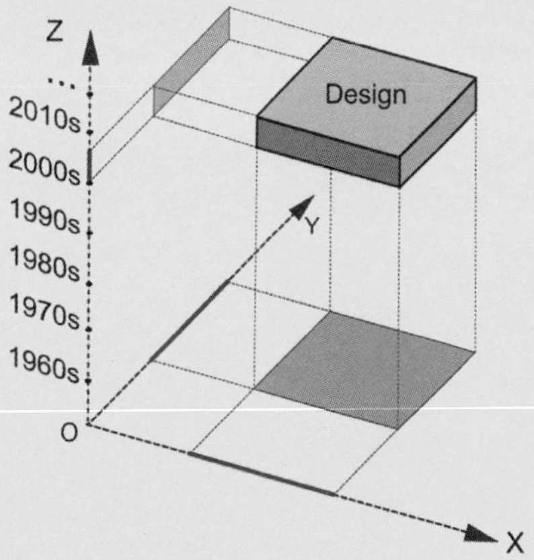

Change, and the Unchanged

Throughout the history of global higher education, many great institutions were at the forefront of the changing times, and contributing their vision for technological, economic, and social development. Various great universities—Gottingen University, Heidelberg University, the University of Chicago, Stanford University, and the Massachusetts Institute of Technology—have played that role with distinction. So is the case for design education—Bauhaus is remarkable because its design education was ahead of the practices of the times, and in sync with the Industrial Revolution. It is imaginable that should Walter Gropius and his colleagues be alive to create a school of design today, it would look nothing like the Bauhaus schools of that time.

When discussing what design is, we must frame the discussion in a time-space "box"—in other words, take historical time and context into consideration. (Figure 1) In the 1940s, several outstanding professors laid the foundation for Tongji's architecture and design education. One of these was Professor Zuoshen Huang—Gropius's only Chinese student—who systematically introduced the ideas of the Bauhaus School to Shanghai. There was a banner at Tongji that read "New architecture is architecture that keeps progressing and evolves with objective conditions, manifesting the progress of history while preventing itself from stalling in any historical stage."[5] This design idea from nearly 70 years ago vividly interprets "change," the unchanging truth, and the true essence of the spirit of Modernism.

The definition of "design" at any given time is only valid within a certain time-space box.[6] Changes in the role, mission, connotation, and method of design are not a linear process but a process with ups and downs—as is the process of design development. (Figure 2) Some ideas may no longer be in fashion, which does not mean that the ideas quit the stage of history forever, given that new technology or a change in other external conditions may revive these ideas, giving them a rebirth.[7] The development

Xiaowei Luo and Dehua Li, "原圣约翰大学的建筑工程系, 1942–1952" [Department of Architectural Engineering of St. John's University, 1942–1952], 时代建筑 [Time+Architecture], no. 6 (2004): 26.

Yongqi Lou, Pius Leuba, and Xiaocun Zhu, ed. 环境设计 [Environmental Design] (Beijing: Higher Education Press, 2008), 13.

Lou, *Environmental Design*.

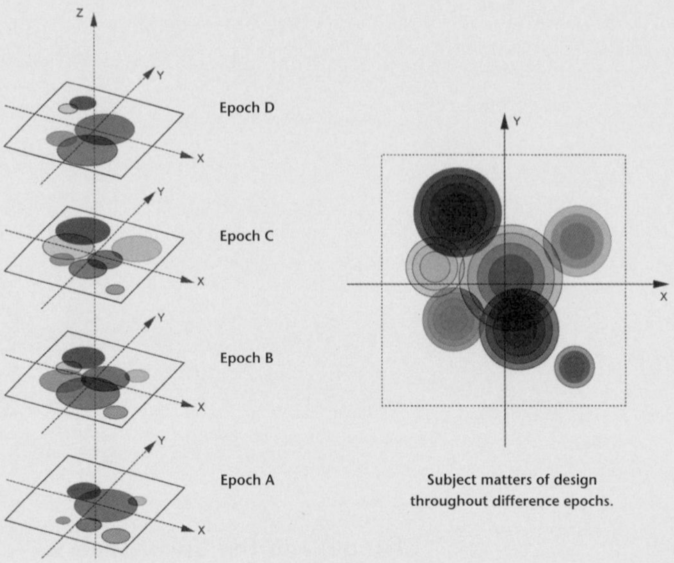

Figure 2 Mapping design to various epochs, it clearly reveals which areas are the main subject matters of modern design in a given historical period. Different colors represent different subject matters, whereas the size of the circle represents the significance of the subject matter. Copyright ©2008 Yongqi Lou.

Figure 3 A classroom scene of the design course taught at Tongji University. Copyright © 2017 Tongji University College of Design Innovation.

of new technologies—such as Big Data, cloud computing, social computing, and AI—sends the discussion of systems engineering in a new direction.

Simultaneously, it takes time for certain forward-looking ideas to be appreciated by the general public. For example, only after his death did the value of Victor Papanek's ideas gain increasing recognition.[8] In a contemporary example, "physical design" is suffering from harsh criticism at the theoretical level but still occupies a major position in many areas at the practical level—a feature shared by almost all "practical theories."[9] Regardless of how technology, society, and the economy change, there are always unchanged principles deep inside after the phenomena on the surface are seen through, which is why the humanities—philosophy in particular—treat design with such a high regard.

8 Victor J. Papanek, *Design for the Real World: Human Ecology and Social Change* (New York: Pantheon Books, 1972).

9 For more on this idea, see Lou et al., *Environmental Design*, 10.

Let us pause our discussion about design for a moment, and instead talk about marksmen—a seemingly unrelated profession. What is a marksman? A marksman is the person who was most accurate in throwing stones in the Stone Age, who handled the bow and arrow with the most skill in the cold weapons era, or who shot most accurately in the firearms era. In the era of modern warfare, who is a "marksman"? The answer is the person who is best at programming. When shooting, the programmer does not pull the trigger; instead, he/she enters a password to run a program that starts an attack. The skillful performance of this "marksman"—particularly the associated technology, methods, and tools—is drastically different with the development of the times. However, the mission to "hit the target with absolute precision" has never changed. The same logic also applies to the discussion of the "artisan spirit" that currently receives much attention in China. In terms of specific techniques, a good carpenter in the handicrafts era was judged by his or her artifacts, his/her ability to operate machines in the industrial era, but by his or her "programming" ability in the information and network era. "Programming" is becoming the most important "new craft" in the future. For this reason, since 2014, the undergraduate program at Tongji University College of Design Innovation has mandated that all freshmen take our "open source hardware and programming design" course (Figure 3) in the first semester of their college life. The ultimate creativity and imagination behind artifacts, as well as an awareness of the best possible standards of quality, are precisely the everlasting soul of the "artisan spirit."

As a folk adage puts it "the only thing that remains unchanged is change itself." Here, it is necessary to review the term "design" in Chinese —"设计," which consists of two characters: "设" (She) and "计" (Ji). "设" refers to planning, being associated with language and labor; "计" refers to strategy, calculation, and calculating ability.[10] "设计" (She Ji) means "planning a strategy"—in other words, a process of manual planning, predicting the outcome, and performing objective instructions.[11] This establishes connections to two of the most important issues in the field of design. First, it is related to people; "being associated with language and labor" relies on talking and action, and not only acting by oneself but also mobilizing

Shen Xu, 说文解字新订 [Shuowen Jiezi Xinding], ed. Kehe Zang and Ping Wang (Beijing: Zhonghua Book Company, 2002).

Ken Friedman, Yongqi Lou, and Jin Ma, "Shè Jì: The Journal of Design, Economics, and Innovation," *She Ji: The Journal of Design, Economics, and Innovation* 1, no. 1 (2015): 1–4, DOI: https://doi.org/10.1016/j.sheji.2015.09.002.

others. Second, it is related to calculation; from the ancient abacus to the modern-day computer, the tools that are used have been continuously evolving, but the nature of calculation has not changed. Computers not only provide more tools for assisted design, management, and construction but have also become increasingly more intelligent and capable of assuming tasks that used to be performed by humans. For example, parametric design has been widely used in modeling and has provided support for designers to better address and solve problems characterized by ambiguity and complexity. Through the presentation of correlations, the combination of big data and computing reveals many patterns that could not be previously found. Although design has undergone tremendous changes, its two essential features— association with people and association with computing tools—have not been altered. Naturally, this does not mean that "设计," the two Chinese characters, have already foreseen many trends in the development of contemporary design but, rather, that compared to the English term "design," the Chinese term "设计" provides a framework for understanding design from a different perspective. For this reason, I named our journal "The Journal of Design, Economics, and Innovation" (Figure 4) as "She Ji."[12]

12 *She Ji* is published by Tongji University in corporation with Elsevier. For more information, see https://www.journals.elsevier.com/she-ji-the-journal-of-design-economics-and-innovation/.

Figure 4 Covers of *She Ji: The Journal of Design, Economics, and Innovation*. Courtesy of *She Ji*.

From "Form Giving" to "Innovation Driving"

For decades, from "form giving" in the 1950s, to "teamwork" in the 1960s, "human understanding" in the 1970s, "coordinated management" in the 1980s, and "experience creation" in the 1990s all the way to "innovation driving" in the twenty-first century,[13] dramatic changes have occurred to design as a collection of professions and as a discipline. Here are some of the dominant trends.

- From creation to strategy;
- From material design to non-material design (service, experience, relationship, etc.);
- From specialty to interdisciplinary;
- From design to design thinking;
- From creativity to innovation.

In this changing process, the discipline of design has begun to take on larger issues that highlight the significance of its contribution. Design thinking combined with scientific thinking connects design to the future by transforming feasible design results into consumer value and market opportunities through more viable business strategies. This enables design to enter a remarkably broad field. This new type of design puts higher demands on the depth, breadth, and comprehensiveness of knowledge. These expanded roles make design not only a unique way of thinking but also an engine driving innovation.[14]

In October of 2015, the International Council of Societies of Industrial Design (ICSID) proposed a new definition for design: "Industrial design is a strategic problem-solving process that drives innovation, builds business success, and leads to a better quality of life through innovative products, systems, services, and experiences."[15] What is more important than the content of the definition is the question of which time-space background should define the contours of today's design practice.

Both design and technology are important driving forces for creating radical innovations. Donald Norman and Roberto Verganti propose two innovation models—incremental innovation and radical innovation.[16] They use hill-climbing as a metaphor: "[while] incremental innovation tries to reach the highest point on the current hill, radical innovation seeks the highest hill."[17] The implication for design is: human-centered design, with its emphasis on iterated observation, ideation, and testing is ideally suited for incremental innovation and unlikely to lead to radical innovation. Radical innovation comes from changes in either technology or meaning.[18] Design triggers changes in meaning; these can resemble technological changes and are important source of new industries. In Roland Barthes' words, what people actually consume is frequently the meaning behind the product. The "meaning behind the product" represents a massive economy, which is society-oriented, service-oriented, spirit- and culture-oriented, and experience-oriented, and can come into being via design. Through changes

13 Lou et al., *Environmental Design*.

14 Lou, "On Innovation: Creativity, Innovation and City."

15 For more information, see http://wdo.org/about/definition/.

16 Donald A. Norman and Roberto Verganti, "Incremental and Radical Innovation: Design Research vs. Technology and Meaning Change," *Design Issues* 30, no. 1 (2014): 78–96.

17 Ibid, 79.

18 Ibid, 80.

Figure 5 The *Design Harvests* project at the First China Design Exhibition. Copyright © 2012 Yongqi Lou.

in meaning, design can not only drive innovation but also promote social lifestyle change and new economic transformation.

In his book "Innovation and Entrepreneurship," Peter F. Drucker notes that during the period from the start of the 1980s to the mid and late 1980s, 4,000 jobs were created in the United States.[19] Where did they come from? Everyone believes that they were created by the IT wave of the 1960s, but in fact, the new jobs created by IT did not even compensate for those lost in the "smokestack industries." A large number of new jobs were created in the fields of middle technology, low technology, and even zero technology. For example, Starbucks, Wal-Mart, KFC, and so on—which have long become symbols of American culture—are by no means high technology; nevertheless, they redefined the original market by firmly grasping the needs of customers and creating a good experience for them. These companies miraculously created a large number of jobs and a brand-new economy as well, while becoming an important part of American culture and changing the world.

In 2007, the US subprime mortgage crisis erupted and spread widely, as a result of which solid industries suffered heavy losses. Subsequently, people began to re-examine the value of design and existing production models. In the same year, Apple launched the first-generation iPhone, and the advent of smart phones and mobile terminals went on to change the fabric of our everyday lives. New business models, ways of thinking, and social relationships were created on and through the platform it provides.[20]

19 Peter F. Drucker, *Innovation and Entrepreneurship: Practice and Principles* (New York: Routledge, 2015).

20 Xiaofeng Fang and Xiaomo Wang, "主动办学,永续发展—访同济大学设计创意学院院长娄永琪" [Education Activism for Sustainability-Oriented Development: Interviewed with Lou Yongqi, Dean of College of Design and Innovation, Tongji University], 装饰 [Zhuangshi], no. 10 (2015): 55–59.

Multiple players—the iPhone, the App Store, and licensed manufacturers—constitute an enormous innovation ecosystem that is redefining and even invading every corner of our lives. Design has become the core competency in that ecosystem—the system, its elements, and relationships are the product of design, while the relationships between this system and other actors and stakeholders are increasingly becoming the subject matter of design.

Efforts to reshuffle today's world economies is intensifying; in the world's top five hundred enterprises, the proportion of those engaging in manufacturing continues to diminish, whereas that of the service industry is gradually increasing. Design has become a powerful tool for the new economy, particularly for innovation and entrepreneurship. According to a 2015 "Fast Company" report, in Silicon Valley approximately one-fourth of the partners in start-ups have a design background, and among the twenty-five companies that have attracted the most capital, approximately forty percent of their founders or co-founders have a design background.[21] In the manufacturing industry, distributed and personalized manufacturing systems have brought about dramatic changes to the traditional manufacturing industry, including a radically reduced production time per product, hardly any impact on production capacity, no costly warehousing and logistics management, the immediacy of the D2U (designer to user) business model, and more generally, an avoidance of intermediate links and intermediate costs, among others.

In the era of the networked knowledge economy, design is playing a dual role. On one hand, it is becoming a contributor to the social and industrial development at the strategic level. On the other, it is becoming the driving force for social innovation and industrial transformation by gradually veering away from the role of passive service provider. Design has begun to partially transform the traditional employer-employee relationship between capital and design into a partnership. Practitioners have moved from simply providing design services to providing "integrated strategies" that offer greater future value to businesses, and further to investing in these services as an investment in "intellectual capital" dedicated to future innovations. With a new, more proactive attitude, design is becoming involved in economic and social changes.[22] For example, in 2007, I initiated the *Design Harvests* project,(Figure 5) a social innovation initiative without clients. *Design Harvests* re-examines the innovative solutions to urban and rural issues using design thinking, and implements novel ideas through innovation and entrepreneurship.[23]

21 John Brownlee, "Four Reasons Why Design Is Taking Over Silicon Valley," *Fast Company*, March 17, 2015, http://www.fastcodesign.com/3043740/4-reasons-why-design-is-taking-over-silicon-valley.

22 Yongqi Lou, "从'追踪'到'引领'的中国创新设计范式转型" [From Catching to Leading: The Paradigm Shift of China's Design and Innovation], 装饰 [Zhuangshi], no. 1 (2016): 72–74.

23 Yongqi Lou, Francesca Valsecchi, and Clarisa Diaz, *Design Harvests: An Acupunctural Design Approach Towards Sustainability* (Gothenburg: Mistra Urban Futures, 2013).

DesignX: Design of Complex Socio-technical Systems

As the paradigm shifts from "form giving" to "innovation driving," the object of design has been extended to interactive design, service design, systems design, organizational design, and mechanism design, among

Figure 6 The DesignX Manifesto was initiated at Tongji Design Week 2014. It was further discussed during the 2015 DesignX workshop. As a result, Don Norman and PJ Stappers's article on DesignX was published in the second issue of *She Ji*. Left: photo © 2014 by Tongji University College of Design and Innovation; Right: image courtesy of *She Ji*.

others. The scope of what design can do has expanded to such an extent that it makes contributions to the system and the entire process of its emergence—whereas before it was regarded as only a link in the industrial and innovation chain, its contributions now sit at the high end of the value chain. Design has become an important means of creating a "sustainable," "human-centered," and "creative" society.[24]

"Everyone designs who devises courses of action aimed at changing existing situations into preferred ones."[25] The most charming part of this definition by Herbert Simon is its optimism. The process of our coping with challenges and exploring a better future is a process of grand design. "The major problems facing humanity today involve complex systems of stakeholders and issues. These challenges often involve large numbers of people and institutions intermingled with technologies, especially those of communication, computation, and transportation."[26] If design needs to turn from creation to these larger issues and systems, then it must transcen a design tradition characterized by intuition and perception, and explore a completely new design culture.

As one of many explorations, in 2014 Don Norman, Ken Friedman, and I (and several other scholars) issued the "DesignX" Manifesto.(Figure 6) [27] In it, we list several characteristics of future design. Here I provide an upda ed brief list based on my interpretation of DesignX.

- Evidence-based design;
- Design that directly faces real-world challenges;
- Design that is interdisciplinary;
- Design that targets complexity, ambiguity, ambivalence, and uncertainty;
- Thinking in a relationship-based, systematic manner that links nature, humans, and the artificial;

24 Yrjö Sotamaa, "The Kyoto Design Declaration: Building a Sustainable Future," *Design Issues* 25, no. 4 (2009): 51–53.

25 Herbert A. Simon, *The Sciences of the Artificial*, 3rd ed. (Cambridge, MA: MIT Press, 1969), 130.

26 Friedman, Ken, Yongqi Lou, Don Norman, Pieter Jan Stappers, Ena Voûte, and Patrick Whitney, "DesignX: A Future Path for Design," *jnd.org*, last modified December 4, 2014, accessed November 11, 2015, http://www.jnd.org/dn.mss/designx_a_future_pa.html.

27 Donald A. Norman and Pieter J. Stappers, "DesignX: Complex Sociotechnical Systems," *She Ji: The Journal of Design, Economics, and Innovation* 1, no. 2 (2015): 83–106.

- Increasing diversity of "designers," from individual to collaborative; and
- Design activism and treating design as an investment for the future.

DesignX is meant for complex socio-technological systems. We believe that design must be gradually freed from the intuitive-based cultural tradition and re-promote an evidence-based design culture. Ours is not an understanding entirely based on the paradigm of scientific research; it also includes exploratory methods and iterative approaches that can enable rapid assessment, testing, and improvement by inferring and creating prototypes. Computer technology will greatly enhance the ability of design to cope with complexity, networked systems, ambiguity, and uncertainty. This new approach to design is more closely linked to the development of digital and other technologies such as the Internet, cloud computing, big data analysis, and AI, among others. Technological advances provide new tools, and although many design activities will gradually be performed by machines, the processes of decision making, intervention, and systems guidance still rely on human brainpower. Humans are becoming an important link between complex systems. The era in which humans and machines with "intelligence" co-design has arrived.

Simultaneously, increasingly complex systemic problems not only need designers as problem solvers in their respective fields, but also need them to foster dialogue and interaction among experts from a wider range of disciplines and functional areas. As the role of design changes, the boundary between designers and implementers must become even blurrier. Designers cannot merely stop at providing a solution strategy—they need to become a part of the solution strategy. Meanwhile, the notion of "designers" is also expanding to include people from all walks of life; through social innovation, the era in which everybody designs has arrived.[28]

28 Ezio Manzini, *Design, When Everybody Designs: An Introduction to Design for Social Innovation* (Cambridge MA: MIT Press, 2015).

Conclusion

The many changes in design are not a process in which "emerging design" replaces "conventional design"—in fact, emerging design is gradually becoming the classic design of the future. By penetrating into different disciplines and work areas, design begins to show many new features—this process is expanding the territory of design. Behind the expanded field of design is a new ecosystem, which allows classic design to have a wider range and a freer space of application. In addition to the understanding at the specialty or discipline level, design has also become a way of thinking and a way of doing things in the world—finding problems, solving problems, creating experience, and adding new value. Design is growing closer to its original meaning: priming and preparation for all the conscious creative activities that humans do.[29]

29 Yongxiang Lu, "设计的进化与面向未来的中国创新设计" [The Evolution of Design and the Future-Oriented Chinese Innovative Design], 全球化 [Globalization], no. 6 (2014): 5–13.

It is worth noting that the potential of design understood beyond the notion as an academic discipline is far from being fully explored. "In design thinking, problem and possible solutions are explored and developed and evaluated simultaneously in an interactive process: A 'design process involves finding as well as solving problems' so that 'problem and solution co-evolve.'"[30] Future societies may increasingly become important "offline platforms," closely linked to online information, knowledge, capital, resources, and communities. Additionally, design creation is a completely new mentality that is able to travel between the online and offline systems at will. Craig Vogel notes that today's graduates can no longer ensure a lifelong career merely with a certificate, and the licenses that students need must be renewed once every five to ten years. Active designers must quickly grasp new trends in professional development so that they can reconstruct existing knowledge and abilities.[31] Has design education prepared future designers with strategies that help them cope with future changes and developments in their fields? Regardless, in the future, when design reconstruction and the expansion of design territory become the general consensus, perhaps another round of examination of the nature of design will onc again be placed on the agenda.

30 Marc Steen, "Co-design as a Process of Joint Inquiry and Imagination," *Design Issues* 29, no. 2 (2013): 18.

31 Craig Vogel, "On Service Design: Understanding How to Navigate between Systems and Touch Points," in *Emerging Practices: Professions, Values, and Approaches in Design*, ed. Jin Ma and Yongqi Lou (Beijing: China Architecture and Building Press, 2014), 354.

Making Things Happen: Design for Inclusivity, Diversity, and Humanity

Sooshin Choi

The Modus Design, USA

Design has been about making things. Design is now about making things happen, and designers are creating systems, services, and strategies besides things and products. In essence, design has become a change agent in the industry and society. The roles of design have expanded, and designers have better tools and processes. But the core value of design is often overlooked. We spend lots of time for what we design and how, but we often forget why we design. This keynote outlines the core values of design and presents examples of designs that address such important matters.

Sooshin Choi is an award-winning industrial designer, design educator, and leader. Choi has a professional career of 26 years in automotive, system furniture and innovative product in Korea and the US. He also has been in academia for 14 years including 4 years at the College for Creative Studies as the Provost & Vice President for Academic Affairs and 10 years at the University of Cincinnati as a Professor of Design and Director of School of Design. Since 2018, he is the CEO and CDO at The Modus Design, a Detroit-based institute offering professional design education. Choi is a frequent speaker at a number of international venues and a judge at numerous design award programs including IDEA, BraunPrize, and Car Design Awards China. He is a member of Michigan Design Council and was the IDSA Education Vice President, awarded IDSA Educator of the Year 2014 and was the IDSA International Conference Chair in 2016.

Designers Are Makers of the Future

Seismic technological, economic, and societal shifts are making designers work harder than ever. True, designers are problem solvers, but many other people solve problems who are not designers. And designers do more than that—in the process of solving problems, we inadvertently create many more. Designers are not alone in this constant struggle. Many other disciplines share similar experiences. Is all of the hard work we do to improve the future actually improving the future?

Every day, we enjoy technological developments that would have been unimaginable even 50 or 60 years ago. For example, some of today's most incredible automobiles have over 100 horsepower, while the greatest emperors in China rode in carriages powered by only four or eight horses. Another example is the iPhone. Who would have thought a mobile phone could work like a computer, or be more powerful than many computers were in the past? These are only a few examples, but overall, we reap a multitude of benefits from leaps in technology, energy, and wealth.

So, looking back, it is easy to assume that our future will be a paradise fuelled by better technology. But are we really making a better future? Consider autonomous driving, for example. Autonomous cars will probably drive better and more safely than many human drivers do today. We also know that computers can beat human beings at complex games such as chess and go. So the question is—which improvements will create a better future?

In 2008, Walt Disney's Pixar Animation Studios released the film *Wall·E*, which tells the story of a robot trash compactor on an abandoned Earth who inadvertently becomes our planet's last hope for renewal. Despite being a children's story, *Wall·E* manages to convey two distinct messages. The first is that our environment is valuable, yet we have been consuming it unsustainably in the name of economic growth and greater comfort. The second message is that we will become much less capable human beings because of the convenience, automation, and entertainment that technology provides. Advances in technologies such as augmented reality, virtual reality, artificial intelligence, and autonomous driving all point to this possibility becoming a reality. Even though the dystopian future depicted in the film may be slightly exaggerated, there is some truth to it. It *is* going to be difficult to bring our environment back to what it used to be; and we *have* already become much weaker physically, and perhaps mentally, thanks to advances in technology. These are two extremely important themes for the innovators of the future. Yet our success as designers is not defined by how environmentally sustainable or uplifting to the human condition a product is. Our success is still defined by how well our designs will sell.

Although humanity is not quite at the stage where we have to leave the planet, it is no longer possible to ignore the negative effects of the "buy more, sell more, earn more" global business model. While it is important to keep businesses going, it is also important to know that the more we produce, the messier the state of our environment will become.

The second part of the movie is even more interesting. Away from the trash heap that is Earth, the humans reside comfortably on massive, convenience-laden airliners. Everything is organized, intelligent, and automatic. Desires are fulfilled at the touch of a button. Robots clean up messes and respond to emergencies seamlessly. AI instantly repairs technological glitches.

The problem is that nobody has to *do* anything. The people have become obese to the point that they can no longer stand. Instead of using the muscles in their legs to move, people use mobile chairs. Instead of having a face-to-face conversation, they video chat with someone three feet away. The film is an unnerving caricature of our reality because it is so familiar! As smartphones get smarter, we get dumber. When our phones' batteries die—and we are suddenly cut off from the lives they contain—we scramble to find the energy they require so that we ourselves can go on living. As technology evolves, we devolve and, unfortunately, become less capable. Technology brings convenience at a cost. Whether it affects our personal lives and experiences or our skills, we have become so reliant on technology that if it breaks, we lack the ability to function as we did before the convenience was introduced in our lives.

But this is not to say that technology is completely evil and its advance spells the end of humanity. There are many examples how technological advancement has made our lives convenient and powerful. In 1993, the original hard drive of a Mac IIci was 12 MB. It was quite a powerful computer back in those days. Now, in just a little over two decades, the iPhone comes with 256 GB of memory. That's 3,200 times more than the Mac IIci. Floppy disks had a storage capacity of 1.4 MB—big enough store the entire Bible. Now an iPhone can store over 180,000 copies of the Bible. Who could have imagined this would be possible?

Technology indeed is evolving, and we should celebrate that. But when we deliver an advancement of any kind to people, we should be aware and deeply conscious of its impact on the environment and the human condition, because these are the last things that we want to destroy.

The Evolution of Design

To get an idea of the role designers should play in creating the future, here is a brief review of how design has evolved up to now, and what each stage means to designers and designing.(Figure 1)

We could call the eighteenth century through the early nineteenth century—the time before industrial design became a formal profession—the Pre-Industrial Design era. Notable movements of this time include Arts and Crafts, De Stijl, and Art Nouveau. As these names suggest, the focus was on art, craft, style, and decoration. For example, Singer sewing machines of that era had beautiful angels and flowers on them. The decorations made the machines look beautiful and likely helped them sell, but had no effect

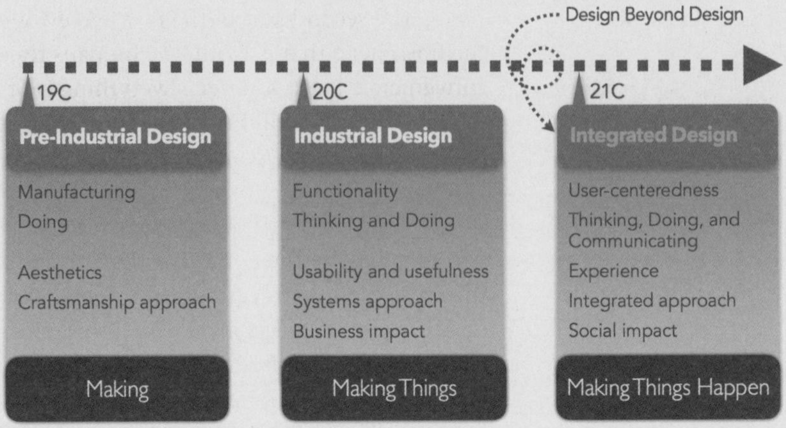

Figure 1 The Evolution of Design. Copyright © 2017 Sooshin Choi.

on the function of the product. In that period, design's role was to add craftsmanship and aesthetic appeal to products.

As we moved into the mid-twentieth century, the importance of improving functionality through design emerged, and the term Industrial Design became popular. Making products look good was not enough; designers used form and function to develop more complete products.

This expanded focus, which included functionality and usability, became crucial to improving product marketability. Designing involved the two main activities of thinking and doing, and designers main efforts were dedicated to making things.

Now, we are in the twenty-first century and designers' focus has expanded even further. Designing a great product is not enough. Designers need to be aware of the responses their products and services elicit from users, and the impact designs have on society, the economy, individual experience, and the environment. Designers and non-designers are working together, and so designing now involves thinking, doing, and communicating. Designers' increased responsibility and influence requires them to develop an integrated view and approach that leads to more valuable and comprehensive outcomes. Industrial Design has become outdated. We are witnessing the emergence of Integrated Design, Now, a designer's job is not merely to make things, but to make things *happen*.

We are now at the era of design beyond design, when designers are dealing with much broader and more complex problems, and joining forces with a wider spectrum of stakeholders The good news is that we can bring more valuable impact to society as the scope of our influence widen, if we do not let ourselves get distracted by the minutia and forget the main goal of design.

Making Things Happen—Designing for Inclusivity, Diversity, and Humanity

The IDSA International Conference 2016 in Detroit had the theme of "Making Things Happen." The theme was a manifesto that we used to spark a wider dialogue about the ever-expanding role of design. The keynote speeches, presentations, and workshops challenged attendees to consider the changing role they would play in this new era of Integrated Design, and led to active self-reflections about how much we have been narrowly focusing on brands, corporate profit, technology, and mass consumption while forgetting the real substance of design. We began to rethink who we are and how we could make the future much more meaningful. To do this, there are three areas we can choose to focus on and design for—inclusivity, diversity, and humanity.

Design for Inclusivity

Designs should serve everyone, let no one be excluded—this is the premise of inclusive design and universal design. Yet there are many products and services today that exclude large portions of society.

To me, design is communication—our designs "talk" to people. For those who cannot remove the sometimes slippery cap of a water bottle, the cap says, "You are not strong enough." For those in wheelchairs, staircases, curbs, poorly placed handles, and narrow openings say, "You are not the person I am designed for." There are unlimited examples of designs that are exclusive.

Inclusivity is understanding and respecting as many differing kinds of needs as possible. When designers define *target user groups*—those who can understand, afford, and use a product—they automatically exclude anyone outside those groups.

If you go to a gym, you probably rarely see people in wheelchairs. Why? Because the target user group for the exercise equipment did not include people in wheelchairs.

Ryan Eder, an industrial design student at the University of Cincinnati, took design for inclusivity seriously. During his daily workout at the gym, he would see a person in a wheelchair. This person brought various straps specifically designed to help him grab handles or bars more easily. He had to request that his wheelchair be secured to the floor before each exercise. Some machines he could not use at all because they included built-in seats. Ryan thought this was unfair, and that wheelchair users deserve the same ability to use exercise equipment. This became his senior year capstone project.(Figure 2)

Ryan was already a design student with a robust design process and skillset, but he found extra motivation from the opportunity to make his design inclusive. He met a number of wheelchair users, physical trainers, and medical doctors to learn more about the challenges surrounding this problem. After discovering and defining seven key issues that exclude wheelchair users, systematically developing solutions, and refining his execution, he designed an adaptive fitness machine that anyone can use. Behind his elegant solution was a beautiful intention—health and fitness for everyone, regardless of physical impairment.

He then submitted his design to the International Design Excellence Award in 2007. His concept won the Gold Award in the Student category, the Best in Show Award, and the People's Choice Award. I was surprised to see a student design winning the Best in Show Award over all other categories, even without considering that inclusive design projects seldom receive such a high award as they are typically not appealing enough. Ryan's inclusive fitness design not only received three honorable awards. He moved the audience to tears when he spoke and showed a video of why he designed it. The impact created by his design and story was so great that he was able to raise funds to turn the design into a reality. After 9 years, the final design shown in **Figure 2** is ready for production. It is beautiful, and his original design concept shines through.

The impact of design for inclusivity goes beyond our everyday expectations. Ryan's design will encourage people with physical impairments to achieve the fitness they deserve. It will help the fitness business to widen its target user group, and open up new opportunities in the fitness machine industry. Ryan's design did more than just fulfill the school's requirements for a capstone project. The *Include Fitness* machine demonstrates the power inclusive design has to help individuals *and* the community, business *and* industry.

Design for Diversity

Some cultures encourage people to share the same or similar ideologies. There are certainly benefits when everyone is thinking, seeing, and acting in similar ways. There may be more cohesion, more productivity and efficiency, and perhaps less trouble. But these benefits come with the risk that people with different beliefs, thoughts, cultural backgrounds, and abilities may be ignored and even rejected. The prevailing virtue in my native Korea—a highly homogeneous society—is unity, while in the USA it is diversity.

Design in this age of integration should serve people equally regardless of difference—cultural, socio-economic, or otherwise. This doesn't mean *ignore* differences, but respect and support difference rather than exclusivity.

Veronika Scott was a graduate student in the Product Design program at Detroit's College for Creative Studies (CCS) when she took a hard look at the city's homeless community. She realized that no designs existed specifically to alleviate the basic difficulty of their living conditions. They are ignored and rejected by society. They use, eat, and wear anything that they can find. In winter, they have nothing to protect them from the elements—no coats, no shelter.

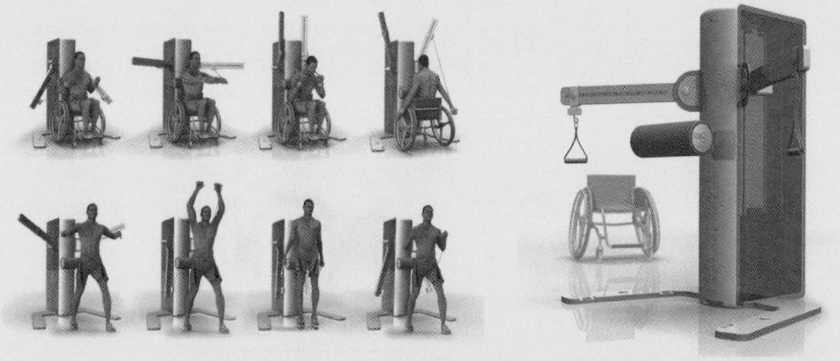

Figure 2 The *Include Fitness* weightlifting machine, designed by Ryan Eder. Copyright © 2017 Ryan Eder.

Figure 3 Veronika Scott's inclusive design idea has now become a successful nonprofit called *Empowerment Plan*. Copyright © 2017 Veronika Scott.

As her graduate thesis project, Veronika designed a coat that could turn into a sleeping bag. At first, it seemed unlikely that any company would be willing to make a product with no commercial value. But Veronika brought the coat to Carhartt, a Detroit-based clothing company, to seek support. Impressed with Veronika's goodwill and the ingenuity of her design, Carhartt donated a massive amount of fabric and several sewing machines to her personally. Veronika began producing coats from home until it became too much to handle there. Several years after her graduation, she turned her project into a non-profit organization called Empowerment Plan.(Figure 3) [1] She uses materials donated by local business giants Carhartt and General Motors, among others. And she hires and trains homeless people to make the coats, providing them with an income, a sense of stability, and the ability to help others. The utility and quality of her design has inspired people from across the USA to request coats for their homeless populations.

For more information, see http://www.empowermentplan.org/.

Veronika's project went far beyond concerns for aesthetic quality or market value. The emergence of her Empowerment Plan non-profit reveals the true goal of designing—to empower people regardless of their physical abilities, education levels, culture, or socio-economic status. That is the power of designing for diversity.

Design for Humanity

"Humanity" means "the quality of being human" and also "being humane."[2] Designing for humanity means respecting human beings and human dignity, and preserving the dignity of other beings, including animals. By extension, it might also mean preserving the integrity of our planet, as it sustains human life.

Our lives are filled with confrontations to our humanity. From sprawling urban developments to complex healthcare systems to automation, the changes that affect and improve our lives can feel less like they are happening for us, and more like they are happening to us.

Even though hospitals are places intended to preserve human life, hospitalization is fraught with dehumanizing experiences. Aware of this, Detroit's Henry Ford Hospital and Henry Ford Innovation Institute invited CCS students to identify something they thought they could improve at the hospital. The students chose the gowns. No designer has improved upon the notorious hospital gown, with its fussy ties and gaping back, for decades. The students found that the patients, doctors, and nurses all hated the gowns, because they leave patients' backs uncomfortably exposed, provide zero warmth, and do not give medical staff the access they need to provide patients with proper treatment. Of course, any redesign would also have to be cheap to make, easy to wash, and one-size-fits-all.(Figure 4)

2 *Merriam-Webster Online Dictionary*, s.v. "humanity," https://www.merriam-webster.com/dictionary/humanity.

Figure 4 A hospital gown designed by CCS students in conjunction with the Henry Ford Innovation Institute. Copyright © 2017 CCS and Henry Ford Innovation Institute.

The CCS students uncovered six aspects of the gown they could improve, and made a number of prototypes to find ways to address these problems. The final design not only looks good, it is functional. Doctors, nurses, and lab technicians can easily unfasten various sections of the gown to provide treatment. But the patients enjoy the greatest benefit. The gown is warmer than the flimsy shifts of yore, and preserves their dignity and modesty by keeping their backs covered. Given the enormous promise of the gown's design, the Henry Ford Innovation Institute has developed it into a real product that they anticipate will be used at hospitals across the USA.

The Designers We Need

So we need designers—good designers.(Figure 5) A good designer is a *conceptor*, a *conductor*, and a *connector*. A conceptor is someone who can see what others cannot—someone who can create a vision and share it with others to make a concept. We all have ideas as reactions to what we experience and understand. When others accept these ideas, the ideas can turn into concepts. As a conductor, a designer should have good design skills and be able to direct and combine the team's efforts proficiently, imaginatively and productively, in the same way that a conductor leads an orchestra. And as connectors, designers must find relevant connections among different areas and cultures of the world so that what they create will be meaningful.

Good designers need these three qualities, and, when designing, must also be mindful of the *soul*, *skeleton*, and *skin* of the design.(Figure 6)

The first layer, the skin, defines the unique aesthetics and identity of the design. The second layer is the skeleton, or the form that facilitates the function of the design, just like our skeletons. But a human is not made of skin and bone alone. Dead bodies and zombies have them too! What makes each one of us unique and valuable is a soul, the essence of who we are as individuals. The skin delivers the visual characteristics, the skeleton brings function and performance, and the soul is the unique value of the design. Finally, for good designers to be able to utilize those three skills and focus on the three aspects of a good design, we must use our brains, hearts, and guts.(Figure 7)

The first key organ in a good designer is the brain. We think, analyze, and dream thanks to our brains. With our designer's brain, we see people as users, customers, and operators. Then, we need a warm heart, which leads us to see these users, operators, and customers as real human beings. With a warm heart, we can stand in other people's shoes and design for them. And finally, we need to have guts. A good brain makes you smart, a warm heart makes you empathetic, and a strong gut gives you intuition and the courage to follow it.

Thousands of years ago, Confucius said, "Life is really simple, but we insist on making it complicated." It is true that we live in a very complicated world. As designers, we must avoid making things even more so. Richard Buchanan said "It is not about making things simple or complex, it is more about making things clear." I totally agree. When we designers deal with complex problems, we need to focus on making our design meaningful and valuable. Only when our designs have a positive impact can we say with confidence that our designs are making things happen.

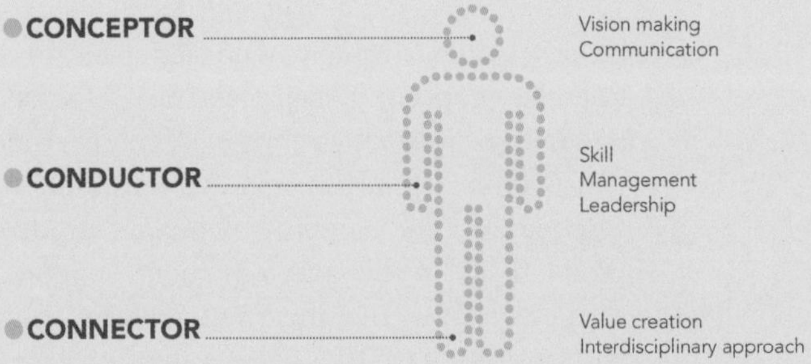

Figure 5 The good designer. Copyright © 2017 Sooshin Choi.

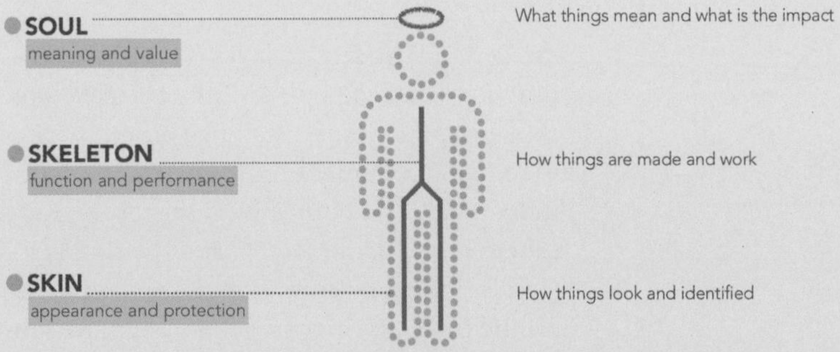

Figure 6 The soul, skeleton, and skin of a good design. Copyright © 2017 Sooshin Choi.

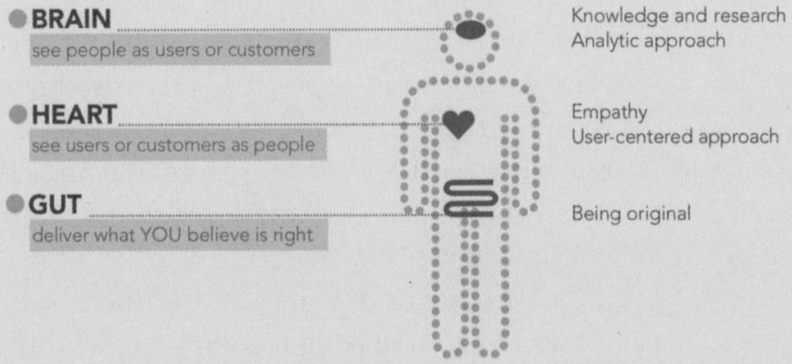

Figure 7 The brain, heart, and gut of a good designer. Copyright © 2017 Sooshin Choi.

The Ethics of Ignoring Rashomon: All Choices Involve Ethics—Simplification Is No Exception

Michael Lissack

Institute for the Study of Coherence and Emergence (ISCE), USA

Our personal ethics are the sum of the processes we evoke while making choices. When we attempt to simplify what we are dealing with, we do so by making a series of choices. Those choices tend to take the form of a *black box*, where only inputs and outputs are observable and the mechanisms and processes which link input and output are hidden from view. It is imperative that we attempt to articulate the ethics of those very choices. Simplification rests upon one's ability to shift explicit representations of meaning onto situationally- and environmentally-cued exformations—meaning is derived from a decoding of the cued and attended-to signal. Such *offloading* represents yet another set of choices, whose ethics again need to be made observable. The key to rendering simplification mechanisms observable is making explicit note of the four *shareds* upon which successful simplification depends—shared context, shared boundaries/constraints, shared history, and a shared sense of what an *explanation* is. By questioning the degree to which each of the four shareds is present, and asking how that could be changed, it becomes possible to render simplification mechanisms transparent enough for ethical inquiry. Simplification is NOT just a design choice. It is a series of ethical choices highly revelatory of the values and beliefs of the simplifying designer.

Michael Lissack is the executive director of the Institute for the Study of Coherence and Emergence (ISCE), President of the American Society for Cybernetics (ASC), the ISCE Professor of Meaning in Organizations, Visiting Professor of Design and Innovation at Tongji University (Shanghai), a Visiting Fellow at the Hull University Business School, an Affiliate Member of the Center for Philosophy & History of Science at Boston University, and a serial entrepreneur. He was the first Walter J. Hickel Professor at Alaska Pacific University. He founded both a non-profit research institute and a charity for artists, launched an international Ph.D. program in corporate anthropology, has written half-dozen books, been a successful Wall Street banker, and a candidate for public office. *Worth* Magazine recognized Dr. Lissack as one of "Wall Street's 25 Smartest Players" in 1999 and as one of the 100 Americans who have most influenced "how we think about money" in 2001. His most recent invention—an Internet research reference librarian replacement can be found at http://epi-search.com. His most recent academic work can be found at http://remedy101.com.

Introduction

Few scientific papers—and even fewer in the social sciences—begin by acknowledging the limitations placed upon us as humans. We speak and write as if we have access to much more of the world than we really do. Since this is a paper about ethics, it is essential to begin by recognizing the limitations and their consequences.

Humans have limited cognitive capabilities. We cannot process the complex, interwoven, infinite string of things that make up whatever it is that reality might be. At best, we can hold five to nine ideas in our minds simultaneously. Most of us have lots of trouble with the idea that what matters may be one or two steps removed from what we are observing. We know we are limited in this way—but we ignore it.

We tend to speak as if we have access to something called "the truth." The point above limits whatever access we have, however. We cannot process the whole truth. We can only process bits and pieces. The truth we are so sure we have access to is a narrative created by our minds to render the world somewhat coherent. Our mind's goal is coherence—not truth

For every situation we find ourselves in, we pick out some aspects of what we are dealing with or encountering and, using those three to nine data points, we tell ourselves a story. We then refine that story so that it fits into our current understanding of the world—an understanding which itself is the result of the years of prior story telling gone before and our immediate perception of the situation or context we find ourselves in. Our story of coherence is built upon those data points, but we will tell the story as if it is based upon some revealed truth.

In order to avoid exhaustion, we also rely on our prior stories to explain current situations. If one or more of our chosen data points lines u with a previously told narrative, it requires a lot less energy to just go with the existing story rather than try to tell a new one. (Which, by the way, is why it is so much easier just to tell the truth—there is no need to either come up with a new story or remember what story you may have told previously.) We allow these chosen data points to trigger some meaning in ou heads, and we then rely on the triggered meaning, unless or until the prior narrative fails to render the present situation coherent.

Figure 1 The "same" object triggers differing interpretations. Copyright © 2017 Michael Lissack.

Throughout this process, we ignore the simple fact that we are choosing which of the infinite data points and observations available to us to pay attention to. This fact needs repeating. *We choose what we pay attentio to, and then we weave our narrative aroun those choices*. Different people encountering the very same situation are high likely to make different choices of data points.(Figure 1)

The ethical questions which follow stem from that very observation. Akira Kurosawa's 1950 film classic *Rashomon* (Figure 2) was about how a single incident could support multiple truths. The *Rashomon effect* is "a term used to describe the circumstance when the same event is given contradictory interpretations by different individuals involved."[1]

The Rashomon effect makes our efforts to simplify questionable. When simplicity works, it can be a very powerful tool. In 1862, while on vacation, Victor Hugo wanted to know how his novel *Les Misérables* was selling. He sent a one character telegram to his publisher—"?." The publisher replied with a single character, "!," telling Hugo of its success. This was simplification at its best. A single character conveyed all the information needed to each of the two participants.

Many of the millennial generation try this same approach to "communicating" with their peers. Their one-character expressions are called emoji. Emoji can have many meanings—a concept which most of their users overlook. Instead, they expect the same results as Hugo and his publisher. Sometimes, when the communication is only within a small tight knot circle, they are pleased. Oftentimes when they include someone who is just a bit outside the circle, they are embarrassed. The curse of ambiguity strikes their single character "communication." The ghost of multiple meanings appears. And, simplicity is lost.

When we simplify we are asking others to accept our interpretation of the world. Is that an ethical request?

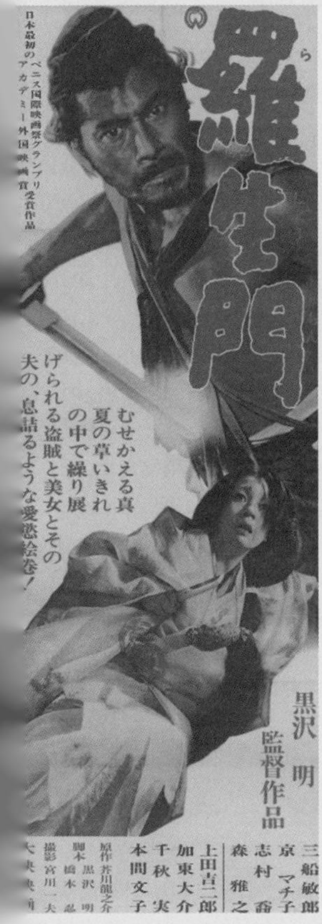

gure 2 The poster of *Rashomon*, directed Akira Kurosawa, released 1950. Source: ikipedia, https://en.wikipedia.org/wiki/ shomon.

Simplification

Simplification is our shortcut to coherence so things make sense and we know what to do. Simplicity is also a great equalizer—the simpler something appears to be, we believe that more people can both do and understand it. However, the shorthand assumptions such simplification is based on may describe a belief system that others do not hold. Simplification leads to a conflation of labels and the things so labeled—such that we overlook the subtleties and nuances that give the actual things significance. Some of this problem stems from our reliance on computers and our use of the *mind as computer* model to govern how we think and learn—as evidenced by our use of keywords, sound bites, texting, and Twitter. It is exacerbated by society's tendency toward dis-intermediation and a lack of curation.

Books and articles about simplicity have tended to be about the virtues of ever more simplification and/or attempts to describe how one goes about simplifying. Simplicity and simplification are posed as the solution to information overload and complexity. When we perceive the world as coherent, we just get on with things. When our perception of coherence is shattered, things no longer make sense and we do not know how to act. We ask questions, and worry about our inability to find answers. We may

1 "Rashomon effect," *Wikipedia*, last modified July 24, 2017, https://en.wikipedia.org/wiki/Rashomon_effect.

react to our loss of assurance with a loss of self-confidence, and we may retreat to "the way it was" or address the new situation by simplifying it.

Simplification usually involves five choices.

1. Decide that some distinctions about the item, situation, or thing in need of simplifying are important and others are not.
2. Discard information that fails to convey meaning when viewed through the filter of those "important distinctions."
3. Look for representations or other signals (which can be words, pictures, anecdotes, movements, etc.) as icons for each important distinction.
4. Choose a set of representations to use.
5. Substitute the chosen representations wherever possible.

This process can be summarized as a shift from explicit elucidation to a reliance upon contextually dependent cues—what Nørretranders[2] termed "exformation." Exformation is meaning which is "offloaded" into the environment or the context in a manner that is capable of then being called back when needed.

The risks we face in relying on simplicity are many. Emergence—the encounter with the new—eventually overwhelms any complexity reduction including simplifications in the form of labels, categories, frameworks, and models. By acting based on simplifications, we rely on models lacking in degrees of freedom, and we are unable to perceive, account for, or attend to adjacent possibles and useful affordances. Such models are usually fragile rather than resilient. This reduces to our ability to cope with change, prosper with emergence, and innovate.

Our goals for simplicity and simplification are *lossness* and *robustness*. Lossness—the opposite of *lossiness*—is the idea that the essential meaning, the essence of the whole in all its details, remains preserved when simplification occurs. To the extent that essence is lost in the process of simplification, the resulting representation is considered to be lossy. Holograms, for example, are mostly lossless.[3] Lossiness is to be avoided. Lossness is the goal. But lossness has no value if the representation is not also robust. We simplify to render the essence easier to use, implement, embody, or manipulate. To the extent that the simplified representation is so highly situationally dependent that it becomes lossy as context changes, it offers little robustness. Taleb would call it "fragile."[4] Such fragility is also to be avoided.

In truth, the lossness, robustness, lossiness, and fragility of any simplification will be context dependent. How dependent will vary. What is considered as the context will vary. In that context dependence lies many of simplicity's ethical questions.

The most important observation about simplification is to acknowledge that we can choose to recognize and deal with the multiplicities of meaning in any ambiguity, or to deny the alternatives. We can embrace Rashomon or deny him. We can also deliberately choose to incorporate

2 Tor Nørretranders, *The User Illusion: Cutting Consciousness Down to Size* (New York: Viking, 1998).

3 The concept has its origins in data compression. When you compress a picture from a RAW file to a GIF, for example, you attempt to use a method which minimizes lossiness.

4 Nassim N. Taleb, *Antifragile: Things that Gain from Disorder* (New York: Random House, 2012).

ambiguity when we want others assume their own meaning in a situation. The choice of how we declare and assign meaning is one each of us consistently makes—though we are often as oblivious to the process we employ as to the notion of choice itself.

In making choices for simplification we are, in effect, designing the reality with which we cope. We each have cognitive limits, and cannot process all the information that is present in the world around us. We must choose what to pay attention to, what to allocate energy and effort to, and what to ultimately deal with. We call the result of these choices reality, but that reality is only a subset of the swirl of items, information, people, and environments around us. In making these choices without sufficient deliberation, our trade-off allocations may not attune well to those made by others on which our actions depend. And when that happens, simplifications fail.

The key takeaway here, however, is that of choice. Simplification is a process of choice. All processes of choice involve ethics. Ethics is focused on a few key concepts. The first is respect—the idea that others should be seen as if they will be dealt with repeatedly and not just as a one-time transaction. The second is the ubiquity of choice—we are always making choices, and ethics is the study of how and why we do so. The third is humility—we know less than we think, especially about the context, history, sense of boundaries and constraints, and sense of what constitutes an explanation (what I write about as *the four shareds*) which go into how others will process the choices we make. And finally, there is the importance of questions over answers. Ethics is about asking questions and having the integrity to reflexively ask them again and again as we revisit choice out of respect and humility.

And so to the ethics of simplicity we turn.

Hidden Assumptions

Our minds dislike ambiguity and doubt. Instead, we have an ingrained desire to construct coherent narratives, which leads us to seek confirming evidence while disregarding information that refutes our prior view—a problem known as confirmation bias. What results is a confidence in our understanding that is greater than the circumstances warrant, and a further confidence in the simplifications we have chosen on which we then base our actions. As Nobel Prize winning economist Daniel Kahneman tells us, "We are ruined by our own biases. When making decisions, we see what we want, ignore probabilities, and minimize risks that uproot our hopes."[5] When we simplify, we allow our biases to help determine the very reality we are creating.

Much of the time any two of us may see the same situation differently **(see Figure 3)**.

Regardless, we then use the same words to mean different things **(see Figure 4)**.

5 From Daniel Kahneman, *Thinking Fast and Slow* (New York: Macmillan, 2011), as quoted in Dennis Berman, "So What's Your Algorithm?" *Wall Street Journal*, January 4, 2012, accessed June 18, 2016, http://www.wsj.com/articles/SB10001424052970203462304577138961342097348.

Figure 3 (L) Two of us may see the same situation differently. Copyright © 2017 Michael Lissack.

Figure 4 (R) We talk as if we are talking. Copyright © 2016 Michael Lissack.

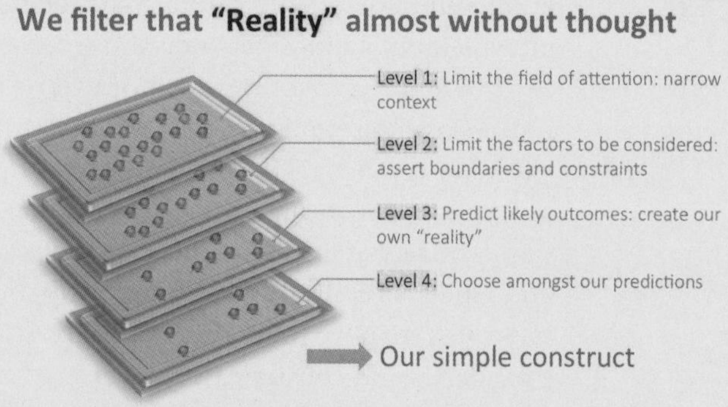

Figure 5 We filter "reality" almost without thought. Copyright © 2016 Michael Lissack.

Figure 6 Simple construct becomes the story we tell. Copyright © 2017 Michael Lissack.

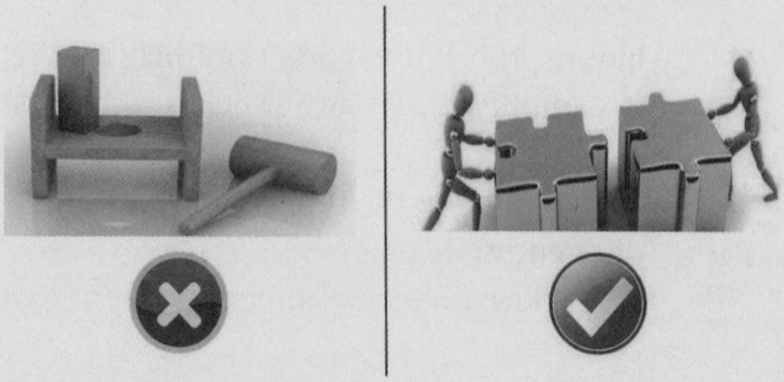

Figure 7 We test that story for coherence. Copyright © 2017 Michael Lissack.

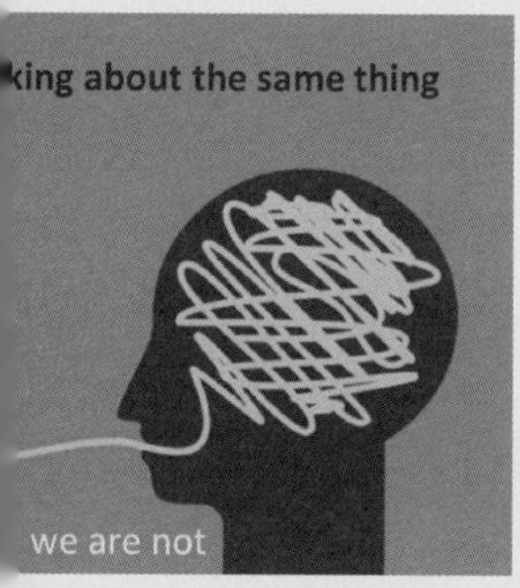

And yet we wonder why our meaning gets lost. The process, all too often, resembles a black box. There is input (the world) and there is output (the simple). We are unaware of the process in between—through either obliviousness or deliberate ignorance. Ethical considerations demand that the black box of simplification be opened to examination. We pick and choose what observations and data points to pay attention to.(Figure 5)

To express that the world, a situation, or a person is "x," we filter the reality that we see. First, we limit our field of attention. We narrow the context of what it is we are dealing with. Then, we limit the factors to be considered. We assert a set of boundaries and constraints. Then, we predict likely outcomes given the boundaries and constraints that we just imposed. In effect, at this point, we have constructed multiple realities in our heads. Finally, we pick among those multiple realities. By choosing from among our predictions, we have taken the complex, complicated reality that we first encountered and turned it into a simple construct. We create a story around those CHOSEN points **(see Figure 6)**.

We test that story for coherence **(see Figure 7)**.

What this means is that the ONLY way to get past the discord and dissonance is for each side to ask lots of questions about which data points everyone is using to compose the narrative around—and to acknowledge that the other side is using different data points. But, that would mean giving up the privilege that is asserted from falsely claiming that one's personal narrative is the truth. Instead, there is the complete nonsense of each side insisting that the other side's narrative is based on lies and distortions.

But notice that fourth step—we CHOOSE what we will pay attention to and to believe. We make that choice based upon our prior history, contexts, and beliefs, and also on our present surroundings, context, and situation.

Our choices of how to simplify are based upon what I call the *four shareds*:

1. shared context;
2. shared boundaries/constraints;
3. shared history; and
4. a shared sense of what an *explanation* is.

Shared Context

When we share context with another, we are capable of referring to that context directly or indirectly. Bourdieu called this kind of context our "habitus,"[6] while Husserl referred to it as the basis for the "Fundierung relation."[7] Shared perceptions of the environment or situation allow for mutuality in representation and reference. If we share a habitus, we share an understanding of some set of repeatable practices, such as waiting for the bus at the bus stop, walking the aisles at a grocery store, or interacting with the desktop metaphor on our PC. Our understanding of the repeatable practice fades into the background such that we pay little attention to it, and

Pierre Bourdieu, *The Logic of Practice*, trans. Richard Nice (California: Stanford University Press, 1990), 53.

Edmund Husserl, *Ideas Pertaining to a Pure Phenomenology and to a Phenomenological Philosophy—First Book: General Introduction to a Pure Phenomenology*, trans. F. Kersten (Hingham, MA: Martinus Nijhoff Publishers, 1982).

instead we pay attention to purposive goal that the exercise of that practice allows us to accomplish.

We walk to the bus stop, have idle conversation along the way, and perhaps get annoyed at waiting for the bus. More often than not we describe this as "going to work." The quality of our walk along Spring Street, its sights, smells, and people are background—unless or until something out of the ordinary is encountered. The same holds for our walk up and down the aisles of the grocery store. We are not noticing the art and colors created by the merchant's displays—whether purposive or inadvertent. We are not noticing the smells of coffee and cheese—again unless unexpected, as a chlorine fish odor might be. We ignore the idle chatter of the ladies we pass in the aisles—with an exception for the one who asked for help in picking a ripe melon.

That which we ignore is what Bourdieu called the habitus—the embodiment of the deeply ingrained habits, skills, and dispositions that we possess due to our life experiences. Habitus, Bourdieu often noted, is so ingrained that people often mistook its *feel* as natural instead of culturally developed. By labeling one's reaction and interaction to the habitus as natural, one can justify ignoring both the conditions which produce and maintain it and one's own role in choosing to be part of that environ and part of those interactions. But, note, we choose to so ignore. The very expression "stop to smell the roses" is a commonplace reminder that we have the ability to make other choices.

Our brains are designed—or have evolved—such that we tend to take the familiar for granted and pay far greater attention to the new or the unexpected. This taken-for-granted-ness is the key idea behind Husserl's Fundierung—the foundation upon which we act or proceed. We seldom pa attention to most of the qualities of the pen with which we write—instead we pay attention to our writing. We mostly share the Fundierung of the per The exceptions are the calligrapher whose focus is on the act of writing, not on the content of what is written—and each of us whenever the pen breaks

When habitus and Fundierung are shared, it is far easier to offload meaning into the environment. Cues will be perceived as coming from the same place. More importantly, that which is to be labeled as different will be recognized as different by those who share the context, habitus, and Fundierung. Shared context becomes a means by which insiders can be identified and outsiders excluded. Such inclusions and exclusions need not be done in a purposive manner. They, too, may be byproducts of the Fundierung behind other choices.

But, there are serious ethical questions that lie beneath the surface. I simplicity and simplification are relying upon shared context, habitus, and fundierung, then they may also be implicitly relying upon hidden definitions of *insider* and *outsider*. When corporate recruiters limit their attention to a small group of colleges, that simplification effectuates choices about insiders and outsiders. When marketers or policy makers simplify their targ by picking labeled groups, implicit in those labels are choices about insiders and outsiders.

It is the implicitness of these choices, the Fundierung of the process by which they get made, which needs to be brought to the surface. Fundierung is about that which is taken for granted and ignored. Choices to include and exclude are being implicitly made when we simplify to the extent that our simplification is itself relying upon shared context, habitus, or Fundierung.

Shared Boundaries/Constraints

Unlike habitus and Fundierung, our notions of boundaries and constraints tend to be articulable. We may have an implicit sense of what a constraint is or where a boundary lies, but when called upon we usually are very capable of expressing the existence of that same boundary or constraint. To the extent that we are unsure of exact location, definition, or condition, we tend to react to that lack of certainty by choosing to stay a safe distance away. Others with whom we are interacting will both likely be exhibiting similar behavior and implicitly observing how we are interacting with the boundary or constraint.

Whether we (or they) are accepting of the boundaries and constraints will be partially determined by our sense of how "appropriate" we perceive them to be—for the situation and for ourselves. Appropriateness is measured by the notion of coherence—how well story, self, representations, and situation fit together into a sense of being one. In the absence of sufficient coherence, dissonance takes over. Such sufficiency demands a "requisite variety"[8]—the notion that we need sufficient ambiguity and degrees of freedom to support adjacent possibilities for action. Appropriateness allows us to recognize that boundaries and constraints are not only limitations but may also function as enablers.

Simplification primarily relies on shared boundaries and constraints in three ways.

1. When the boundaries and constraints are explicit, they need not be otherwise articulated—we instead rely on shared context to tell us how to behave inside or outside of the boundary or constraint. We could not make our way through life if we were continually being told what set of rules or behaviors did not apply because we were on one side or the other of a boundary, the information overload would be crippling. Making a boundary or constraint explicit and obvious is thus one way to simplify. The more obvious and explicit the greater the shared sense of what or where the boundary or constraint is.
2. When the boundaries and constraints are implicit, hidden, or unsure, we will usually attempt to remain a safe distance from them. To the extent that we desire to induce others to stay that safe distance, we will both obfuscate the boundary or constraint and make obvious a significant penalty for violation.

8 W. Ross Ashby, "Requisite Variety and Its Implications for the Control of Complex Systems," in *International Federation for Systems Research International Series on System Science and Engineering*, Vol. 7, ed. George E. Mobus (New York: Springer, 1991), 405–17.

3. Alternatively, when the boundaries and constraints are implicit, hidden, or unsure, some of us at particular times will attempt to probe or challenge what we believe to be the boundary or constraint. Such challenges can vary with respect to how public or private they may be. Battles over boundary and constraint definitions are themselves simplifications of battles regarding the inclusionary or exclusionary effects of implicit reliance on habitus. Thus, the greater the publicness of the battle, the greater the stakes at least one of the protagonists perceives.

The third case happens far more often than we like to believe. At the societal level, and with rather high stakes, boundary issues are raised whenever the slogan "Black Lives Matter" is evoked. One's actual acceptance of the slogan—without the immediate articulation of some form of "don't all lives matter?"—depends upon shared context and habitus, but the slogan's acceptance has become an implicit boundary. The fighting over that boundary takes place at multiple levels—content, symbolism, evocation of history, perceived ritualistic indications of respect, and group identity.

Simplification is assisted to the extent that boundaries or constraints are shared and articulable in common amongst the relevant stakeholders. Ethical issues arise both in the definition of such boundaries and constraints and in the degree of explicitness asserted to be held by stakeholders.

Shared History

"All historical narratives contain an irreducible and inexpungible element of interpretation. The historian has to interpret his materials in order to construct the moving pattern of images in which the form of the historical process is to be mirrored. And this because the historical record is both too lull and too sparse. On the one hand, there are always more facts in the record than the historian can possibly include in his narrative representation of a given segment of the historical process. And so, the historian must interpret his data by excluding certain facts from his account as irrelevant to his narrative purpose. On the other hand, in his efforts to reconstruct what happened in any given period of history, the historian inevitably must include in his narrative an account of some event or complex of events for which the facts that would permit a plausible explanation of its occurrence are lacking. And this means that the historian must interpret his materials by filling in the gaps in his information on inferential or speculative grounds. A historical narrative is thus necessarily a mixture of adequately and inadequately explained events, a congeries of established and inferred facts, at once a representation that is an interpretation and an interpretation that passes for an explanation of the whole process mirrored in the narrative."[9]

9 Hayden White, "Interpretation in History," *New Literary History* 4, no. 2 (1973): 281.

Shared history matters in any process of simplification, because the history possessed and attended to by the interpreter of symbols, labels, representations, and exformational cues has a huge influence on the meaning that that interpreter perceives. White, above, tells us that all of history is a product of interpretation. The obverse is also true—all interpretations are a product of history. Interpretations are not a product of History with a capital H, but instead of the personal and attended to at that moment history of each individual interpreter. The greater the history that is shared in common, the greater the likelihood of similar interpretation.

> "Meaning is given by sets of objects and associations that are invoked when a term is used. Membership of these sets can change....
> In everyday life, words and phrases often emerge from concrete situations in which participants jointly work out ways of describing what is going on. New terms, symbols, or images are situated—they acquire meaning through collective use in real situations."[10]

10 D. C. Gooding and T. R. Addis, "Modelling Experiments as Mediating Models," *Foundations of Science* 13, no. 1 (2008): 20.

The ethical questions here revolve around the idea that what matters are the elements of shared history that are attended to at the moment of interpretation. Because it is attended to history matters, if one can manipulate what is attended to, one can manipulate interpretation. Truth and facts are not what matter. Instead, coherence with pre-existing beliefs and "truthiness" are far more important.

Stephen Colbert coined the term "truthiness" in 2005. Of it, he says "Truthiness is 'What I say is right, and [nothing] anyone else says could possibly be true.' It's not only that I *feel* it to be true, but that *I* feel it to be true.... Truthiness (noun)—the belief in what you feel to be true rather than what the facts will support."[11] More generally, truthiness is defined as the state of intuitive truth without regard for logic, evidence, information, or facts. It is an instinctive truth that is felt deep down in the gut. Truthiness encapsulates how we often make decisions—beginning with a gut feeling and then backtracking, if pushed, to justify the conclusion.

11 Nathan Rabin, "Interview: Stephen Colbert," *A.V. Club*, last modified January 25, 2006, http://www.avclub.com/article/stephen-colbert-13970.

Truthiness is a large determinant of whether attended to history enters into an interpreter's interpretation. While logic and rationality may argue that only if one has well-earned confidence in one's descriptors does it make sense to use them to analyze a situation, truthiness relies on confidence alone. There is no screening for what has been well earned. Metaphors and analogies may be fascinating and tantalizing; objectively, they are very uncertain and questionable. But, metaphors and analogies are simple and lend themselves to truthiness. It used to be—especially amongst academics and journalists—that if one wanted to model or label a situation, one needed to be sure of the definitions, identities, and terms of use one was making use of. In theory, we were all taught to do this at school. Yet, no such epistemic care appears to be the norm any longer. Labels are all too quickly assumed to be accurate depictions of reality. Truthiness wins.

To the extent that we share history, and have that shared history called to our attention, the greater the likelihood that we will accept simplifications in the form of asserted truthiness. "Make the lie big, make it simple, keep saying it, and eventually they will believe it."[12] Thus, the selective telling and retelling of "facts" becomes part of the attended to history that we will recall and make use of in interpretation. Which facts, and how they are told, needs to be looked at as an ethical question and not just taken for granted. If a protagonist is capable of telling what Gould called "canonical stories,"[13] bringing into play "just enough" shared history and truthiness, such a simplification will likely have great power.

> "The organizing power of canonical stories leads us to ignore important facts readily within our potential sight, and to twist or misread the information that we do manage to record. In other words … canonical stories predictably 'drive' facts into definite and distorted pathways that validate the outlines and necessary components of these archetypal tales. We therefore fail to note important items in plain sight, while we misread other facts by forcing them into preset mental channels…."[14]

12 This quotation is usually attributed to Adolf Hitler.

13 Stephen J. Gould, *Triumph and Tragedy in Mudville: A Lifelong Passion for Baseball* (New York: W. W. Norton, 2010), 219–42.

14 Ibid., 222–23.

A Shared Sense of What Constitutes an Explanation

Simplifications only work if they are accepted and used. When they are challenged, they need to be able to withstand the questioning of how, why, and whether these things really matter. To the extent that the challenge is being evaluated by people with similar understandings of what constitutes an explanation, the greater the likelihood that the challenge—with its questions and answers—will be interpreted in a similar manner. But, there are multiple perspectives about what it is that constitutes a good or an adequate explanation.

An analogy may be helpful. There are two ways of learning accounting as a professional field. The traditional approach asserts that the purpose of accounting is to present an accurate snapshot of an organization and its activities through a set of numbers developed via a commonly agreed-upon rule set. This approach asserts that accuracy is the most important criteria with which to judge the accountant's work. A second approach asserts, instead, that the purpose of accounting is to capture a rough, fuzzy Polaroid of the organization and its activity. The goal of the out-of-focus picture is to generate questions, and it is the narrative formed by seeking answers to those questions that is the accountant's goal. Creating the context for the generation of good questions becomes the criteria with which to judge the accountant's work. The traditional evaluation of an explanation as being rooted in provable facts and based on appeals to truth is thus like first kind of accounting. But, if coherence with self-identity and canonical stories is the criterion, then explanations in the pursuit of truthiness can be judged to be more like the second kind.

The truthiness standard for explanation starts from the premise that the goal of simplicity is to construct models, labels, or representations that allow the observers and users thereof to better attune to context, such that they or other observers and users may make use of that model, label, or representation as a guide to next actions. In this view, simplicity is successful when it reveals or calls greater attention to affordances, both good or bad, that were previously—in other words, before application of the simplistic model, label, or representation—unrecognized by the observer, or whose salience was understated. Simplifications fail when they call attention to false affordances—false because, when contextually embedded, the possibility for action is non-existent or infeasible—or overstates the salience of affordances due to the imposition of overly-restrictive boundary conditions or constraints within the context of the situation.

Friedman argued that, in economics, if a model works then we should regard it as "truth."[15] In life, such models often take the form of labels—mere words. Vygotsky noted that the use of such words can be reality changing.[16] Or, as he explains, "It is not merely the content of a word that changes, but the way in which reality is generalized and reflected in a word."[17] And later, according to Hawking and Mlodinow, "The only meaningful thing is the usefulness of the model.... When such a model is successful at explaining events, we tend to attribute to it, and to the elements and concepts that constitute it, the quality of reality or absolute truth."[18]

If there is a disagreement about what constitutes a good explanation, then challenges to simplification will be met with acceptance by some and virulent disagreement by others. Truth has a hard time displacing truthiness—until or unless some physical, real-world entities supervene, and even then the explanations offered for what happened will differ wildly.

The Power of Diverse Opinions

Thousands of CEOs and other business executives test these simplification principles through the mechanism of a peer-to-peer advisory group. This is a group of 12–20 executives who meet regularly for the very purpose of encountering the perspectives of the others. The members of these groups use the Rashomon effect to full advantage, hoping to gain new insights into their own situations and issues. Peer to peer groups work because they embody the following tenets (captured from my own peer-to-peer group):

- The members recognize that most of the time we, and others, operate by the principle of least action—we minimize the effort needed to satisfice our goal. In other words, we find it easier to rely on the initial stories we tell ourselves rather than make the effort to compose new ones. Unless we are made aware of the limitations which our original stories impose upon us, we will not recognize the (high energy) price of staying with the original stories.
- Our understanding will always be based, in part, on the present context as we encounter it.[19] The more insight and self-limitation that becomes evident to us through the group dialogue, the greater

15 Milton Friedman, "The Methodology of Positive Economics," in *Essays in Positive Economics* (Chicago: The University of Chicago Press, 1953), 3–43.

16 Lev S. Vygotsky, *Thought and Language* (Cambridge, MA: MIT Press, 1962), 227.

17 Ibid.

18 Stephen Hawking and Leonard Mlodinow, *The Grand Design* (New York: Bantam Books, 2010), 7.

19 We should note that, by definition, abstract definitions and arbitrary labels are meant to be context free.

the opportunity for us to choose a different context. Because we can only pay attention to a limited number of data points, those we pay attention to will determine our context—context always matters.

- In order to simplify any context we are dealing with, we tend to hide processes that allow inputs to become outputs and treat them as a black box. We can create more possibilities if we recognize when a black box is being used and ask questions in an effort to reveal—at least partially—those hidden processes. The key strength of the group dialogue is found in the questions fellow members ask as they attempt to understand.
- Because the receiver determines meaning, and not the sender, the give-and-take of dialogue allows for the mutual development of reflective understanding. This requires that (1) the sender work very hard to take into account how the receiver may interpret, and (2) the receiver distinguish between a triggered meaning in the self and a meaning that emerges from a process of dialogue. The mutual understandings that surface become the foundation for the next possibility.
- Possibilities are limited by affordances—in other words, only those possibilities that are immediately adjacent (available) to a current situation are capable being enacted. Choices become available as possibilities only when we recognize them as such—an unattended-to choice is incapable of being acted upon. Another contribution of the group process is surfacing adjacent and available possible actions. We should not confuse goals and intentions with adjacent and available actions.
- Collectively, the group serves as a reflective sounding board for each of its members. The reflective part comes from the insight each member gains while discussing issues raised by others. When raising one's own issues, the group process changes how members listen to themselves, which opens a productive opportunity for self-reflection
- Successful group processes become a part of each member's day-to-day interaction with all of their significant others—professionally, personally, and in his or her community. As lessons regarding questions to be asked, openness to the perspectives of others, and recognition of self-imposed limitations are reflexively recognized and then shared, each member is able to help these others grow.
- Peer-to-peer groups thus help members act so as to maximize the choices available to them. The reiteration of this process over many situations creates an opportunity for members to abstract guiding principles from lessons learned.

Implications

Ambiguity is ever present in our world, but all too often we choose to ignore it. We assert the simple in lieu of the complex, the direct in lieu of the nuanced or the subtle, the label or category in lieu of recognizing the portfolio of choices that label/category represents. How we choose to deal with ambiguity is just that—a choice. Often, we opt for simplification. But—and this is a vitally important but—many times that simplification is inappropriate for the situation and leads to negative outcomes. It is a pattern we cannot seem to break. We do not go through life overwhelmed by the apparent complexity continually confronting us. Instead, we make choices about what to deal with, what to see, and what questions to ask. We choose to assert the simple over the complex. And then, we act.

But we have an alternative. We can embrace Rashomon. We can be like the executives in their peer-to-peer groups and seek out alternative perspectives. We can ask questions instead of demanding adherence to some pre-chosen given.

To ignore multiple meanings and ignore context is to assume a stasis to the world that seldom exists. Such a stasis assumes that opportunities are predictable, context is controllable, and emergence is non-existent. The world of practicing managers does not match these oversimplifications. Prediction, at best, is only possible in the short term. Boundaries are always shifting. Team composition, temporary organization, and company, industry, or competitive environment is rarely predictable—in the long term, at least. Identities are unclear. The trade-off between outcome and process does not favor one over the other. In the world we live in, emergence is pervasive, context is seldom controllable, ecologies are emergent, and few affordances are predictable. Situation and context play key roles. In the complex world of today, continuity is but a fragile, temporary, and illusionary notion—the assumption of predictability does not hold.

In 1963, Heisenberg told us "The world is not divided into different groups of objects but rather into different groups of relationships.... The world thus appears as a complicated tissue of events, in which connections of different kinds alternate or overlap or combine and thereby determine the texture of the whole."[20] Simplification pretends to be a means of representing that texture. And, when the four shareds are present, it works. But, to the extent that the four shareds are missing, simplification sets us up for error.

[20] Werner Heisenberg, *Physics and Philosophy: The Revolution in Modern Science* (London: Allen and Unwin, 1963), 107.

We act based on the simplifications we choose regardless of appropriateness. But, as when PT Barnum posted signs proclaiming "This way to the Egress," those who take a shortcut are all too often sorely disappointed. Keywords, emojis, and sound bites are no substitute for careful curation. Labels and categories are no substitute for the fact checking and verification of a trusted intermediary. A sixty thousand-word novel is the equivalent of three thousand tweets. The novel has a title—the tweets do not. The novel has a coherent structure and an ending (or so we hope). The tweets do not. But many of you would nonetheless pay far more attention to the 3,000 tweets.

Part of the problem here is that keywords, categorizations, and labels make it all too easy to express something in a sound bite, text, or tweet. To those in the know, that something may have defined meaning. For others, there are few cues on which meaning can be constructed. The substance of a tweet equaling one hundred and forty characters is, at most, twenty to twenty-five words, or a ten-second sound bite. Those ten seconds are the cue to the other part of the problem. As more and more of our supposed conversations occur in sound bites, texts, and tweets, our attention span draws shorter and shorter—approaching that same ten-second mark. It is the rare member of Generation Z and beyond who will happily spend hours reading a book. Those same Gen Zers will spend time on an activity—rollerblading, working out, shopping—but engaging in deep thought seldom counts.

The old solution for much of this part of the problem was to rely on intermediaries and curators to do a preliminary sort of the information for us. Fifty years ago, we watched the network news, listened to the radio, and read newspapers, magazines, and books. In each of these there was someone—or some few—who acted as a filter. They were our intermediaries, standing between each of us and the raw sources of information. They were our curators, picking and choosing which items they deemed worthy of our attention. Few of us went looking for primary sources of data unless we were doing academic research or were journalists ourselves. Still fewer of us attempted to put primary data out there, in the world, be it via publishing, letters to the editor, or calling in to a talk show. Instead, we came to depend on a set of curators and intermediaries in whom we trusted—for those my age and older, think Walter Cronkite, Warren Buffett, and the Christian Science Monitor; for the younger reader, think Perez Hilton, Suze Orman, or Barbara Walters. If they thought we should be aware of something, we at least gave it some attention.

Flash forward to today. An ill-timed tweet or Instagram post can circulate to millions in the blink of an eye before any of it is vetted, or any of it is fact checked—often before any of it is reflected upon by its author. It's all just a click away—send, post, tweet, publish. Every day, people share more than ten billion pieces of content on Facebook. Every day, on Twitter five hundred million tweets are tweeted. It is all un-curated and dis-intermediated. It is just raw data—screaming to be simplified and made cogent, at almost any price—all we have to do is simply google it.

Because we have lost the trusted curators and intermediaries who used to sort through information for us, we are stuck doing it for ourselves And we are not very good at it. We mistake popularity for accuracy, and credit ignorant crowds with a wisdom reserved to only the most learned master craftsman. We all know how to look up "cognitive bias" on the Internet but few of us are willing to take the steps required to overcome them.

Instead, we simplify, and rely on our simplifications. The act and processes of simplification have become engrained in our personal habitus. Simplification is the Fundierung that underlies our ability to label and categorize. We do it without much thought. We also do it without reflexively acknowledging that each such choice carries with it a whole host of ethical questions.

The ethical questions affect not only others but also ourselves. By making assumptions (and in so doing restricting ourselves to a set of labels and a model) we predetermine what might be learned, which will limit the options that appear to be open to us. This is because by adopting a particular perspective, and therefore making assumptions consistent with that perspective, we limit what we can see. The perspective acts as a lens that only allows particular features to come into focus—all other features are lost or assumed not to be relevant. Furthermore, in communicating with others, by making use of a particular viewpoint we limit our and their ability to see what is relevant.

We need to embrace Rashomon. Each of us grew up and matured under different circumstances, with different influences, made different efforts, and achieved different results. We each have our own frames for interpreting situations. What we have in common is that we all strive to make sense out of what we encounter—each from our own frame.

If we can learn to give up our claims to know the truth, and instead learn to ask the others to explain what their truth is based on...

If we can learn to explore the factors that go into our assigning something to a category and a label, instead of demanding that others agree with our chosen labeling...

If we can accept that each of us believes that our truth is the truth...
we might find a way to dialogue about our problems and actually act in the common good.

That will demand we accept the lessons of Rashomon. We cannot afford the hubris of self-proclaimed certainty. Rashomon demands that we put the responsibility for interpretation back where it belongs—on ourselves. We choose what interpretations make sense for us. We need to learn to examine those choices, and be willing to discuss the basis on which they were made.

Simplification involves choice. Choices evoke ethics. When your labels, models, or simplifications seem to be working, it may be truthy to ignore the underlying ethical issues. But, the issues remain—and will fester for another day.

Chicken Run: Designing for Complex Food Systems

Clare Brass

Department 22, London, UK

Design is useful to address the complexity of our everyday lives, to unpick and re-think systems that have evolved to be unsustainable and morally questionable, particularly in collaboration with other experts. The poultry industry has evolved to rear fast-growing broilers in the smallest possible area, with low regard for the environment with low regard for the environment, and for the welfare of birds. Chicken Run is a transdisciplinary project that began as a student workshop at the Royal College of Art in 2013. Run with a group of scientists, it explored ways of redesigning the poultry industry with consideration for environmental impact as well as better animal welfare.

Clare Brass, designer, supports the creation of positive social and environmental futures with businesses and young creative talent. She is currently director of Department 22, a London-based educational and training consultancy for the circular economy. She is a skilled business coach, helping young entrepreneurs turn their concepts for sustainable businesses into credible enterprise propositions. Through tutorials and national and international workshops, she helps participants use their creative skills to find circular economy responses to social and environmental issues.

Clare set up and was Head of SustainRCA, a cross-departmental research center for sustainability at the Royal College of Art, inspiring, encouraging and supporting students from across all disciplines at the College to embrace sustainability in their work. She was also Senior Design Tutor in IDE (Innovation Design Engineering), responsible for guiding students in Sustainability and Enterprise, and a mentor for the Ellen MacArthur Foundation. She was formerly Leader of Sustainability at Design Council and founder of SEED Foundation, exploring design-led entrepreneurship.

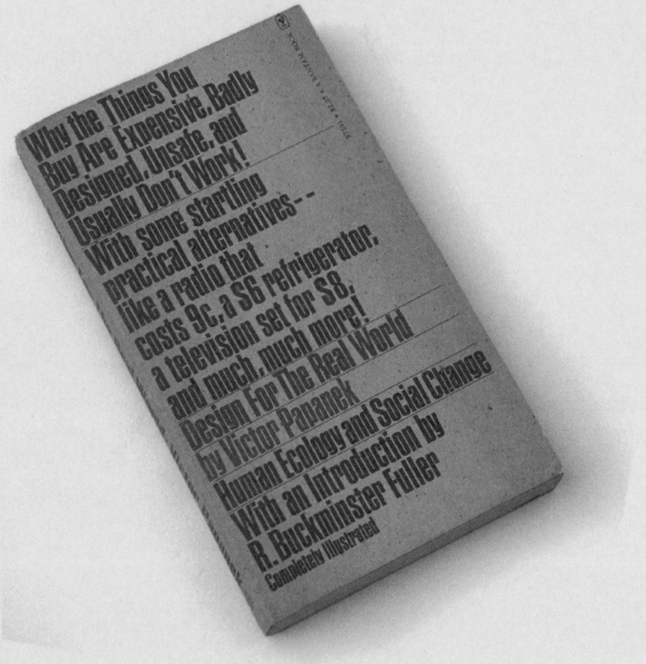

Figure 1 Cover of the first edition of Victor Papanek's book: *Design for the Real World*. Photograph courtesy of Shawn Haze, http://bookworship.com/?p=1017.

Design and Complexity—An Introduction

A complex system can be defined as any system with more than three interacting variables. The real-life systems that organize and facilitate our lives comprise a multitude of interactions between people, social and economic infrastructures, and technology, among many other factors. Behind the scenes of contemporary life, for example, complexity is omnipresent even in our most mundane tasks. Driving a car, buying clothes, working on a computer, and other day to day activities engage us in an unseen network of products, materials, energy, transport, and human labor. Designers have invariably been involved in all of these, and thus have long been accustomed to dealing with complexity, developing some excellent tools and skills to cope with it. Amongst others, these include a focus on people—we carefully forge products and services around the subtleties of unexpressed human needs; systems thinking and mapping—which provides a more comprehensive view of a project's various actors, intermediaries, and stakeholders in context; visualization—which plants the seed for an idea into the heads of managers and consumers; and prototyping—which helps designers and other actors to create designs that suit users' needs as rapidly and accurately as possible.

Until recently, the design profession has been embedded almost exclusively in the economic mechanisms of consumption. Yet our skills are valuable assets when it comes to sustainable design. My interest lies in how designers can use their abilities to break away from their participation in consumerism and bring about positive social and environmental change in other contexts. Food is one such context. The complex networks and supply chains of commercial husbandry and agriculture have resulted in substantial environmental degradation—compromising our health and our future ability to feed the world—plus questionable labor conditions and poor standards of animal welfare.

The idea that design can be applied to creating a better world is not new. In his seminal work *Design for the Real World* (1971),(Figure 1) Victor Papanek suggested that "there are professions more harmful than industrial design, but only a very few of them."[1] Initially widely ridiculed, Papanek's viewpoint was that designers were adept at "persuading people to buy things they don't need, with money they don't have, in order to impress others who don't care."[2] In 2015, Dieter Rams expressed regret at the missed opportunities of his career, and offered a vision for the future role of design. "If I had something to do in this world again, I would not want to be a designer. Because I believe, in the future, it will be less important to have many things and more important to exercise care about where and how we live."[3]

Is it possible to have both? Today we are seeing more and more design courses emerging that encourage designers to take a holistic approach, look for systems solutions rather than product solutions, and encourage designers to look at circular and regenerative systems.

Food—A Complex Issue

Food is more than a necessity—it is a cultural connector with deep traditions, and one of life's great pleasures. It has an enormous impact on our lives economically, socially, and environmentally. Our food systems are the most complex and urgent of all human systems requiring change. But to change them means that people would have to adopt a different world view, one long since forgotten over the last 400 years: our planet is the foundation for our survival. We are a part of nature, and its ways must be respected.

The bigger our cities get, the more removed we become from the source of our food and from the importance of nature. Our contemporary lifestyles have slowly led us to lose the understanding that a healthy ecosystem is essential for our survival.

Around the time of the enlightenment, philosopher Francis Bacon postulated that nature was an abundance that exists to provide man with his needs, to be dominated. The industrial revolution cemented this worldview, one that is now firmly ingrained in the minds of people in industrialized cultures. As Aysar Ghassan says, "the notion that Earth is a vast stockpile of matter waiting to be converted into the material culture shaping human existence is completely dominant in our industrial practice."[4] Science, economics, and mathematics reveal the absurdity of this worldview—nature's abundance is not infinite. We are consuming resources at a faster rate than

1 Victor Papanek, *Design for the Real World: Human Ecology and Social Change* (New York: Bantam Books, 1971), preface.

2 Ibid.

3 Gary Hustwit, "Dieter Rams: If I Could Do It Again, 'I Would Not Want to Be a Designer,'" *Fast Company*, March 18, 2015, https://www.fastcodesign.com/3043815/dieter-rams-if-i-could-do-it-again-i-would-not-want-to-be-a-designer.

Aysar Ghassan, "Earth with Agency: A Thoroughly Queer Notion," *Design Philosophy Papers* 12, no. 1 (2014): 35–50.

nature can replenish them and disposing of our waste faster than nature can decompose it. In doing so, we are toxifying the land and air we depend on, and squandering precious resources that we will continue to need. In doing so, we are building a world that is full of inequalities that is destroying our health, and, statistically, making most of us quite unhappy. In short, this is without doubt a most precarious moment in human history. But it is also an exciting opportunity to redesign our future.

In the developed world, we take the abundance of food for granted, but a glance behind the scenes reveals that our complex and globalized food systems are topsy-turvy and loaded with contradictions and absurdities. It's a gloomy picture: a growing appetite for meat means that much of the land used to grow crops is dedicated to feeding animals that feed us, a far less calorie-efficient process. Our love of processed food—in which palm oil is a near-essential ingredient—directly causes the destruction of precious rainforests and their delicate ecosystems. Heavy tilling machinery tears up the Earth—with yearly regularity, it destroys the structure and reduces the fertility of the soil. In spite of vast over-production, one in nine people on the planet are chronically undernourished, while another third are overweight or obese. Meanwhile, we throw way about half of all food produced, with the average family in the UK throwing away the equivalent of about £60 of food per month.[5]

5 Rebecca Smithers, "Food Waste Report Shows UK Families Throw Away 24 Meals a Month," *The Guardian*, last modified November 7, 2013, https://www.theguardian.com/environment/2013/nov/07/uk-households-food-waste.

Some Principles of Designing for Complexity

All of this makes complexity a great topic for design to get its teeth into! It constitutes one of my favorite topics, and I have worked extensively with designers looking at various issues around the topic of food. Through this work, I have thought a lot about the skills required from designers who address any complex issue. Some of these are mentioned above—a focus on people, systems thinking and mapping, visualization, and prototyping—but a nature-centered approach to design also requires some additional tools, some of which I list here.

- Using a *problems-as-opportunities* approach overcomes the challenge of working within existing limitations, and giving in to clients' demands, a situation that makes it virtually impossible to introduce anything more than incremental changes. Seeing problems as opportunities means focusing on goals and imagining a desirable future outcome. It requires a designer to examine an idea's commercial viability, and hence its potential for sustainability in the real world. The key here is that inside every environmental problem is an opportunity that businesses can leverage to their advantage.
- Taking a *"services" versus "products" perspective* can help you avoid creating physical objects when the desired outcome can be produced without them.
- *Thinking digital* means using digital technologies to connect people

in ways that would have been impossible in the past. Digital technologies enable the sharing of tangible resources—such as tools, cars, and bicycles—and intangible assets—such as digital media. This has given rise to an entirely new "sharing economy," and the prioritization of common goods over ownership. In China, the sharing economy is booming—one need only look at the streets of Shanghai to see how new bike-sharing programs are changing the nature of transport in the city.

- Having a *bio centric or animal-centered mindset* encourages designers to see things from the viewpoint of other non-verbal stakeholders such as animals, plants, and the wider ecosystems they exist within. This does not mean we should replace human-centered design, but rather that we must add another layer to it. A bio centric mindset includes biomimicry—observing how nature has evolved solutions to deal with specific challenges that might be similar or comparable to those encountered in the design process. Bio centric thinking helps designers address the fact that, in our current food systems, the animals we eat are merely aspects of a system engineered for practicality. We seek to promote their growth with added hormones, keep them free from disease with antibiotics, and reduce the costs related to their husbandry by keeping them in cages, pens, and battery farms. By incorporating animals' experiences into the design process, interesting innovations can result in improving welfare conditions and environmental impact. From a design perspective, bio centric thinking is a shift away from our currently anthropocentric worldview—where humans take center-stage and environmental concerns often come as an afterthought—towards an approach where humans are part of an interconnected and inter-dependent system of living beings. (Figure 2)

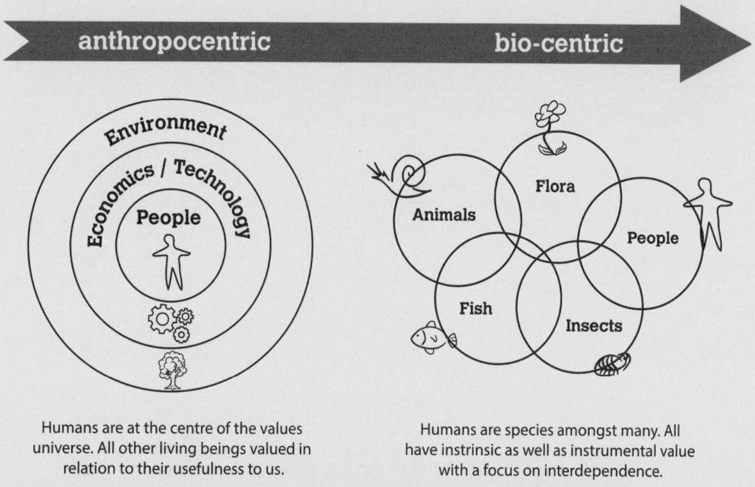

ure 2 Transitioning from our current sign process, where humans are at the nter of an anthropocentric worldview vards an approach where people are nsidered part of an interconnected and er-dependent system of living beings. pyright © 2017 Clare Brass.

Figure 3 The *Growframe* proposal makes use of empty containers travelling back to Asia from the UK. Image courtesy of Philippe Hohlfeld.

Figure 4 The *Growframe* is a collapsible, hydroponic, vegetable cultivation farm that can be installed in an empty shipping container. This entirely autonomous, low-tech system functions in the container's sealed environment for the duration of its three-week journey. Courtesy of Philippe Hohlfeld.

Figure 5 A 1:1 scale model close-up of Growframe's hydroponic growing units. The project's ecological and economic impact remains low throughout its lifecycle. Courtesy of Philippe Hohlfeld.

Cases

Below are some examples of projects that have applied these approaches to create groundbreaking projects that address one or more aspects of human nutritional needs. Each example is followed by a set of keywords representing the principles of designing for complexity described in the previous section.

Vitamins—Growframe, by Philippe Hohlfeld

(Keywords: services versus products, problems-as-opportunities, thinking digital.)

Due to massive imbalances in global trade practices, half of the shipping containers returning to Asia from the UK are empty. The Growframe proposes to utilize the space in these empty twenty- and forty-foot shipping containers as a resource to create new business opportunities. The project takes an innovative approach to existing hydroponics—it is a shippable, collapsible, low-tech hydroponic system that works autonomously in a completely sealed environment. Although most hydroponic farms have farmers checking up on them every day, Growframe works for three to five weeks without supervision. Growframe aims to tackle the challenges related to autonomous farming through novel designs for new growing mediums, watering systems, support structures, and lighting.

On top of creating innovative hydroponic technology, the Growframe's ecological and economic impact is low at every stage in its lifecycle. The ultimate goal of Growframe is to turn the empty spaces being shipped around the world today into the sustainable farms of tomorrow. (Figures 3–5)

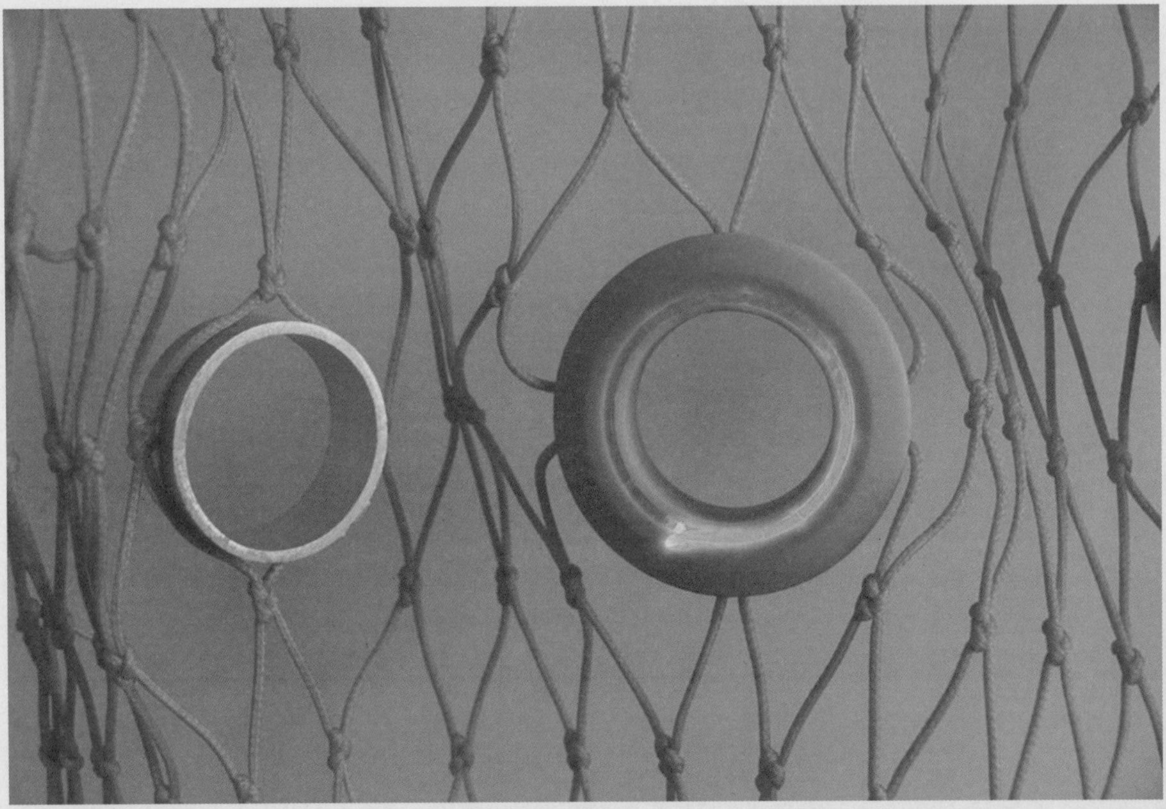

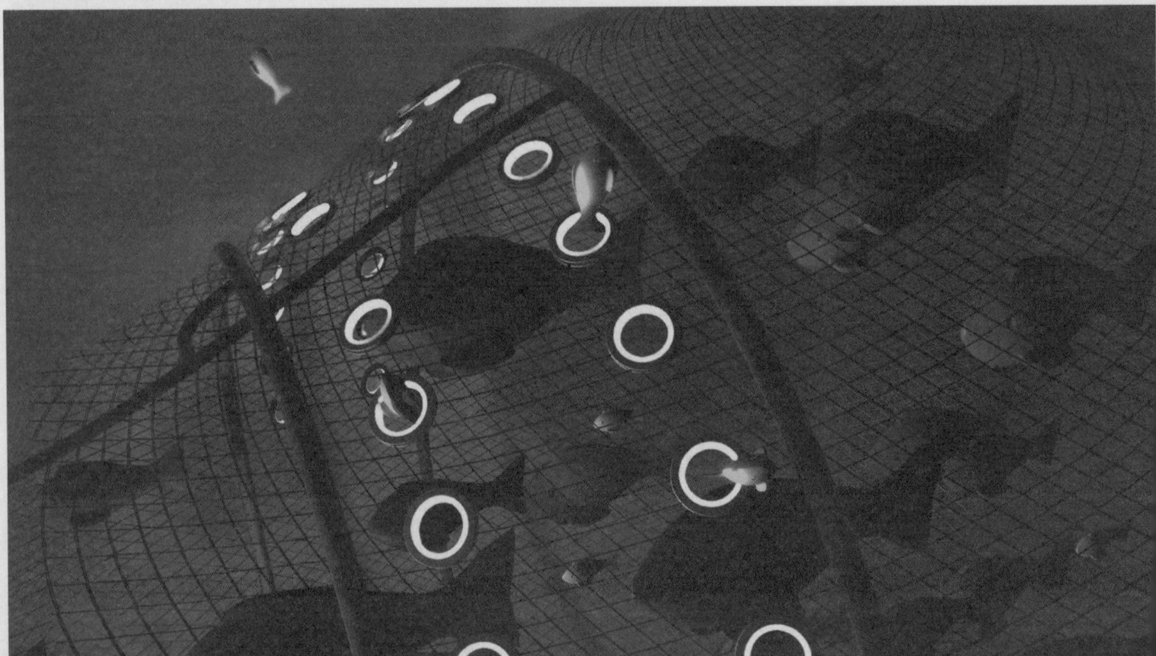

Protein—Pisces, by Dan Watson

(Keywords: bio centric/animal-centered, problems-as-opportunities.)

Pisces designer Dan Watson noticed the way regulation-sized holes in trawler nets become longer and narrower when the nets are dragged through the water. This prevents smaller fish from escaping the net—resulting in a phenomenon known as *bycatch*. In the UK, two out of every three fish caught are discarded, dead, as bycatch. Many of these discarded species are also the most threatened.

When researching fish behavior, Watson discovered that panicked fish tend to swim towards light. His response was to design a lighted ring that can be fitted into the holes of existing netting. Pisces rings keep the holes completely open and lit at all times, signaling and providing an escape route to tiny, trapped fish(**see Figures 6, 7**).[6]

6 Pisces is currently the subject of a crowdfunding campaign. For more information, see https://www.indiegogo.com/projects/pisces-the-light-which-reduces-fish-bycatch-environment.

Figure 6 Pisces is part of an integrated system whose goal is to reduce unnecessary deaths in the fishing industry. Courtesy of Dan Watson.

Figure 7 A lighted ring is fitted into regulation-sized net holes. The ring remains open, allowing tiny fish to escape even when the net is dragged through the water. Courtesy of Dan Watson.

Figure 8 A 1:1 scale prototype of the Enrichment Feed System. Pigs nibble at food blocks mounted onto a concrete base, causing crumbs to fall onto the base where the pigs can root them out. Image courtesy of Anne Sophie Lefevre.

Figure 9 Omlet is a product/service platform that helps anyone with a small outdoor space to keep chickens and produce eggs. Courtesy of Omlet Ltd.

Protein (Pigs)—The Enrichment Feed System, by Anne Sofie Lefevre
(Keywords: bio centric/animal-centered, problems-as-opportunities, thinking digital.)

There are over one billion pigs in the world, and over ten million slaughtered every year in the UK alone. China consumes almost half of the world's pigs, with 672,344,610 slaughtered in 2011.[7] To reach these numbers, ninety-eight percent of pigs are reared on industrial-scale farms where they are kept in close confinement and cannot engage in natural pig behavior such as sniffing, rooting, and chewing. In the wild, they rub their bodies against trees to remove parasites and roll about in mud wallows to regulate their body temperature. Without the ability to engage in these behaviors, industrially-reared pigs often injure each other.

This project explored pig welfare on commercial farms to find ways of allowing pigs to engage in natural behavior.[8] Designer Anne Sophie Lefevre created edible blocks made from supermarket food surplus, which she fed onto poles embedded into heavy cement bases. Pigs use their snouts to play with the blocks, which gradually crumble into a concrete tray shaped to encourage rooting. A movement sensor at the top of the pole alerts the farmer when the blocks need replacing. The project outcome did not intend to disrupt the entire system, but rather to facilitate the farmer's work while improving the daily life of pigs confined for human consumption.(Figure 8)

7 "Statistics: Pigs," *Farm Animal Welfare Compendium*, updated January 03, 2013, https://www.ciwf.org.uk/media/5235115/Statistics-pigs.pdf.

8 For more information, see: https://www.rca.ac.uk/more/our-history/college-history/sustain/sustain-rca-show-and-awards-archive/pig-welfare-enrichment-feed-system/.

Protein (Eggs)—Omlet, by Johannes Paul, Simon Nicholls and William Windham
(Keywords: service design, thinking digital.)

Chickens provide a regular flow of eggs, and they eat everything, so they are a great way to recycle food waste. Three Royal College of Art graduates set up Omlet,[9] a product-service platform that makes it easy for urban and suburban inhabitants to rear their own chickens. The Omlet service concept is aimed at people who have even the smallest of gardens, providing them with everything they need to keep their own egg-laying hens. When you invest in Omlet, you receive not only a fox-proof chicken coop—essential in UK urban environments, where foxes thrive—but also two hens and a one-month supply of chicken feed.(Figure 9)

9 For more information, see: https://www.omlet.us/misc/about_us/.

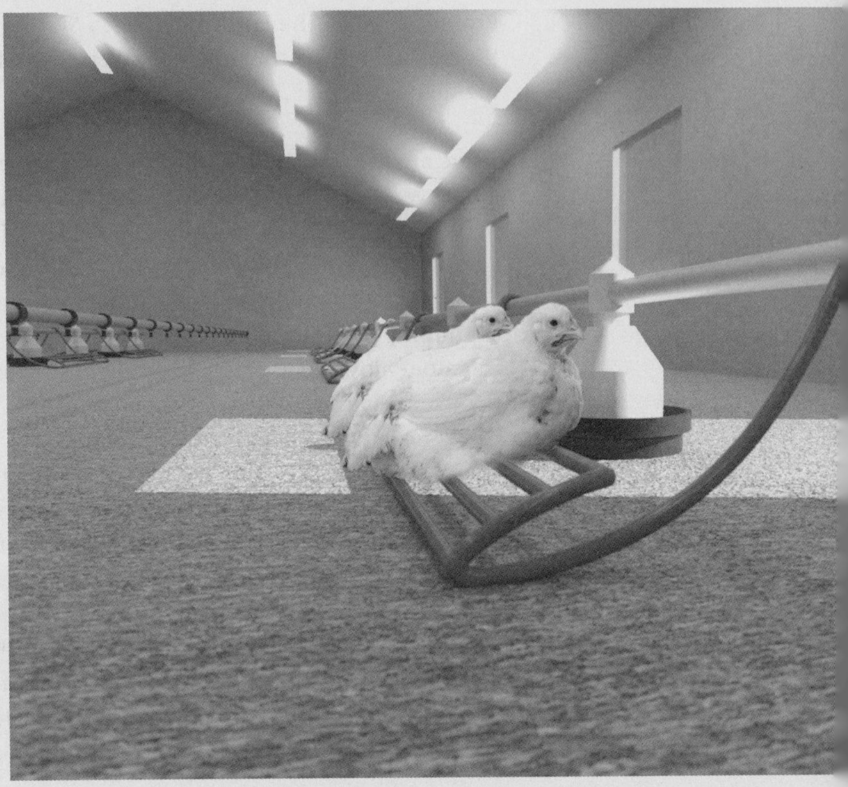

Figure 10 Chicken Run—the Enrichment Perch. Copyright © 2017 Clare Brass.

The SustainRCA Team, and Chicken-Centered Design

In 2013, a high street retailer and a fast-food company asked SustainRCA to redesign the way poultry is produced. We organized a one-week workshop called "Chicken Run," and recruited 25 students to go with us on a deep dive into the world of poultry. An initial visit to two poultry farms allowed us to meet farmers and understand a chicken's life at close range, and working closely with two scientific advisors taught the team more about the life of a commercial broiler chicken. Two retailers provided information about the commercial end of the chicken industry. A period of research and mapping followed, with brainstorming sessions, designing, and development. Students were split into teams, and over the course of a week, the teams generated a number of different concepts under four different systemic themes: feed, enrichment, barn design, and customer engagement. Each team was tasked with tracking the entire lifecycle of a chicken from egg to plate, from the perspective of three main stakeholders: the farmer, the consumer, and the chicken. The methodology we used for this project came to be known as "chicken-centered design."

Many new and interesting ideas emerged, several of which were taken forward for a period of prototyping, testing, and further development. Here I will talk about some of the most innovative and promising concepts.

The Enrichment Perch

(Keywords: bio centric/animal-centered, systems thinking.)

Natural chicken behavior includes pecking, scratching, and perching. At rest, birds tend to lock their feet onto a branch, allowing them to sleep in safety. They cannot do this in the commercial chicken environment, where up to forty thousand birds are cultivated on the floor area of a single barn and constantly fed, and up to eighteen thousand liters of water are consumed per day. As a result, over the course of the crop, the bedding becomes increasingly soiled, and the chickens' feet often become damaged. Perches alleviate this problem, allowing the birds to rest off the floor and engage in natural perching behavior. Perches, however, must not interfere with routine checks that the farmers perform through the shed. The team created a concept for a perch connected to the feeding lines, which would remain out of the way of the farmer and become more accessible to the birds as they grow increasingly immobile because of their size.(Figure 10)

Black Soldier Flies and Supersprouts

(Keywords: bio centric/animal-centered.)

During project research, this team discovered that chickens in the UK eat mostly protein in the form of soya imported from South America and Asia.

Figure 11 Chicken Run—Black Soldier Fly. Protein-rich Black Soldier Fly (BSF) larvae are an alternative food source with an added benefit: BSF larvae happily consume waste products including chicken waste, so would clean the litter. Courtesy of Sara Zarakani, Julia Georgallis, Zhujing Jiang, Wei-Che Chang, and Duck-Soo Choi.

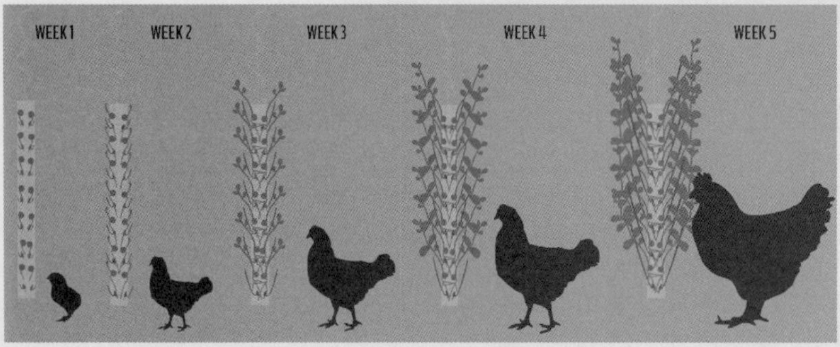

Figure 12 (L) Chicken Run—Supersprouts. Sprouting seeds are embedded on a roll of matting and connected to the water system in the chicken shed. They grow as the chickens do. Courtesy of the Royal College of Art.

Figure 13 (R) A Supersprouts prototype. Courtesy of Clare Brass and Bobby Petersen.

Figure 14 MeatUp is an app dedicated to informing customers about how to eat better meat. Courtesy of Clare Brass and Dejan Mitrovic.

An increase in demand for soya—caused by a growing demand for chicken and other barn-bred meat—is causing deforestation to create more lucrative, arable farm land. We found there is a growing interest in some parts of the world in the Black Soldier Fly (BSF), an insect whose copious and protein-rich larvae have an insatiable hunger for what we humans consider to be waste, including food waste, human waste, and chicken waste. As it turns out, the BSF lifecycle echoes almost perfectly that of the broiler chicken. The design concept was to create fly incubation systems that protect the larvae as they spend time cleaning the litter, before exposing them for consumption by the chickens, who could engage in natural scratching and pecking behavior when eating them.(Figure 11)

The student design team discovered that the environmental conditions in which so many chickens are raised lead to increased incidence of *campylobacter*, a bacterium that multiplies in the chickens' intestines. Although this bacterium is destroyed during cooking, it still causes considerable health problems for humans. Recent research has suggested that chicken gut health can be improved by supplementing their feed with probiotics,[10] leading the team to develop a concept that would allow poultry access to sprouting seeds, naturally high in probiotics.[11] They embedded seeds into a roll of matting set on a vertical frame and connected the frame to the water lines in the shed. After a few days, the seeds begin to sprout, providing fresh greens to the chicks, who peck higher and reach more mature green sprouts as they grow each day.(Figures 12, 13)

10 Yan Wang et al., "Effect of Probiotics on the Meat Flavour and Gut Microbiota of Chicken," *Scientific Reports* 7, Article number: 6400 (2017), DOI: https://doi.org/10.1038/s41598-017-06677-z.

11 Manju Pathak, "Germinating Seeds: Source of Probiotics," *World Applied Sciences Journal* 26, no. 2 (2013): 224–31.

MeatUp—Customer Engagement via App

(Keywords: services versus products, thinking digital.)

Without educating consumers, improvements in food animal welfare may be impossible to sustain. One of the groups involved in the Chicken Run project was tasked with finding a way to get customers on board with a food animal system upgrade. Any potential changes to the system would have been useless if people buying chicken could not differentiate between high- and low-welfare meat, particularly due to the inevitable higher cost of high-welfare meat. The team observed customers' buying behavior, and noted that there is considerable confusion as to what constitutes high-welfare meat. Furthermore, even in those customers who expressed a preference for higher-welfare meat, cognitive dissonance sets in when it comes to actual purchasing decisions—higher welfare meat may cost up to six times as much as its lower-welfare equivalent. The app the team created attempted to inform a wider range of customers about how to locate, select, purchase, and prepare "better meat" via a set of measurable welfare criteria, in addition to offering users information about shops, restaurants, and recipes (see Figure 14).

Conclusion

It is clear from these examples, and many others not mentioned here, that the food production sector is a domain where there is enormous scope for designers to intervene, and to change the status quo in our current food systems. Food system issues are multifarious, complex, and interconnected, and innovative solutions may change the future of the human and natural world. Many examples of design-led approaches to complex challenges in our food systems are emerging, leading to exciting new changes in the way we will cultivate, catch, grow, and process our food in the future.

Information Visualization: Where Design Meets Engineering

Nan Cao

College of Design and Innovation, Tongji University, China

Information visualization is one of the most important research areas in the field of data science. It plays an important role in supporting a better understanding of the big data. A picture worth a thousand words. An effective and intuitive visualization reveals the insights of the data and illustrates data evidence to help users make a better decision or help analyzers more precisely formulate a scientific hypothesis. The field of information visualization is a seamless combination of both design and engineering. In this essay, we will review the development of visualization techniques in the past decades, introduce new challenges in the era of big data, and illustrate its applications in the field of information security domains as an example.

Nan Cao is a professor at Tongji University College of Design and Innovation. He is also an adjunct professor at NYU Shanghai and NYU Tandon. Before joining Tongji University and NYU Shanghai, he was a research staff member at IBM T.J. Watson Research Center and has worked for IBM for 10 years during 2005–2015. Dr. Cao received his Ph.D. degree from the Hong Kong University of Science and Technology. Dr. Cao's primary expertise and research interests are information visualization and visual analysis. He is specialized in producing novel visualization techniques to represent and analysis complex (big, heterogenous, multidimensional, dynamic) real-world data. Referring to http://nancao.org for more information about him.

In 2011, the US Navy killed Osama Bin Laden. The event instantly made the headlines of every major newspaper and magazine in the US and was the subject of breaking news bulletins on TV stations nationwide. Interestingly, the very first report about Bin Laden's death appeared on Twitter. That single tweet instantly influenced so many people across space and time. But how is it possible for a simple message broadcast on social media to achieve such a massive impact?

New York city startup SocialFlow is a social media company that helps its clients control the information diffusion process to increase their advertising and marketing impact. The question is: how do they achieve this? In the case of the Bin Laden story,[1] the first thing they did was try and understand how the information was being spread on Twitter. A group of engineers and scientists in the company represented the diffusion pattern of the first tweet using a graph visualization.[2] It depicts the rate and scope of the "Death of Bin Laden" Tweet across the platform. The graph shows that a network was formed based on users' retweeting behaviors. Each dot in represents a user on Twitter, and each line between them represents a retweeting. They found that the original message, highlighted by the red circle, was tweeted by an opinion leader, which influenced its exposure. The graph visualizes more than 14M users who were involved in spreading the message. This is an excellent example of the power of big data visualization. As Scottish engineer and economist William Playfair—a forerunner in the field—famously said, "The best way to capture the imagination is to speak to the eyes."[3] The bandwidth offered by information visualization is enormous.

What exactly is information visualization? Basically, it is a computer-supported technique that transforms data into various kinds of interactive visual representations. In this definition, "computer-supported" plays a very important role; however, research into information visualization started long before the advent of the computer.

1 "Breaking Bin Laden: Visualizing the Power of a Single Tweet," *SocialFlow*, May 6, 2011, http://www.socialflow.com/breaking-bin-laden-visualizing-the-power-of-a-single/.

2 See the visualization at http://www.socialflow.com/breaking-bin-laden-visualizing-the-power-of-a-single/.

3 Cited in Jefferson Bailey and Lily Pregill, "Speak to the Eyes: The History and Practice of Information Visualization," *Art Documentation* 33, no. 2 (2014): 168–91, DOI: https://doi.org/10.1086/678525.

A Very Brief History of Information Visualization

William Playfair was the first to visually represent statistical data, nearly two and a half centuries ago. He invented the majority of the statistical charts that we use nowadays, including the bar chart, pie chart, and line chart.

Later, Charles Joseph Minard, a French civil engineer, created visualizations to help with storytelling. The one shown in **Figure 1** is his most famous—a visual representation of Napoleon's invasion of Moscow and its eventual retreat in defeat. This picture has been used in many textbooks as representative of effective visualization design.

About a century ago, Austrian philosopher of science Otto Neurath and artist Gerd Arntz invented Isotype, a pictorial language they used illustrate statistical data. It was the first time anyone had tried to standardize the components of graphic visualizations.

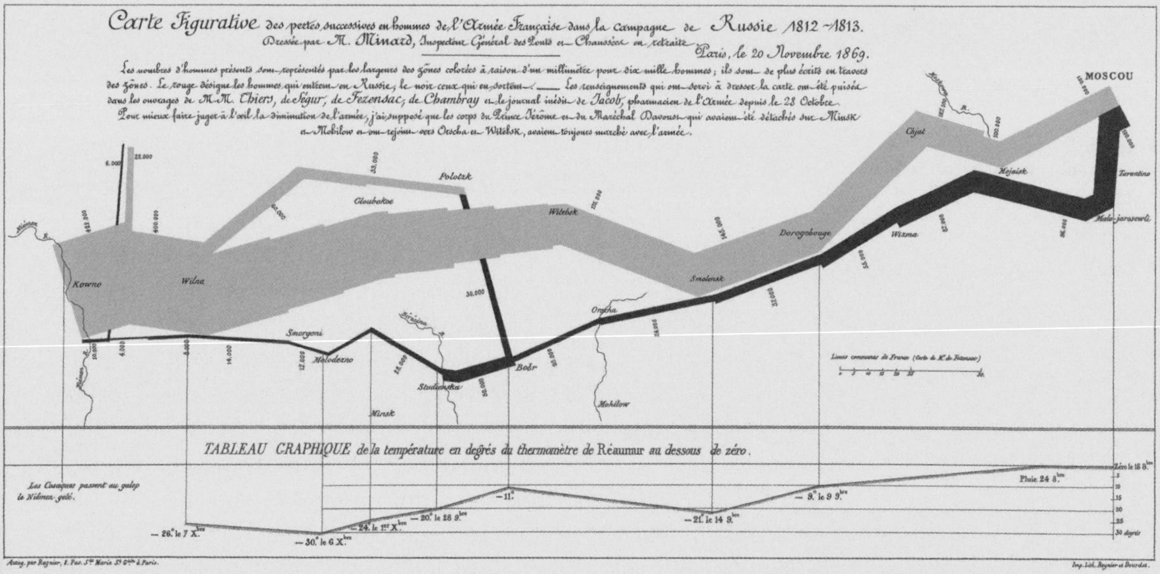

Figure 1 (A) Charles Joseph Minard's flow visualization about Napoleon's invasion of Moscow. Charles Joseph Minard, *Tableaux Graphiques et Cartes Figuratives de M. Minard*, 1845–1869, 1869. Public domain. Source: Wikimedia Commons, via Internet Archive, https://web.archive.org/web/20140301150547/ https://commons.wikimedia.org/wiki/File:Minard.png.

Figure 2 (R) Two charts by Nigel Holmes: "Monstrous Costs: Total House and Senate Campaign Expenditures, in Millions" and "Diamonds Were a Girl's Best Friend." Images courtesy of Nigel Holmes.

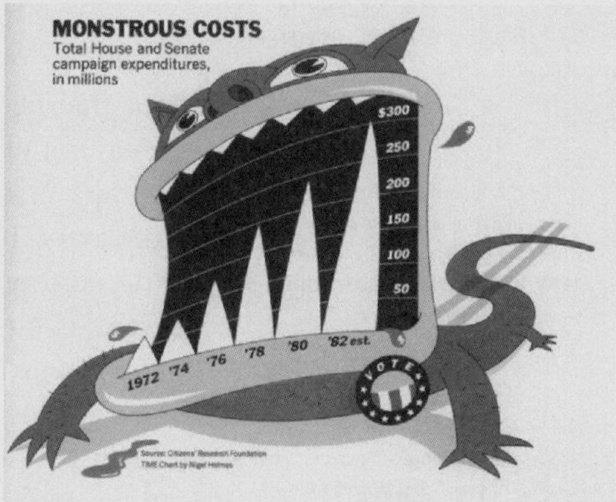

Around 60 years ago, designers began to get involved in information visualization. Nigel Holmes, a British/American designer, used graphic tools and techniques to make text-based data easier to understand.[4] He created a series of charts that were published in various magazines in the United States—visualizations that later became known as "infographics." Among the rich collection of his work, there is a category that is of particular interest here. "Monstrous Costs"[5] and "Diamonds Were a Girl's Best Friend"[6] are two examples.(Figure 2) The first one uses a monster's teeth to illustrate total US House and Senate campaign expenditures in millions of dollars. The second uses the curve of a woman's leg to shape a line chart that illustrates the change in the average price of a one-carat D-flawless diamond. Later on, Edward Tufte—a statistician and professor at Yale University—criticized this type of design, calling it over-decorated which makes the information hard to understand. Tufte dubbed these kinds of visualizations "chart junk."[7] While people debate over the decades on whether visual embellishments are detrimental to understanding the information or they may have other benefits,[8] there is no doubt that we look forward to obtaining clear, rich, and meaningful information in visualizations.

In 1992, Ben Shneiderman—a computer scientist and a professor at the University of Maryland—introduced the "treemap," a data tiling technique that he later extended together with his colleagues.[9] The word "tree" is a metaphor used to explain the way information is hierarchically structured in computer science. Each rectangle of the treemap has an area proportional to the amount of data it represents. The arrival of treemapping is considered as the starting point of modern information visualization. From that time onward, computer science would play an important role in the field.

About 10 years ago, German professor Daniel Keim, one of the most important founders of the visual analysis field and also one of the most influential researchers in the field, broke new ground by combining visualization with data analysis techniques. According to Keim and his colleagues, "visual analytics focuses on handling ... massive, heterogeneous, and dynamic volumes of information by integrating human judgment by means of visual representations and interaction techniques in the analysis process."[10]

4 For more information see Nigel Holmes' website: http://www.nigelholmes.com.

5 See, for example, Nigel Holmes, "Monstrous Costs," *Visualoop*, June 22, 2017, http://visualoop.com/infographics/monstrous-costs.

6 See the original chart used in Alexander L. Taylor III, "A Gem That Lost Its Luster," *Time* 120, no. 9 (August 30, 1982): 66.

7 Edward R. Tufte, *Envisioning Information* (Cheshire: Graphics Press, 1990), 34.

8 Scott Bateman et al., "Useful Junk? The Effects of Visual Embellishment on Comprehension and Memorability of Charts," in *Proceedings of CHI 2010*, April 10–25, 2010, Atlanta, USA (New York: ACM, 2010).

9 Ben Shneiderman, "Treemaps for Space-Constrained Visualization of Hierarchies: Including the History of Treemap Research at the University of Maryland," University of Maryland, December 26, 1998, http://www.cs.umd.edu/hcil/treemap-history/.

10 Daniel A. Keim et al., "Visual Analytics: Scope and Challenges," in *Visual Data Mining: Lecture Notes in Computer Science*, vol. 4404, ed. Simeon J. Simoff, Michael H. Böhlen, and Arturas Mazeika (Berlin: Springer, 2008), 76, https://link.springer.com/chapter/10.1007%2F978-3-540-71080-6_6.

Designing Visualizations

When we review the historical development of information visualization (see Figure 3), we find engineers and computer scientists have driven the field since the very beginning. Nevertheless, I believe the field holds vast potential for designers.

Since the creation of the treemap, a staggering variety of visualizations have been created for different purposes and domains. Ten years ago—while I was still a research and development engineer at IBM—I started my career in the field. The principal challenge I faced was defending the usefulness of my work. My colleagues believed that visualization techniques

Figure 3 The key figures responsible for the development of information visualization practice. Copyright © 2017 Nan Cao.

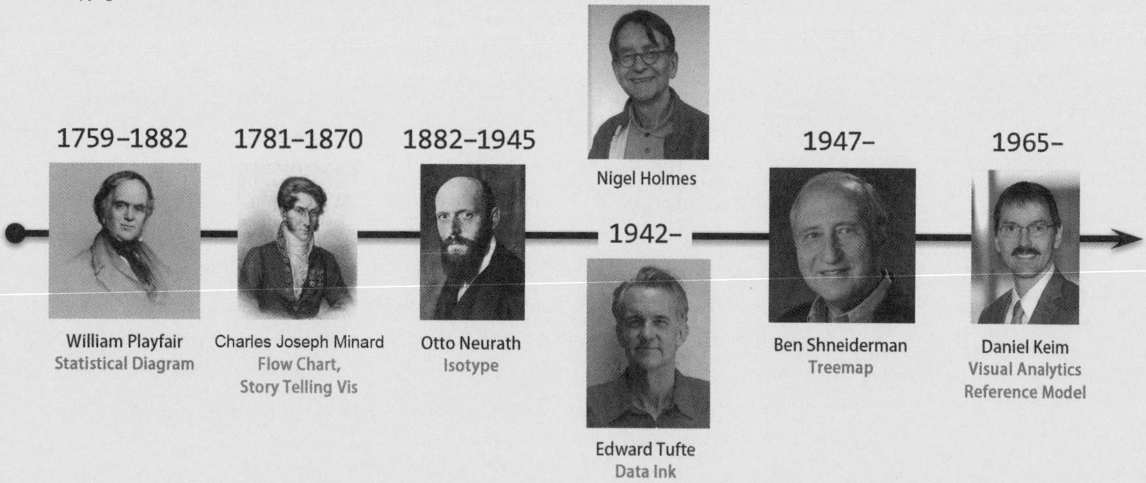

were nice to have, but not necessary. Thanks to rise of big data, visualization nowadays is considered very important. People are starting to realize that visualizations can help users with little to no background knowledge quickly grasp the meaning of the data they represent, and perceive insightful patterns within them.

In 2010, for example, Paul Butler, then an intern on Facebook's data infrastructure engineering team, created a great visualization of "the locality of friendship," using R—an open-source statistics environment. He was keen on seeing "how geography and political borders affected where people lived relative to their friends." The resulting plot turned into a world map with surprisingly rich details and patterns.[11] Similarly, a visualization of all 13,000-or-so McDonald's franchises in the United States by Stephen von Worley vividly revealed the distribution of the population centers and the highway grids across the nation.[12]

Let us consider for a moment the ways that visualizations can impact popular involvement in the kinds of issues facing our planet. In November of 2011, the UN invited representatives of 194 countries to Durban, South Africa for the 17th conference of the climate change group COP17. At that time, American cable news network CNN didn't just broadcast the climate change conference to the world—it brought the world to the climate change conference by visually tracking the hashtag #COP17. The CNN COP17 "ECOSPHERE" is a digital ecosystem that designers constructed from thousands upon thousands of tweets related to climate change; each information diffusion process was presented as a growing sphere.[13] The ECOSPHERE is an evolving digital garden depicting the global discussion

11 Ties between Facebook users. See Paul Butler, "Visualizing Friendships," Facebook, December 13, 2010, https://www.facebook.com/notes/facebook-engineering/visualizing-friendships/469716398919/.

12 See Stephen von Worley, "Where the Buffalo Roamed: How Far Can You Get from McDonald's," *Data Pointed*, September 22, 2009, available at http://www.datapointed.net/2009/09/distance-to-nearest-mcdonalds/.

13 For more information, see "CNN Ecosphere Project Case Film," *vimeo*, 2:38, from Ecosphere, https://vimeo.com/35955609.

on the Internet. Every tweet tagged with #COP17 became part of one of the "plants" which represented topics such as sustainability or carbon footprinting. The plants' size and color reflected the intensity of the online exchanges. In the week before the conference, CNN called for contributions with an online and broadcast promotional campaign. The project spread around the world via social media, and the ecosphere flourished. Inside the conference, CNN connected the 20,000 delegate attendees with the global discussion via a dynamic digital installation—a live 3D hologram showing the developing ecosphere with an inset broadcasting incoming tweets. CNN also brought the global discussion to international viewers by broadcasting tweets on air. At the end of the conference, delegates represented with the digital route, documenting the growth, significance, and most popular content from the project. As a result, the ECOSPHERE project got more people involved in a climate change conference than ever before. CNN went on to use the same technique to connect the world to Rio+20, the UN sustainable development summit, in 2012.

Visualizing big datasets is not an easy thing to do, because the designer has to squeeze billions of data points emerging from millions of nodes into the mere thousands of pixels that an everyday computer display can handle. So how can we solve this problem? and what kind of challenges do we face?

The first challenge comes in the form of visual clutter—the unavoidable overlap of nodes or line crossings that tend to cause a lot of "noise" on the screen. What can we find in the mess of data? It is often difficult to tell.

A second challenge is related to performance. Even with a very large data set, we still want to render all the data in real time to support interactive exploration and feedback collection. How to address the related performance issues in terms of rendering a large data set?

A third challenge is that even when we adequately address the two previous challenges—in other words, visualize the data clearly and efficiently—we still have no way of knowing whether the users will be able to understand it, and the kind of patterns they will be able to perceive. Showing too much information always makes it difficult to understand.

Nowadays, there are standardized solutions for each of these issues. When we have a raw dataset, the first thing we do is preprocess it using data mining and analysis techniques, which makes the data understandable and reveals aspects we wish to visualize. After that, we transform the data we have selected for visualization into an abstract—structured—form. From the transformed data, we then design visual encoding schemes and layout algorithms to represent the data in appropriate ways, and in the right places on the screen. Finally, we present the results of this visual analysis to users. Users explore the data and provide feedback based on their interactions with the visualization. This process follows the "reference model for information visualization and visual analysis," depicted in Figure 4. Most of today's visualization systems have been designed in line with this model.

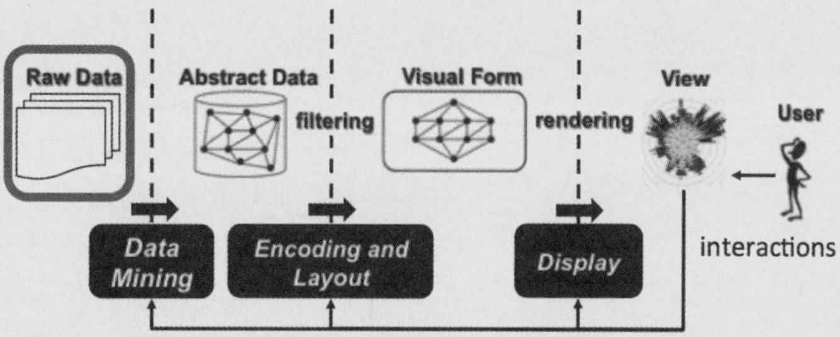

Figure 4 Reference model for information visualization and visual analysis Copyright © 2017 Nan Cao.

Visualization and Information Security

Social media has become part of our everyday lives, and there are more and more users every day. One significant problem with using it is establishing trust in and among users. Do we really know who our contacts and "friends" are? How do they behave online? It is still possible for users to completely conceal—or fabricate—their online personas. There are a huge number of anonymous users on Twitter, for example. Such anonymous users are potential threats to society because they are not accountable for egregious behavior—spam, phishing, and rumors abound. The research goal is trying to detect those people who have anonymous behaviors on Twitter.

The problem lies in the area of anomaly detection. This is, in fact, a very important field in data mining, whose experts try to detect the data instances that do not conform to an expected pattern, or to the other instances in a dataset.

Traditional outlier detection techniques have two major challenges: (1) It's very difficult to define what is "normal" and what is "abnormal." Their definitions are usually based on some human standard—there are no formal definitions in mathematics. (2) Machine-learning techniques usually rely on a "ground truth"—empirical data—for training the analysis model or validating the analysis results. But this kind of ground truth data is usually missing from real-world cases. So how can we solve these problems?

Visualization techniques may offer a useful solution. My colleagues and I have designed a visualization system that collects live Twitter data in real time and stores them in a database.(Figure 5) We also designed a visualization that monitors the diffusion of these messages in real time. Once the data are collected, they can be processed in parallel by a computer cluster—a group of computers that have been configured to operate as a single system—for later analysis. After that, we conduct anomaly analysis and visualize the result in an intuitive visualization. Finally, expert users review the analysis results via visualization and mark and label the suspicious user account as feedback to supervise the previous analysis procedure.

Based on this system, we developed the set of visualization tools

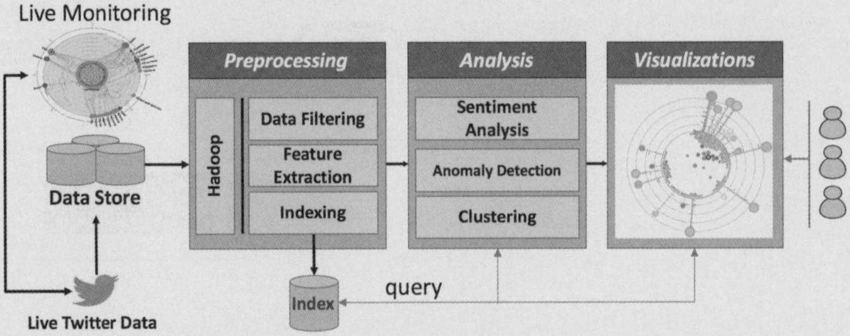

Figure 5 A visual analysis system designed to detect users with anomalous behaviors. Copyright © 2015 Nan Cao.

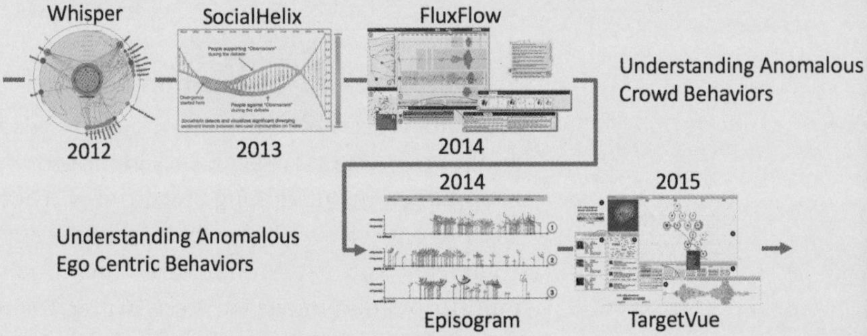

Figure 6 A visualization system designed and developed to reveal users' collective and egocentric behaviors on social media. Copyright © 2015 Nan Cao.

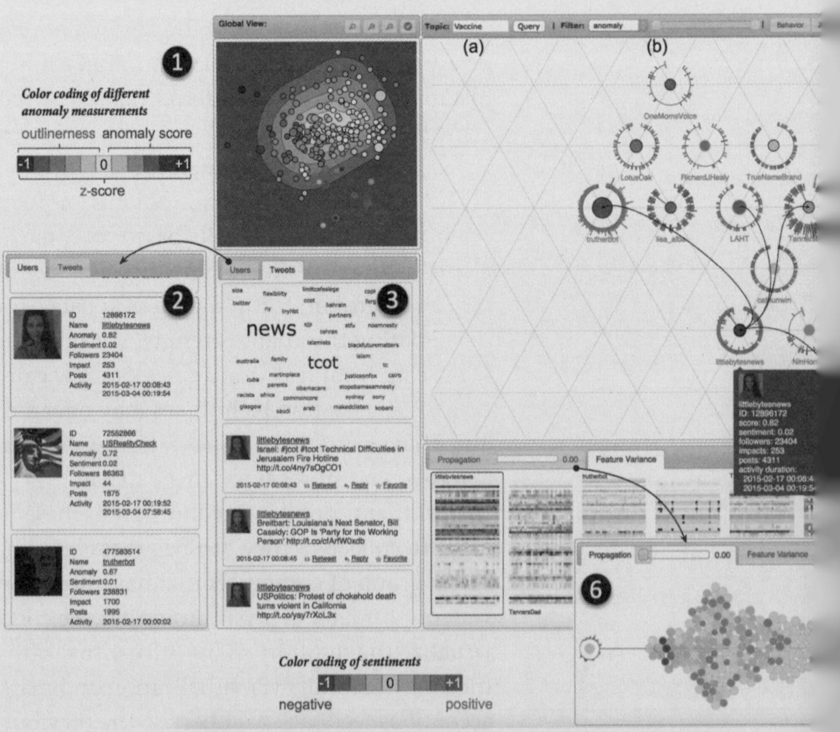

Figure 7 The user interface of the TargetVue System. Copyright © 2015 Nan Cao.

depicted in **Figure 6**. In 2012, we introduced "Whisper," which we use to convey how information is spread on Twitter. In 2013, we built "SocialHelix," a visualization system we use to represent sentiment divergence—conflicts of opinion—on social media. The SocialHelix in **Figure 6** shows the sentiment divergence associated with "Obamacare" during the presidential debate that took place on October 3, 2012. Obama had announced new strategies to improve the Affordable Care Act; by visualizing the associated Twitter data, we found a significant conflict trend between two user communities.[14] In 2014, we developed "FluxFlow." We use this system to illustrate how rumors are spread over time—a first in the field of data visualization. In 2015, we designed visualizations that can illustrate individual user behaviors on Twitter. Based on this system, we developed "TargetVue" to visually convey anonymous user behaviors.

There are, generally speaking, two types of user behaviors on social media. One is posting, which typically takes the form of tweeting, uploading an image, or publishing a message. The other is responding—retweeting or replying to messages posted by others. Imagine that you want to analyze these two types of behaviors; how can a visualization help?

First, you would need to convert the posting and retweeting behaviors into data form so that the computer can understand them. To this end, we extracted a set of features based on the tweets of a given—"focal"—user account. These belong to five principal categories: statistical features, which represent the number of the user's posted or retweeted messages; content features, including keywords or salient sentiments extracted from the tweets; temporal features, which represent posting frequency and retweeting patterns; network features, such as user centrality; and profile features. These features are converted into numbers that describe the key behavior properties of a user. Features change over time, forming what is known as a "feature vector time series." Anomaly detection algorithms are designed to assign each user an anomaly score indicating the degree of outlierness of their behaviors in relation to their features.

To help interpret the results—the meaning behind users' anomaly scores—we have developed a number of modes that visualize their data. **Figure 7** is an image showing TargetVue's general user interface. It includes a view of the dataset's most anomalous users;[(Figure 7-1)] for example, the top 300 ranked according to their anomaly scores. Each circle represents a user; its size indicates the user's importance—defined by the number of followers—and its color illustrates the anomaly score computed by the algorithm; the darker the red, the higher the score. The users and their behaviors are shown in the middle, while their profiles are listed on the left.[(Figure 7-2)] When a user is selected, his or her tweets are shown in the tweet list,[(Figure 7-3)] and more details will be shown in the context view at the bottom of the user interface.[(Figures 7-5, 7-6)]

14 Nan Cao et al., "SocialHelix: Visual Analysis of Sentiment Divergence in Social Media," *Journal of Visualization* 18, no. 2 (2015): 221–35, DOI: https://doi.org/10.1007/s12650-014-0246-x.

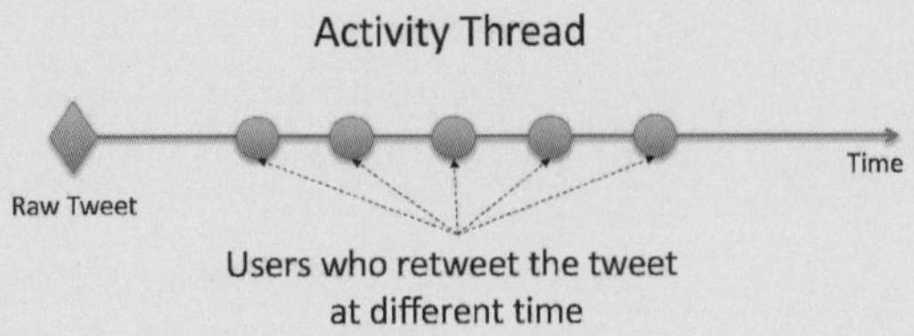

Figure 8 An "activity thread" plots a raw tweet and the subsequent users who retweet it on a timeline. Copyright © 2015 Nan Cao.

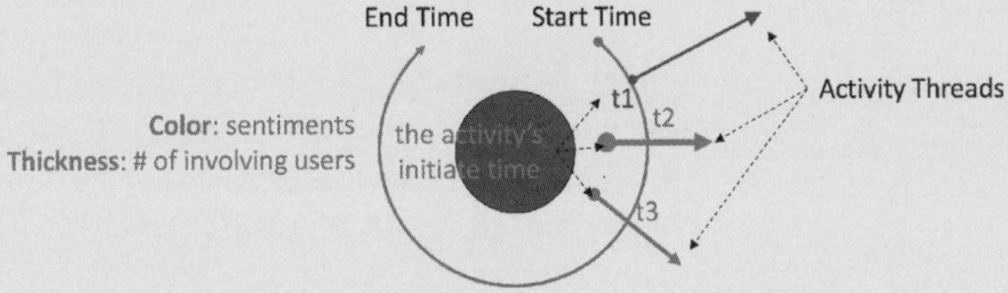

Figure 9 A behavior glyph. The user is represented as a circle in the middle surrounded by a circular timeline recording all his or her posting and retweeting behaviors. Copyright © 2015 Nan Cao.

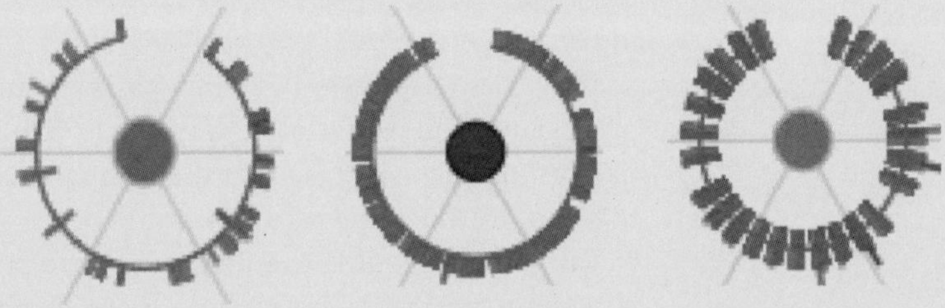

Figure 10 The behavior glyphs of three example users. Copyright © 2015 Nan Cao.

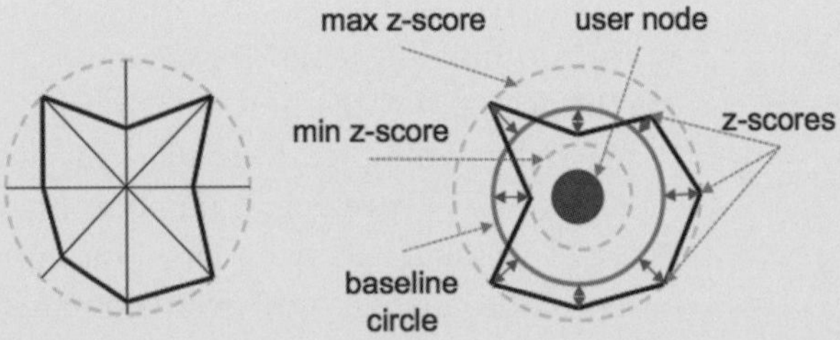

Figure 11 The design of a feature glyph. Copyright © 2015 Nan Cao.

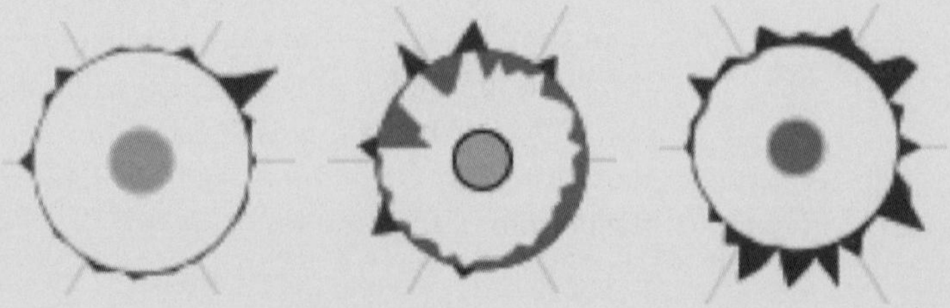

Figure 12 The feature glyphs of three example users. Copyright © 2015 Nan Cao.

Three Ways to Illustrate User Behavior

We have designed three types of glyphs to exemplify three types of social media user conduct—behaviors, features, and connections.

Behaviors

The "behavior glyph" illustrates a user's posting and retweeting behavior. To design the glyph, we created a symbol we called an "activity thread." An activity thread is a timeline that records users' retweeting behaviors after an original tweet (situated on the leftmost end of the timeline).(Figure 8)

First we depict a user as a circle whose size indicates his or her importance and whose color indicates his or her anomaly score.(Figure 9) We use a circular timeline—a time "arc"—to record the focal user's activity history during the given period of the time. Whenever the users posted or retweeted a tweet, we draw a corresponding activity thread perpendicular to the time arc at the point when the activity occurred. The color of the thread indicates its sentiment; for example, red means negative and green means positive. The thickness of the activity thread indicates the number of people who became involved in the thread.

A posting behavior corresponds to a thread that is situated directly on the circular timeline at the point in time when the posting occurs. A retweeting behavior related to a thread intersects with the timeline at the point when the focal user retweets the original tweets. In this way, we intuitively show two types of behaviors clearly and distinctly.

Figure 10 shows examples of three different users. The user on the left only posts but never retweets, while the user in the middle only retweets but never posts. Neither resembles typical human behavior. A normal person would post or retweet in an irregular fashion. The design is simple yet information rich.

Features

In addition to the behavior glyph, we also want to show a user's features. Figure 11 shows how we design individual feature glyphs for a given period of time.

First of all, we again visualize the user as a circle whose size represents importance and whose color represents the anomaly score. A baseline circle is drawn surrounding the focal user indicating the mean feature values across the entire dataset. Feature axes are then radially arranged. We plot the focal user's feature value around the baseline along the feature axes. Feature values below average we visualize inside the baseline circle and those that are above average we show outside the baseline circle. A user with regular human features has a feature glyph with a regular shape close to the baseline circle, whereas those with abnormal features are revealed to have irregular shapes commensurate with their irregular behaviors. Figure 12 shows three example users. These features in the middle glyph are below average, and those in the rightmost glyph are above average. Only the leftmost glyph looks like a normal user, as its shape is relatively regular.

Connections

TargetVue also shows the interactions between different users, which we call "connections." For example, while most users are connected in some way, some are isolated, which makes them suspicious.

Web (Ro)Bot Hunting

Based on our system, we took part in a "bot" detection challenge. A bot is a piece of software that runs automated tasks, such as posting and retweeting, intended to simulate human activity. The challenge had two stages: an influence challenge and a bot detection challenge. In the influence challenge—which we did not participate in—the organizer invited several groups of researchers to design social media bots. The designed bots would be launched on Twitter, and the group whose bots influenced the most people would win the game. This stage lasted a month and the bots launched influenced eight thousand target users—4 million tweets from these users were collected. Our participation began in the second stage of the challenge. Our goal was to detect the social bots that had been designed during the first stage. So, how did we manage this?

Firstly, we loaded a query into the system that searched for users whose posted tweets related to a certain topic. We are able to explore users like these by hovering over each node—the user's profile is shown on a tooltip—also known as a "hoverbox." The most suspicious users we grouped and loaded into the inspection view, which uses behavior glyphs to visualize them in depth. We then explored the user details by zooming or switching to different views.

Using the inspection view, we found that some of the users had only posted but never retweeted. And some users only retweeted by never posted Some users' retweets showed a periodical pattern, and others aggressively posted a lot of tweets. When we switched to the feature view, we found that some of these aggressive users had relatively normal features, but the feature glyphs of others—who had regular behaviors—had very abnormal shapes. All of these, we decided, were suspicious users. We explored details on the temporal dimension by clicking on a node, executing a detailed investigation, and checking the raw tweets of suspicious users; finally, we marked the most suspicious users as bots. The marked data was fed back into the analysis module, which makes the analysis more and more precise.

Finally, through our data visualizations, we were able to find all the bots the competitors had designed. We also found that the bots were designed by two groups of designers or researchers by only observing their behavior glyphs. As shown in Figure 13, the first group is composed of bots that only posted but never retweeted. In comparison, the second group of

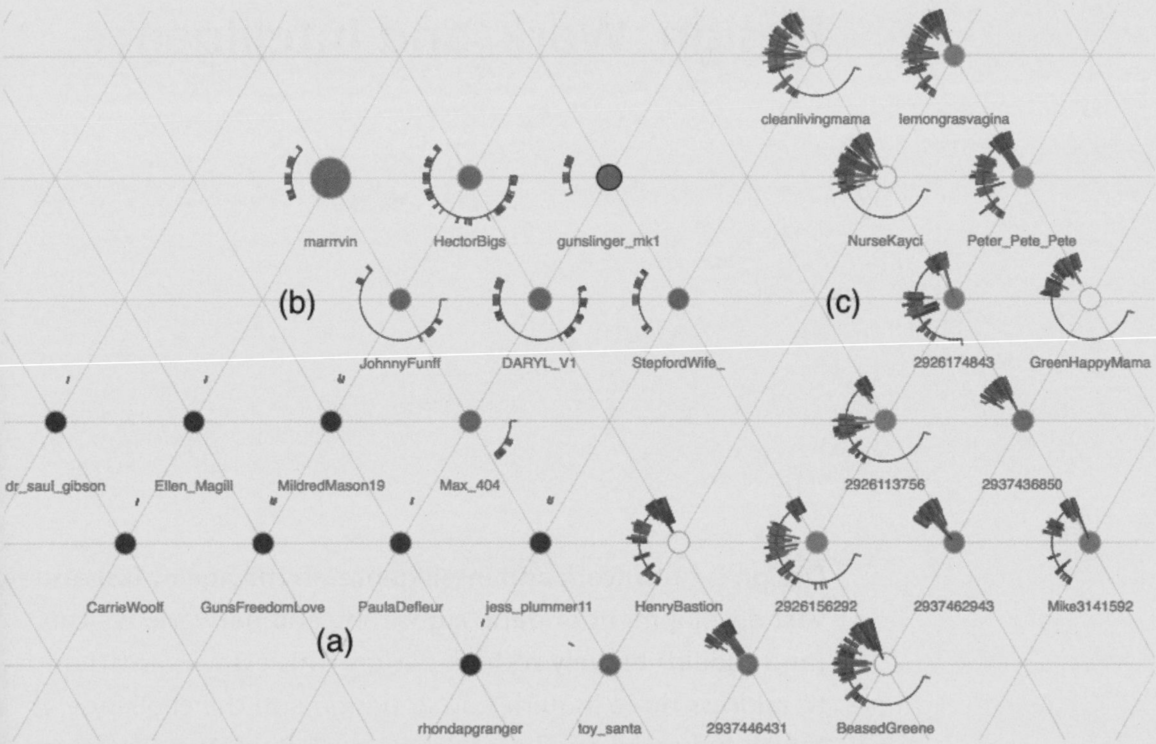

Figure 13 All the social bots we were able to detect using the TargetVue system. These bots can be largely separated into two groups according to their behaviors. Copyright © 2015 Nan Cao.

bots were more smartly designed. They post a message, sleep for a while, and then follow up with a series of retweets. Obviously, this design is the more successful, as the bots in the group have a much longer life circle in comparison to the ones in the first group.

Acknowledgments

The author wish to thank Nigel Holmes not only for his permission to use his work but also for generously sharing the scanned copies of the originals that were created long before the computer.

Design, Work, and Intelligence

Ling Fan

Design and Artificial Intelligence Laboratory, Tongji University, China;
Tezign.com, China

Design is both work and intelligence. In the age of fast and vast development of data, algorithm, and network, we can (and should) bravely rethink design. This essay is an attempt to address three inquiries: first, design and the challenge of fourth industrial revolution; second, digital talent platform and design as work; lastly, machine intelligence and design intelligence.

Ling Fan is a scholar, entrepreneur, and catalyst to bridge design, technology, and business. He has taught and researched at the University of California at Berkeley, Harvard University, China Central Academy of Fine Arts, and Princeton University. Ling earned his Doctor of Design from Harvard University, a master from Princeton University, and a Bachelor from Tongji University. In 2015, Ling founded tezign.com, a venture-backed Internet startup to match designers with pressing real-world business and social problems. He also founded "Design Matters," a non-profit devoted to bringing design values and humanity to technology, in the form of conferences, seminars, and workshops, drawing the attention of over 40 media outlets and commanding aggregate audiences of 200,000. Hong Kong M+/Design Trust granted Ling the inaugural design fellowship in 2015. He is a World Economic Forum Young Global Leader, a fellow of Aspen Institute China Fellowship and a member of Aspen Global Leadership Network.

Design is both work and intelligence. In the age of fast and vast development of data, algorithms and networks (also known as the fourth industrial revolution), we can (and should) be brave and rethink design. This paper is an attempt to address three inquiries: firstly, design and its new challenge; secondly, distributed design talent platform; and lastly, machine intelligence and design intelligence. This is written from my position as a founder of a technology startup (tezign.com) and a research leader for the Design and Artificial Intelligence Laboratory at Tongji University. I do wish to note that, what is presented here is still a work in progress and open to critique.

Design and the Challenge of the Fourth Industrial Revolution

The industrial revolution has transitioned from the second industrial revolution which emphasized the productivity of material goods through the third industrial revolution which emphasized the production of knowledge to the present fourth industrial revolution which emphasizes data and intelligence. Such a transition is evident in the dynamic between the supply and demand sides of production. In the second industrial revolution the supply side emancipated the productivity of goods by means of standardization and industrialization. As such, the price of goods dropped dramatically and the circulation of goods became global. For the demand side, the goods were widely available, albeit the choice was very limited (large in number/small in variety). In the third industrial revolution the internet and the information revolution greatly emancipated the "immaterial production,"[1] the production of ideas, designs, content, copyrighted material, patents, code, music, and so on. This mode of production redefines productivity from solely quantitative to qualitative. Fundamental to immaterial production is diversity. The diversity in supply leads to high diversification in demand (small in number/large in variety). The accumulation of data from both supply and demand leads us to the fourth industrial revolution. The demand side data has made each individual: a unique user ID stored in the cloud. Every individual can be treated as an individual with services, products, information, and marketing truly personalized (minimum in number/maximum in variety).(Figure 1) With the help of data and machine intelligence, a human economy is not so far from us. The human economy is based on those human traits that we cannot gain from data and machine intelligence, such as creativity.

Over the past forty years, the Internet has grown considerably to bring different layers of humanity *online* and *connected*. The process starts from the externality of humanity (information, social relationships, and tangible objects) to internality of humanity (skill and mind).(Figure 2) In order to connect, one needs to have protocols that standardize the interface between the two. The second industrial revolution unified the industrial standard that enabled the globalization of production. A part manufactured in one place of the world can be assembled in another place. Internet of

1 Michael Hardt and Antonio Negri, *Multitude: War and Democracy in the Age of Empire* (New York: The Penguin Press, 2004); Michael Hardt, "The Common in Communism," *Rethinking Marxism: A Journal of Economics, Culture & Society* 22, no. 3 (2010): 346–56.

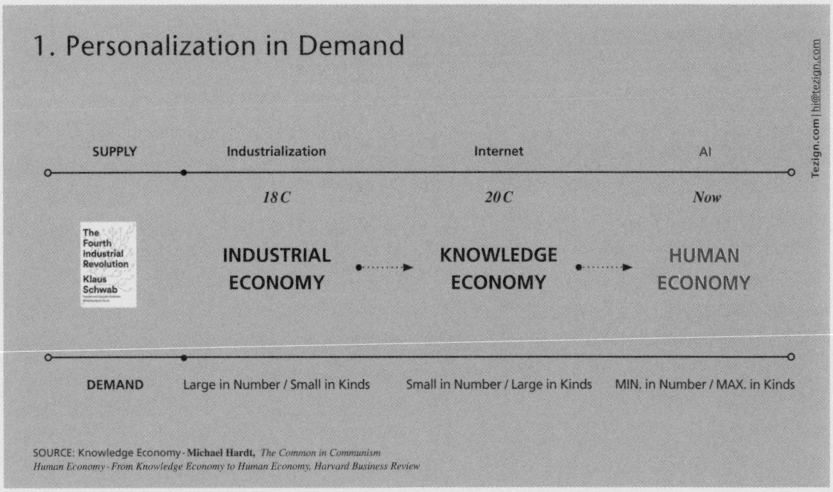

Figure 1 Personalization in Demand. Copyright © 2017 Ling Fan.

Things (IoT) also attempts to unify the interface between data and objects to connect different "things". Can the connection of skill and mind also be possible? Can we capitalize on skill and mind beyond its own territorial limitation to be global? How to build the protocol for connecting the skill and mind? These are profound questions that are currently being explored by global visionaries.

Design as a skill would be reconsidered in such a context. MIT professor Thomas Malone proposed there was a tendency of "hyperspecialization" in the skill development. Historically, human skill was a localized concept that could only be accessed in relation to local needs. However, with the development of internet and working online, certain skills can be used in a global context. Hyperspecialization means someone can do a highly unique job very well. Where once a hyperspecialized skill might have been too niche and, therefore, less useful in a small region now with the availability of the network this skill can be understood, found and deployed globally.(Figure 3) In another word, one can look for a place to apply their skills in the broader world. This does not only apply to rethinking of the way skills are deployed but also applies to a critique to education as well. What used to be regarded as good education was to give students a standardized, average capacity. But if skills can be matched in a larger scope, standardized and average capacity means people are easy to be replaced. To meet the demands of a hyperspecialized world, education system needs to address requirements for specialized practitioners. To achieve such specialization schools and universities should turn to student-centered approaches where each student's needs can be treated differently.

For these skilled individuals, the challenge will be to penetrate enterprises and collective organizations. An article published earlier this year by McKinsey Quarterly called "Organizing for the Future"[2] said that while organizations used to hire full time employees, today's bigger, more complex tasks should be divided into smaller projects and smaller tasks. Some

2 Aaron de Smet, Susan Lund, and William Schaninger, "Organizing for the Future," *McKinsey Quarterly*, January 2016, http://www.mckinsey.com/business-functions/organization/our-insights/organizing-for-the-future.

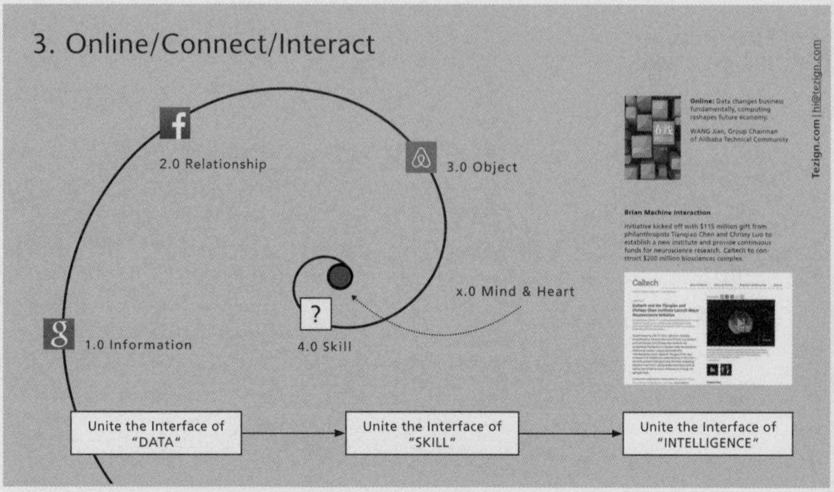

Figure 2 Online / Connect / Interact. Copyright © 2017 Ling Fan.

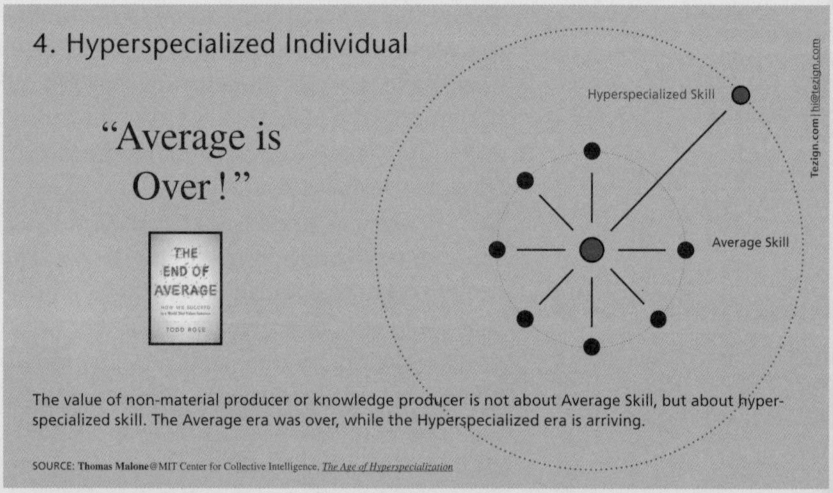

Figure 3 Hyperspecialized individual. Copyright © 2017 Ling Fan.

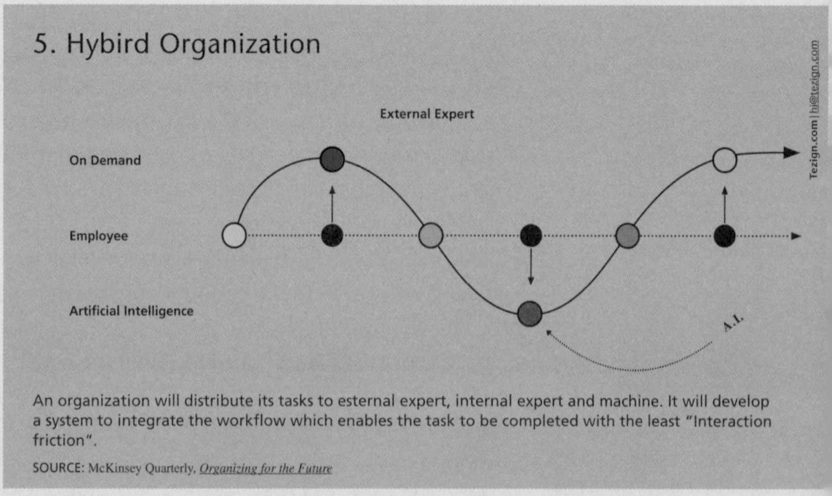

Figure 4 Hybrid Organization. Copyright © 2017 Ling Fan.

of the tasks can be—and need to be—performed by full time employees in the traditional way. The organization should, however, try to match some of the tasks with the right specialists. These specialists—call them designers, immaterial workers, knowledge workers, consultants, or simply freelancers—are everywhere. They want to work independently, for themselves. It is entirely feasible that organizations can profitably match work with specialists directly, on a task-by-task basis, instead of hiring them as ongoing employees.(Figure 4) In a parallel development, there have been improvements in technology intelligence and automation intended to streamline the execution of tedious or repetitive tasks at the same time some of the more complex work can be done with machines. The New York Times, The New Yorker, Chinese internet company Tencent, and Toutiao (今日头条, a Chinese search engine and news outlet), have all begun to use robots to write simple pieces. You may ask how a robot could write a moving news story, but for now they are only writing the simplest—and most brainless—items. This kind of piece used to be written by humans, nevertheless. In this scenario, future organizations, entities, or collectives will combine three kinds of workers. For example, IBM employs two thirds of its workforce full time, but the other third is composed of agile workforce, on-demand specialists, and automated machines.

A Distributed Talent Platform

This brings us to next question: how can innovative organizations tell that an on-demand specialist is the most suited to a particular job? This is the research I am currently undertaking at tezign.com—the technology startup I founded.(Figure 5) Economist Ronald Coase used to say that before hiring outsiders, a company needs to compare the costs of producing something internally versus outsourcing not only in terms of transactional costs but also in terms of organizational costs.[3] At tezign.com, we believe that for organizations to work more closely with on-demand specialists, they need to fully comprehend what the specialist is good at, especially when the work is immaterial and subjective. Some of the criteria people use to judge immaterial service providers are fairly standard—things like the candidate's name, current job title, education, work history, and the like. But some criteria are actually very elastic. For example, if you have been working for a carmaker, then you are likely adept at designing transportation, or you are proficient in some way with matters of speed, mobility, public infrastructure, etc. The flexibility inherent in this kind of experience can be supported and promoted through data mining, including user behavior mining. On our platform we try to understand our users' behavior by monitoring their activity on the site. Which job postings do they click on? What kinds of jobs do they track? Which jobs do they apply for, accept, or reject? By tracking user behavior, we understand which kinds of things he or she is passionate about, because they are active in their areas of interest, track developments there, and

Ronald H. Coase, "The Nature of the Firm," *Economica* 4, no. 16 (1937): 386–405.

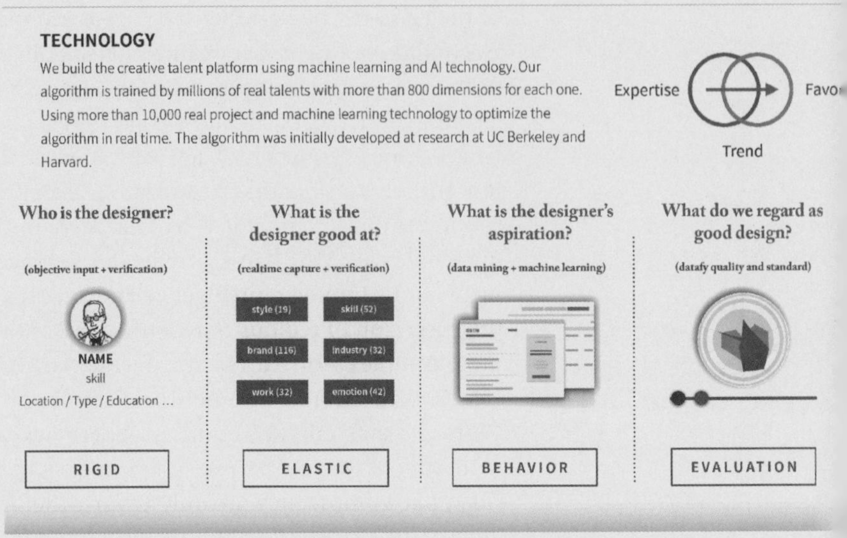

Figure 5 The interface of Tezign.com platform. Copyright © 2017 Ling Fan.

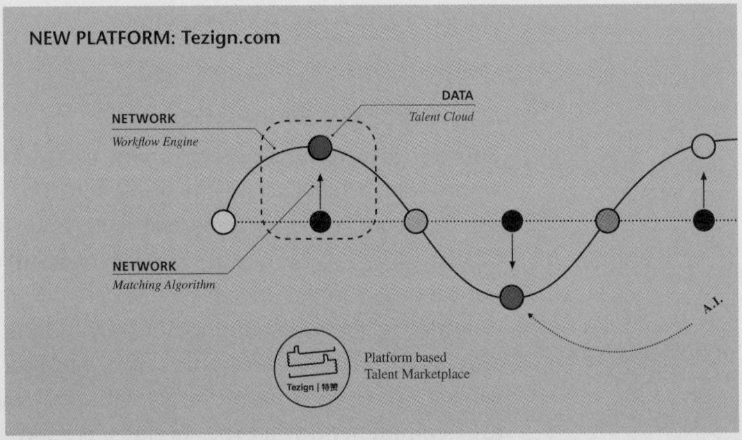

Figure 6 Three aspects of the Tezign talent platform. Copyright © 2017 Ling Fan.

POTENTIAL IMPACT OF "TALENT PLATFORM"

Higher Labor Force Participation	1.27	*work for current inactive people and increased hours for current part-timers*
Greater Emplyment	0.11	*New matches*
	0.70	*Faster matches*
Improved Productivity	0.29	*Reduced informality*
	0.34	*Best matches*

Source: MGI

By 2025, boost global GDP by $2.7 trillion

Figure 7 The potential economic impacts of talent platforms. Source: McKinsey Global Institute (MGI). Copyright © 2017 Ling Fan.

actually spend a lot time talking to people they might work with. We believe that their behavior will help us to match not only the enterprise with the right specialist, but also the specialist with the right kind of job—something he or she is passionate about.

One of our clients is an automobile website. As many can testify, Internet company employees tend to come and go very frequently. This company is eight years old, but the people who are in charge of design and marketing have only been there six months, and the oldest staff member has been there just two years. They needed designers, so we used our matching system to find candidates for them. One of the candidates had been using their website for seven years—he had used the site to buy and sell five cars over that seven-year period. Mining his data showed us just how passionate he was about cars, and speed, while his portfolio only showed designs for consumer products. The data mining uncovered what was hidden about the specialist—some potential that the specialist might want to develop—and we were able to find a balance between what he is good at, what pays well, and what he loves.

This example demonstrates the advantage of a distributed talent platform. It comprises three aspects—data, computation, and network.(Figure 6) Understanding what the task and organization requires, we examine the talents we have. Then we build a workflow that helps employers assess the appropriate pool of on-demand workers very easily, and decide whether to hire in house or on demand. Imagine that Autohome.com, for example, needs some specialized design skills. Our workflow helps them immediately recognize the potential organizational costs of hiring on-demand talent—if they determine that the potential risk of friction is low, they know they can hire outside the firm. Our platform's workflow helps the company reliably access, hire, and manage design talent; because project workflow activity is also recorded as data input, the matching and data profiling of the talent would become more and more accurate due to the machine learning technology.

This is fundamentally changing both business and society, in three ways.(Figure 7) [4] First of all, this kind of platform encourages greater workforce participation. It helps people who are not ready for full time—or those not even actively looking for work—to find a job they might love, rather than one they might take merely to earn a living. The second impact a platform like this has is that it creates jobs. In the design world, we all know that there is no lack of designs to be created or design budgets to pay for them—sometimes all that is lacking is the right person for the job. Our system actually helps a lot of companies to make decisions about new designs, and make design-related decisions more quickly. We are promoters of design talent. We show companies that whenever they have the budget, we can find the right person to help them. We boost the profile of design and the kinds of roles designers can play within these companies. The third impact is improved productivity. In a lot of cases, getting paid is not even the

4 McKinsey Global Institute, *A Labor Market That Works: Connecting Talent with Opportunity in the Digital Age* (McKinsey&Company, 2015), 6.

Figure 8 The evolution of US employment across four types of works. Source: Federal Reserve Bank of St. Louis. Copyright © 2017 Ling Fan.

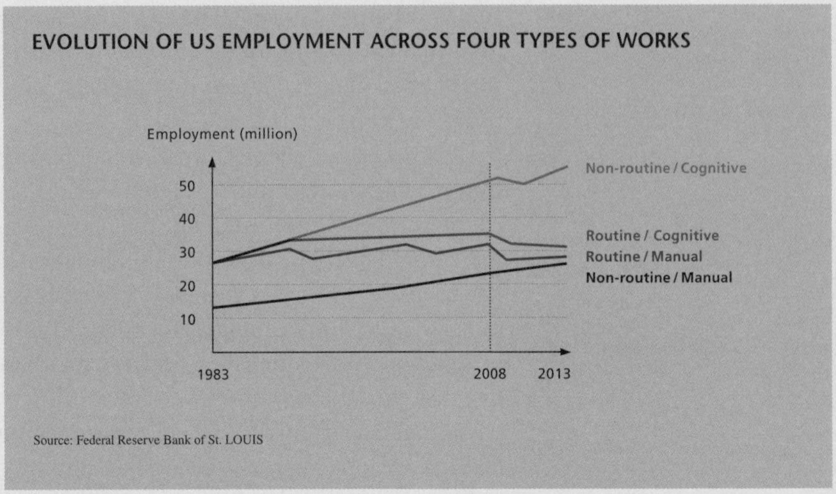

Figure 9 Bottle neck variables of work automation. Copyright © 2017 Ling Fan.

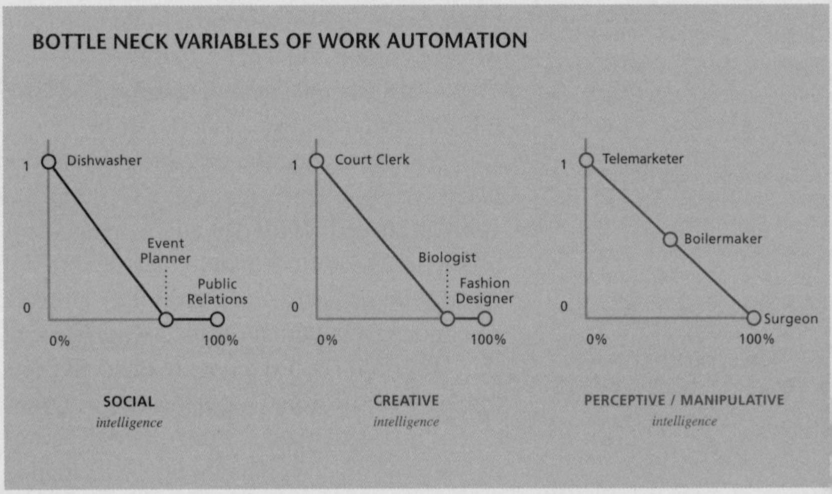

freelancer's problem. Their problem is that their role is too casual—without a formal contract or a full-time position, there has not been enough time to establish trust. During the design project lifecycle, the designer is writing, taking pictures, shooting movies, building models–producing all sorts of immaterial things—and has to establish trust with the employer rather quickly. The platform helps designers to deliver results at the right pace, to the agreed standards, on budget, and on time. And I think using data technology and computation actually facilitates these interactions—the data facilitates trust building. Some statistics indicate that, by 2025, freelance platforms could have a $2.7 trillion impact on global GDP, by creating and filling more roles, doing this more quickly, and generally increasing the bandwidth between employers and the on-demand employees they need.

When we started to collect data and use the matching algorithm to embed the workflow into enterprises, we realized that the matching stage is critical. Boston University economist James Bessen found that alongside graphic design tool development, and increases in graphic design work and graphics-related work, there was a drop in the tendency to hire typographers.[5] In other words, the tool eliminated some jobs and added others. Imagine trying to tell people you were working with VR, or drones, or even a user interface twenty years ago... it would have been unbelievable. Now these domains are creating jobs. Instead of being afraid of automation or artificial intelligence, or any kind of advancement in existing technology, I think about implementation and incrementalism. I would rather see these developments as opportunities to increase jobs—similar to the ways that designers benefitted from the development of graphic design tools.

At the same time, there will be a decrease in employment at a certain point. Routine and manual tasks tend to be those targeted by automation. Derek Thompson used the artwork by Adam Levey to show two examples of the kinds of jobs that automation will replace in ten or twenty years—routine cognitive work and routine manual labor.[6] The evolution of US employment across four types of work (Figure 8) also indicates the implications resulting from such tendency.[7] So economists have a huge column issue on this automation anxiety.[8] The easiest people to replace are not waiters or waitresses—they are telemarketers. (Figure 9) Who uses people to make cold calls anymore?

There is no job that will remain immune to some kind of automation, but, while some roles in the future might be replaced by artificial intelligence, others will still require human intelligence—especially social intelligence. Despite the growing number of graphic design jobs, the need for graphic designers will drop at some point—not because the need is diminishing, but because data collection, better algorithms, and networks boost the productivity of individual workers—not necessarily professionals in the traditional sense, though. The challenge is to apply artificial intelligence in ways that can support human activity. A very good example is Instagram. By collecting data and inventing filters, anybody can become a passable photographer. This is applying artificial intelligence in positive ways that combine data gathering and a network with machine learning and computation.

What part of designing can be replaced with AI? We spend a great deal of time on data collection and data processing, both of which AI can perform quickly and efficiently. But the human heart and mind, or our capacity to form judgments or formulate strategy can hardly be replaced, nor could our social skills. Project stakeholders could not be replaced, but designers could probably reduce 50% of their workload with applied AI.

This year, Professor Liang Ming and I will open the Design and Artificial Intelligence Lab at Tongji in Shanghai. There is a real difference in scale here that I find interesting. My startup, Tezign.com, has one hundred

5 James Bessen, "Computers Don't Kill Jobs but Do Increase Inequality," *Harvard Business Review*, March 24, 2016, https://hbr.org/2016/03/computers-dont-kill-jobs-but-do-increase-inequality.

6 For example, see Derek Thompson, "A World without Work," *The Atlantic*, July/August 2015, https://www.theatlantic.com/magazine/archive/2015/07/world-without-work/395294/.

7 Maximiliano Dvorkin, "Jobs Involving Routine Tasks Aren't Growing," *Federal Reserve Bank of St. Louis, On the Economy* (blog), January 4, 2016, https://www.stlouisfed.org/on-the-economy/2016/january/jobs-involving-routine-tasks-arent-growing.

8 For example, see Carl B. Frey and Michael A. Osborne, "The Future of Employment: How Susceptible Are Jobs to Computerisation?" *Technological Forecasting and Social Change* 114 (January 2017): 254–80.

thousand users and nine thousand specialists, and we serve two thousand firms including Unilever, Alibaba, Coca Cola, and many tech companies. Our job is to connect the right person to the right job, and the right job to the right person. The AI Lab, on the other hand, deals with the issue of applying computation and machine learning more broadly. Instead of matching one hundred thousand specialist users with hyperspecialized tasks, the AI Lab will be addressing a reality that may become the future for roughly ten million Chinese designers.

Cases

CASE 7
DO-IT-TOGETHER:
INFRASTRUCTURING FOR SOCIAL INNOVATION
Xiaolan Wang

CASE 7
Xiaolan Wang

Embedding Designers in Government Innovation Teams: Insights from the Designmatters Fellowship Program at ArtCenter

Mariana Amatullo

Parsons School of Design, The New School, New York, USA.

Jennifer May

Designmatters at ArtCenter College of Design, Pasadena, USA

There is a growing uptake of professional designers joining multi-disciplinary practices in city- and country-level "innovation" divisions of governments around the world. Varying in organizational scope and thematic foci, these new practices are often situated at the intersection of human-centered design, technology, and policy, and share a commitment for citizen-centric public services and societal change at scale. While unequivocal signs of designers taking on stewardship roles in these teams abound, the career pathways leading up to these roles remain emergent. We also know little about designers' team learning experiences and impact in these government settings. This case study helps bridge this gap in articulation. Grounding our analyses on the theoretical framework and established predictive value of the *design attitude construct*, we collect empirical data from a sample of designers and managers affiliated with the Designmatters Fellowship program at ArtCenter College of Design who have participated in Bloomberg Philanthropies' Government Innovation initiative. In particular, we highlight key takeaways from their contributions to the innovation teams (i-teams) from the mayors' offices of Los Angeles and Long Beach. Our study offers new evidence about the unique value designers bring to the work of government innovation.

Keywords **Design attitude, public sector design, social innovation, fellowships, i-teams, team learning, design and government**

Mariana Amatullo is an Associate Professor of Strategic Design and Management at Parsons, The New School, New York, and the Co-Founder of Designmatters at ArtCenter College of Design. She was at the helm of Designmatters from 2001 to 2017, spearheading the award-winning social innovation department and its portfolio of research initiatives and projects for 16 years. Amatullo is a Scholar-in Residence at the Weatherhead School of Management, Case Western Reserve University. She is the lead editor of LEAP Dialogues: Career Pathways in Design for Social Innovation (DAP, 2016); her research focuses on the impact of design on social innovation and organizational practice. Amatullo holds a PhD in Management from the Weatherhead School of Management, Case Western Reserve University, an M.A. in Art History and Museum Studies from the University of Southern California, and a Licence en Lettres Degree from the Sorbonne University, Paris.

mariana.amatullo@newschool.edu

Jennifer May is the Director of Designmatters at ArtCenter College of Design in Pasadena, California, where she oversees the Department's operations and a dynamic portfolio of social innovation projects, including the Designmatters Fellowship program. Jennifer was the Managing Editor of *LEAP Dialogues: Career Pathways in Design for Social Innovation* (DAP, 2016). Jennifer holds an M.B.A. from the Marshall School of Business at the University of Southern California, where she was a Graduate Fellow at the Brittingham Social Enterprise Lab, a Fellow with the prestigious Education Pioneers program and a Forté Fellow.

Jennifer.May@Artcenter.edu

Introduction

A new class of multi-disciplinary practices focused on innovation at the intersection of human-centered design, technology, and policy is emerging in local and national governments around the world. Varying in organizational scope—from satellite nonprofit centers (Public Policy Lab, New York) to labs embedded in government (MindLab, Denmark) to government in-house consulting innovation teams (Bloomberg Philanthropies' Innovation Teams Program)—they share a commitment to creating novel and useful solutions (the very definition of innovation) that address complex challenges, delivering citizen-centric public services, and creating societal change at scale.[1] These practices also embrace innovation as a deliberate process that requires strategic intent, dedicated capabilities, collaboration across disciplines, and the relentless pursuit of citizen engagement as the source of resonant insights for actionable outcomes.[2] Along with this imperative for innovation in government, there are unequivocal signs of a growing uptake of professional designers joining these practices in new stewardship roles.[3] However, the career pathways leading up to these positions and what they might look like are far from evident.[4] Meanwhile, the team learning experiences and value that designers bring to these government settings continues to be poorly understood and in need of further elucidation and assessment.[5]

The present research focuses on understanding how we might elucidate the value designers bring to government innovation practices. Grounding our analyses on the theoretical framework and established predictive value of the *design attitude construct*, which we define as "the holistic conceptualization of the unique abilities and capabilities that professional designers espouse as they problem-solve,"[6] we collect empirical data from a sample of designers and managers affiliated with the Designmatters Fellowship program at ArtCenter College of Design who have participated in Bloomberg Philanthropies' Government Innovation initiative. In particular, we highlight key takeaways from team members who have contributed to the innovation teams (i-teams) from the mayors' offices of the cities of Los Angeles and Long Beach. In order to gain a better understanding of the unique value designers bring to government innovation, we pose the following research questions:

- What is the experience of designers and government innovation teams as they interact and work together in the public sector?
- Can a design attitude capability in problem solving amplify the innovation processes of these practices?
- Are there particular opportunities and/or barriers to designers' effectiveness in these complex contexts for innovation delivery?

Our answers to these questions point to shifts that are taking place in the public sector when it comes to the integration of design as a competency. We also surface key situations that provide evidence of the value of embedding designers in government innovation teams.

1 The Public Policy Lab (launched in 2010) is structured as an independent non-profit organization located in Brooklyn that partners with government to design public services with low-income and at risk communities; their mission is to "work at the intersection of human-centered design and public policy." More on their mandate at http://publicpolicylab.org/. In Denmark, Mindlab is a cross-governmental innovation unit that receives oversight from the Ministry of Industry, Business and Financial Affairs, the Ministry of Employment, the Ministry of Education and Odense Municipality. Their interdisciplinary staff includes designers who collaborate with individuals that have backgrounds in social science, philosophy, journalism and engineering to address strategic public sector challenges that have policy implications. More on their mission and programs at http://mind-lab.dk/en/.

2 Ruth Puttick, Philip Colligan, and Peter Baeck, "I-teams: The Teams and Funds Making Innovation Happen in Government around the World," *Nesta*, last modified June 30, 2014, http://www.nesta.org.uk/publications/i-teams-teams-and-funds-making-innovation-happen-governments-around-world; Mariana Amatullo, "Design Attitude and Social Innovation: Empirical Studies of the Return on Design" (PhD dissertation, Case Western Reserve University, 2015); Christian Bason, *Design for Policy* (Fahnham: Gower Publishing Limited, 2014).

3 Bryan Boyer, Justin W. Cook, Marco Steinberg, and Helsinki Design Lab, *Legible Practises: Six Stories about the Craft of Stewardship* (Helsinki: Sitra, 2013); Leah Armstrong, Jocelyn Bailey, Guy Julier, and Lucy Kimbell, *Social Design Futures: HEI Research and the AHRC* (Arts & Humanities Research Center, University of Brighton and Victoria, and Albert Museum, 2014), available at https://mappingsocialdesign.files.wordpress.com/2014/10/social-design-futures-report.pdf.

4 Mariana Amatullo, Bryan Boyer, Liz Danzico, and Andrew Shea, eds. *LEAP Dialogues: Career Pathways in Design for Social Innovation* (Designmatters at Art Center College of Design, 2016).

5 Amatullo, "Design Attitude and Social Innovation."

In this paper, first we offer some contextual grounding for the study by describing the nature and relationship between the programs highlighted in this case—the Designmatters Fellowship program at ArtCenter and its partnership with the Los Angeles and Long Beach i-teams. Second, we frame our research questions in the context of the design-theoretical framework that grounds our observations. We then provide an overview of our methodological approach, describing our research design and data collection strategy. We conclude by sharing salient findings and reflecting on the implications as well as the limitations of this study.

The Designmatters Fellowship Program at ArtCenter College of Design

Designmatters at ArtCenter College of Design in Pasadena, California was established in 2001 with the mandate to bring real-world and real-time issues into the curriculum of the College as the source of experiential learning about the role of the arts and design disciplines in catalyzing social innovation.[7] Throughout its 16-year history and considerable growth trajectory, the department's philosophical orientation has remained consistent—foster an open, forward-thinking, entrepreneurial culture of socially-responsible design through a range of learning activities, both curricular and co-curricular.

Launched in 2006, the Designmatters Fellowship program is one of the signature initiatives of the Department.[8] The fellowship is an honors internship that places an average of six to eight of the most talented ArtCenter students annually in international development organizations, government agencies, and social enterprises. Designmatters Fellows are selected first and foremost based on merit—they are students who stand out in their discipline and have the required skills and versatile set of competencies to excel at meeting the challenges of the strategic design assignments they are typically handed. Importantly, they are also chosen based on their interpersonal skills, leadership acumen, and ability to navigate successfully what are often complex organizational environments that have little or no design fluency.[9] In this sense, they are often considered ambassadors of design in organizational settings, where in many situations they are the sole design experts on their teams and are responsible for extending a design mindset to problem solving.

Over time, the Designmatters Fellowship program has become an effective framework for building partnerships. Through the Fellowship, Designmatters mobilizes the design expertise of ArtCenter students as a key resource that can be leveraged by host organizations as an influx of creativity and innovation for program development and delivery. In commenting about the program, Julienne Chen, former Deputy Director of the Los Angeles i-team noted, "The support of the Fellow helped to elevate our conversations from theory and concepts into practical shapes and forms

6 Richard J. Boland and Fred Collopy, *Managing as Designing* (Stanford: Stanford University Press, 2004); Richard Boland, Fred Collopy, Kalle Lyytinen, and Youngjin Yoo, "Managing as Designing: Lessons for Organization Leaders from the Design Practice of Frank O. Gehry," *Design Issues* 24, no. 1 (2008): 10–25; Kamil Michlewski, "Uncovering Design Attitude: Inside the Culture of Designers," *Organization Studies* 29, no. 3 (2008): 373–92; Amatullo, preface to "Design Attitude and Social Innovation."

7 The Designmatters Department adopts the following definition of social innovation put forth by the Skoll Centre for Social Entrepreneurship: "new products, processes, environments, and systems that satisfy unmet needs and enhance society's capacity to act." See Geoff Mulgan, Simon Tucker, Rushanara Ali, and Ben Sanders. "Social Innovation: What It Is, Why It Matters and How It Can Be Accelerated," (working paper, Skoll Centre for Social Entrepreneurship, Oxford Saïd Business School, 2007), http://youngfoundation.org/wp-content/uploads/2012/10/Social-Innovation-what-it-is-why-it-matters-how-it-can-be-accelerated-March-2007.pdf.

8 The initial rationale of conceiving the Designmatters Fellowship was to have a mechanism to offer funded internship opportunities for the most talented ArtCenter students within United Nations agencies as part of the non-governmental organization status of the college and Designmatters' commitment to integrate a design capability into the organizational setting of the UN's family of funds and agencies. In the first two years of the program, Fellowships were made possible by a philanthropic fund from ArtCenter College of Design that placed fellows at organizations in the following agencies and funds of the UN system: UNESCO, UNICEF and the UN Department of Public Information (DPI). Starting in 2008 and to date, the Fellowship program evolved its funding model to be less dependent on philanthropic support and instead focused on a reciprocal partnership framework, with most Fellows now funded by the organizations that host them.

9 The Fellowship placement is comprised of a multi-step rigorous vetting process that includes a written application, followed by cross-departmental internal-panel interviews to identify semi-finalists as well as a final set of interviews with the host organization leading

and helped people to start seeing the art of the possible. This opened up new opportunities in terms of partnerships and projects."[10] In turn, Fellows experience firsthand the tangible outcomes of their contributions. Chase Airmet, the first Designmatters Fellow placed with the City of Long Beach i-team in the summer of 2015, reflected on this influential dimension of his Fellowship experience, stating "I loved my time working not only with the wonderful people in Long Beach but also with Designmatters. Designmatters gives students an amazing opportunity to focus on difficult problems that are often hard to find singular solutions for. My life and perspective have changed due to my experience, and I hope to continue to work in the public sector."[11] The reciprocal dynamic of value added by the Fellowship program represents a win-win. It illustrates the notion that partnerships can "create spaces for individuals and communities to seek different types of leadership that were not possible in traditional models of organization and governance."[12]

An important observation culled from the experiences of Fellows over the 11-year span of the program is how often the Fellowship has been a conduit for the integration of design capabilities into the institutional fabric of organizations that welcome the Fellows. This happens in two ways. It occurs at the level of the relationship between Fellows and host organizations, where a continuum of engagement is created after the Fellowship ends, with approximately 35% of Fellows receiving offers for freelance assignments or full-time positions post-Fellowship.[13] This integration of Fellows into longer-term contractual agreements is a direct way for organizations to increase their design fluency, and in turn for Fellows to craft novel career pathways after graduation. Additionally, and more indirectly perhaps, the Fellowship often serves as an introductory engagement for organizations to experience the value of adding design competencies into their operations and projects. In this regard, the Fellows play a key role in their ability to demonstrate the value of design contributions to their supervisors and peers in these organizations. The Designmatters staff also establishes a close rapport with the host organization to mentor and track the Fellows' progress, and a relationship of trust often builds as a result. Once mutual trust has been built, organizations are open to exploring more strategic design engagements.[14] As a result, the Designmatters department has seen a number of successful Fellowships lead to comprehensive and team-based collaborations with faculty and students through joint research initiatives and externally funded curricular projects that follow that initial Fellowship engagement.

The Government Initiative at Bloomberg Philanthropies

Government Innovation is one of five areas of focus Bloomberg Philanthropies, the charitable organization established by former New York City Mayor and philanthropist Michael Bloomberg.[15] Starting with the premise

up to the selection of the candidate (graduate and undergraduate ArtCenter students may qualify). Candidates are evaluated for excellent academic record, strong interpersonal skills, motivation and fit with the organization. Placements last the length of the academic term (14 weeks) and occur up to three times a year with most Fellowships scheduled during the summer academic term. For more information see http://designmattersatartcenter.org/fellowship-program/.

10 Statement made by Julienne Chen in response to the December 2016 survey of i-team members. See Appendix B, p. 175.

11 Statement made by Chase Airmet in response to the December 2016 survey of Designmatters Fellows. See Appendix B, p. 175.

12 Jane Nelson, *Building Partnerships: Cooperation between the United Nations System and the Private Sector* (New York: United Nations Department of Public Information, 2002), 4.

13 Examples of freelance assignments such as branding campaigns and documentary films include Adriana Crespo's (Illustration, 2014) experience with the Pan American Health Organization (PAHO) in the spring of 2015, and Benjamin Weiss (Film, 2013), a Fellow with the Aquarium of the Pacific in the summer of 2014 who produced several short films for the organization post Fellowship. Examples of Fellows more permanently seeing their career pathways after graduation influenced by their Fellowship placements and being granted full-time offers have included Jonathan Goldman (Advertising, 2006) with a new in-house design position created at the Organization of American States to take advantage of his skillset; Geoff Brewerton (Graphic Design, 2013) hired shortly after his Fellowship by his host organization Proximity Designs to oversee their Graphic Design Department. Mari Nakano (Graduate Media Design Practices, 2009) was a Fellow with the United Nations Population Fund (UNFPA) in the summer of 2008 and continued to work on a freelance basis, which led her to her current full-time position with the Innovation Office at UNICEF, one of the first divisions in the UN system to pursue an intentional strategy of hiring designers into their teams. More on Nakano's professional role with UNICEF at: http://unicefstories.org/2016/02/24/unicef-innovation-team-spotlight-mari-nakano/.

that innovation involves taking risks and trying new ideas—which doesn't often come easy to government—Bloomberg's foundation has invested in a series of programs that encourage public sector leaders to gain the capabilities and confidence needed to embrace the challenge of innovation in government. One facet of this programming takes the form of innovation teams, or i-teams, which are typically embedded in City Hall and help city leaders drive innovation, change culture, and create an ongoing ability to tackle systemic problems and deliver citizen-centric services.

This case study highlights a set of designer journeys and discreet design contributions to the i-teams working with the mayors' offices of the cities of Los Angeles and Long Beach, both grantees of the Government Innovation initiative portfolio. Focused on distinct high priority challenges in their cities, these i-teams are pursuing activities in four broad categories—(1) creating and developing solutions to respond to the priority area(s) identified; (2) engaging citizens, business and partners outside government to seek new ideas outside the system and enabling these ideas to take hold within government; (3) transforming the skills, process and norms of practice of government, bringing in new approaches that can result in a lasting innovation mindset; and (4) developing a blueprint for system level change that can have actionable policy implications.[16] We briefly describe below the focal activities that Fellows encountered in each i-team.

14 A case in point is the multifaceted engagement with the City of Long Beach i-team. After integrating four consecutive Fellows into their projects, the i-team secured the evidence to invite Designmatters to partner on a large scale proposal for a city-funded public health communication and awareness initiative on the rising rates of STDs—including HIV/AIDs—in the city. Learn more about this project at https://designmattersatartcenter.org/proj/engage-envision-empower-longbeach/.

15 The foundation oversees all of Bloomberg's charitable giving. The other focus areas that the foundation is intent on creating lasting change include public health, arts and culture, the environment, and education. Learn more about the foundation at https://www.bloomberg.org/about/.

16 Puttick, Colligan, and Baeck, "i-teams."

Raising Awareness of the Rent Stabilization Ordinance—a Los Angeles i-team Initiative

One of the principal designers placed with the Los Angeles i-team helped conceive and develop a new marketing and awareness campaign about the city's Rent Stabilization Ordinance (RSO). The campaign aimed to help tenants and landlords better understand and access city resources so that vulnerable populations can afford to stay in their homes during a compressed housing market with rents rapidly rising.[(Figure 1)]

A human-centered design process, inclusive of a pluralism of perspectives from stakeholder interviews, together with a comprehensive analysis of target audiences and messaging allowed the i-team to develop an effective multi-platform campaign.[(Figure 2)]

Outcome implementation began 2016 in communities vulnerable to displacement. The design interventions leverage highly-visible assets including transit shelters, bus interiors/exteriors, subway stations, and city facilities like library and WorkSource centers.[(Figure 3)]

Integrating Design Thinking Processes in the Day-to-Day Practices of the Long Beach i-team

The Long Beach i-team focuses on identifying how the City can make it easier for entrepreneurs to start and grow their business in the City of Long Beach. Since the i-team's inception in 2015, five designers from the Designmatters Fellowship program were placed in consecutive quarterly

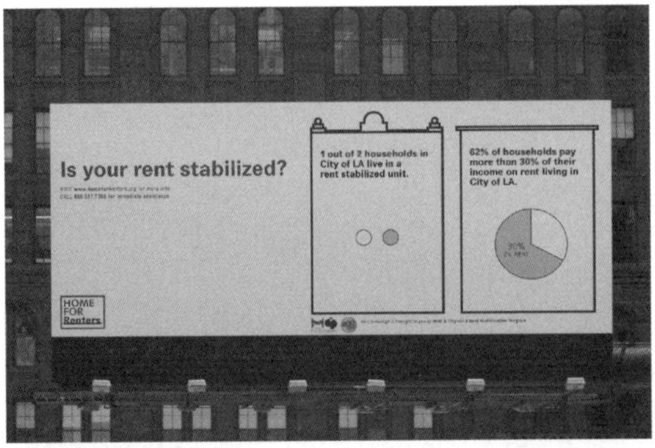

Figure 1 Rent Stabilization Ordinance campaign billboard designed by Los Angeles i-team member and ArtCenter Alumna Bora Shin. Copyright © 2016 City of Los Angeles.

Figure 2 Rent Stabilization Ordinance handbook for renters. Copyright © 2016 City of Los Angeles.

Figure 3 Rent Stabilization Ordinance campaign bus stop poster installed in Boyle Heights, California. Copyright © 2016 City of Los Angeles.

appointments to support this mandate. Through a variety of design interventions—including the creation of a branding system for the i-team, infographics and data visualization tools, design thinking workshops for staff in City Hall, and human-centered design toolkits for fieldwork—the Fellows worked to converge many elements of the i-teams processes and amplify their impact.(Figures 4–7)

Theoretical Framework

Our study draws broadly from the literature streams of design attitude, social innovation, and public sector design. Importantly, our research builds on the design attitude body of literature as it offers new evidence of the significance of the construct as key to furthering innovation outcomes in the public sector. The following section provides a brief overview of these streams as a backbone to our research.

The Design Attitude Construct

Design attitude is a multidimensional construct first coined by management scholars Richard Boland and Fred Collopy.[17] It has been defined as "a composite of distinct abilities (skills, capabilities, aptitudes) that designers apply during the process of designing."[18] One of the important implications of a design attitude approach to problem solving is that it allows designers to be agile when faced with discontinuous change, leading to outcomes that are not necessarily envisioned at the onset. This conceptualization highlights the capabilities of designers as a distinct set of heuristics that "fosters an acceptance of and a comfort with a problem-solving process that remains liquid and open, celebrating new alternatives as it strives to develop a best design solution."[19] This approach is conducive to innovation aims, as it is opposed to a decision attitude—one often dominant and favored in bureaucratic government environments, and which assumes that alternative courses of action are ready to hand or, at the very least, readily obtainable.[20] There are five salient dimensions of the design attitude construct first identified by Michlewski in his research of design consultancies such as IDEO and companies such as Phillips who have a robust track record of design expertise.[21] These key dimensions were extended and operationalized as (1) empathy, (2) tolerance to ambiguity, (3) connecting multiple perspectives, (4) creativity, and (5) aesthetics; and show robust statistical results (positive and significant relationships) that demonstrate the very strong explanatory power of design attitude to further innovation outcomes in projects as well as impact team learning.[22] In this study, we develop a survey that tests several dimensions of design attitude as well as techniques commonly used by designers—such as prototyping and visualization—with the aim of drawing a more precise picture of what might be the skillsets and approaches designers bring to the public sector that stakeholders perceive and accept as particularly valuable (see Appendix A, p. 174).

17 Boland and Collopy, *Managing as Designing*.

18 Boland and Collopy, *Managing as Designing*; Michlewski, "Uncovering Design Attitude"; Kamil Michlewski, *Design Attitude* (Farnham: Gower Publishing Limited, 2015); Amatullo, "Design Attitude and Social Innovation," 15.

19 Richard J. Boland and Fred Collopy, "Design Matters for Management," in *Managing as Designing*, ed. Richard J. Boland and Fred Collopy (Stanford: Stanford University Press, 2004), 10.

20 Boland and Collopy, *Managing as Designing*.

21 Michlewski, "Uncovering Design Attitude."

22 Amatullo, "Design Attitude and Social Innovation."

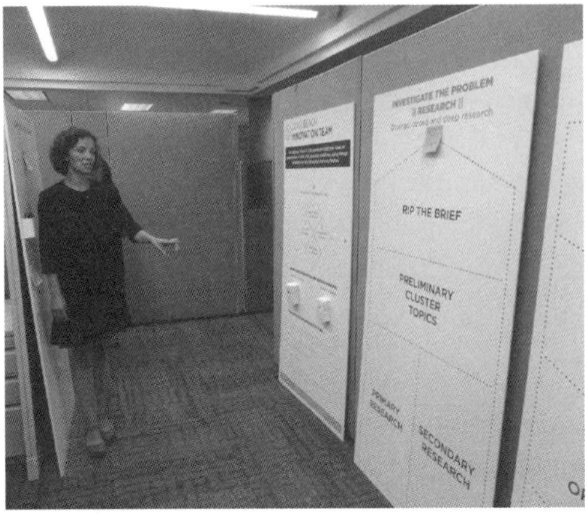

Figure 4 Designmatters Fellow, Justine Esquivel at work during her Fellowship with the Long Beach i-team. Photo courtesy of Justine Esquivel.

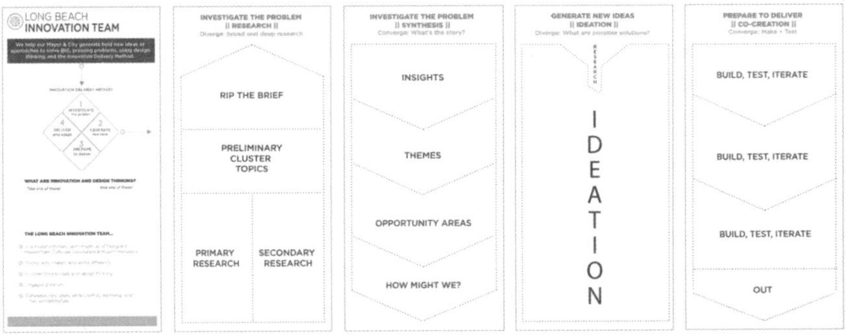

Figure 5 Long Beach i-team toolkit designed by Designmatters Fellow Justine Esquivel. Copyright © 2016 City of Long Beach.

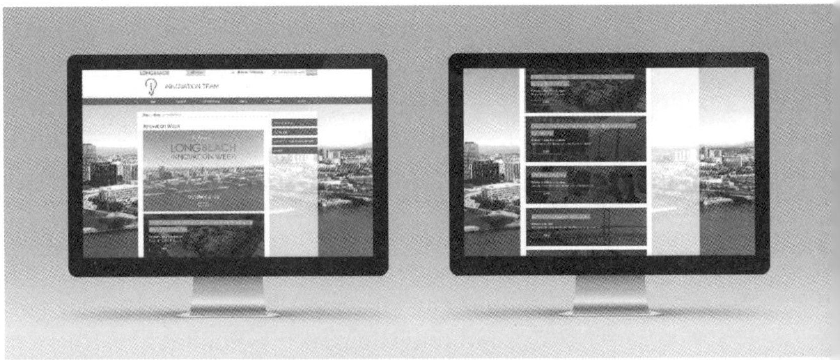

Figure 6 *Long Beach Innovation Week* website designed by Designmatters Fellow Karen Davison. Copyright © 2015 City of Long Beach.

Figure 7 Long Beach Citizen Police Complaint Commission Report designed by Designmatters Fellow Karen Davison. Copyright © 2015 City of Long Beach.

Social Innovation and Public Sector Design

Social innovation is considered a "practice-led field" wherein understandings, definitions, and meanings have partly emerged through people doing things in new ways rather than thinking about them in an academic way.[23] Therefore, a precise conceptualization of the term is challenging. This study does not aim to offer a comprehensive literature review of the social innovation field. For the purposes of our research, we define social innovation as "a new solution (product, service, model, process, etc.) that simultaneously meets a social need (more effectively than existing solutions) and leads to new or improved capabilities and relationships and better use of assets and resources ... enhance society's capacity to act."[24] This definition of social innovation encompasses three core elements that are relevant to the experiences of the Designmatters Fellows surveyed in our study and the contributions they have made in the government i-teams that we analyze. These elements are (1) novelty—social innovations that are new to the field, sector, region, market or user and represent an intervention that can be applied in a new way and imply invention; (2) societal impact—social innovations that are explicitly designed to meet a recognized social need and enhance society's capacity to act;[25] and (3) a move from idea to implementation—social innovations that imply the application and implementation of ideas and new value creation.[26] As a field of research and practice, social innovation can overlap with a category of design practices that have been proliferating in government settings that touch public life.[27] These practices are often referred to as "public sector design" practices. They bring a user-centered approach to the development of social service delivery and augment the relevance of government agencies in the lives of their citizens.[28] Our case study is squarely situated within this growing body of research and design practices.

Methodological Approach

Since 2015, Designmatters has placed a total of eight designers in i-teams working in the mayor's offices of the cities of Los Angeles and Long Beach. This case study compares and contrasts Fellows' experiences as well as the perspectives of their supervisors and team members. Data sources include qualitative interviews, documents, design artifacts from each i-team, and a survey—all of which allow for a rich description of the phenomena studied. We have guided our analyses using an inductive approach to pattern building from the data along with emergent theory generation about how design as a knowledge domain is manifesting in government innovation practices.[29]

Research Design

Between September and December 2016, we conducted open-ended qualitative interviews with Fellows and i-team members, gathered documentation of the Fellows' design interventions, and followed up with a survey

23 Julie Caulier-Grice, Anna Davies, Robert Patrick, and Will Norman, *The Young Foundation Social Innovation Overview: A Deliverable of the Project: The Theoretical, Empirical and Policy Foundations for Building Social Innovation in Europe* (TEPSIE), European Commission—7th Framework Programme (Brussels: European Commission, DG Research, 2012), also available at http://www.tepsie.eu/index.php/publications.

24 Grice et al., *The Young Foundation Social Innovation Overview*, 18; Frank Moulaert, Flavia Martinelli, Erik Swyngedouw, and Sara Gonzalez, "Towards Alternative Model (s) of Local Innovation," *Urban Studies* 42, no. 11 (2005): 1969–90.

25 Robin Murray, Julie Caulier-Grice, and Geoff Mulgan, *The Open Book of Social Innovation* (London: The Young Foundation, 2010).

26 Grice et al, *The Young Foundation Social Innovation Overview.*

27 Eduardo Staszowski and Scott Brown, eds., *(New): Public Goods, The Journal of Design Strategies* 8, no.1 (2016).

28 Bason, *Design for Policy*; Geoff Mulgan, "Design in Public and Social Innovation: What Works and What Could Work Better," *Nesta*. January, 2014.

29 Kathleen M. Eisenhardt and Melissa E. Graebner, "Theory Building from Cases: Opportunities and Challenges," *Academy of Management Journal* 50, no. 1 (2007): 25–32; Robert K. Yin, *Case Study Research: Design and Methods*, 5th ed. (Sage Publications, 2013).

instrument. The purpose of the survey was to build and extend emergent theory about the shifting roles of designers in the government innovation practices they were embedded in. Key questions were designed to gain insights into (1) the contributions and value designers brought to the i-teams; (2) any shift in perspectives about design's role in the public sector, and (3) opportunities and barriers to design adoption in the public sector.

Sample and Data Collection

Due to the nature of the survey's goals and the groups identified, we worked with a very small sample size (four respondents from the i-teams and five respondents from the Fellows group) and followed a strategy of purposeful sampling. The surveys were not meant to gather statistically significant data for quantitative or qualitative evaluation. Rather, the surveys were used to produce transparently observable phenomena[30] as an exploratory tool to add support to the empirical evidence gathered through the case study methods previously described, and help gain deeper insights and identify patterns among and across the groups surveyed.

The surveys for the i-team members and the Fellows asked similar questions and followed a similar order to help identify potential patterns of commonalities and differences between the perspectives of the two groups. Appendix A presents an explanatory summary of the survey's key sections and aims, and Appendix B presents the full results of the survey.

30 Kathleen M. Eisenhardt, "Building Theories from Case Study Research," *Academy of Management Review* 14, no. 4 (1989): 532–50.

Findings and Discussion

In this section we discuss three key themes that emerge from our analysis of the survey responses and comment on patterns in the data that show commonalities and differences both among and across our two groups, design Fellows and i-team members. We also triangulate this data with other secondary research from these case studies and existing theoretical insights to arrive at the conclusions we offer.

Finding 1—Assessing Fellows' Activities and Contributions

In order to assess where Fellows brought value to the i-teams and how their design expertise was deployed in the government innovation context, the respondents were asked to rank how strongly they agreed with the statement "The Designmatters Fellow/I made significant contributions to the i-team." One hundred percent of respondents across both i-team members and Fellows agreed or strongly agreed with this statement, which is indicative of both groups positively embracing the experience. A second set of survey questions asked Fellows and i-team members to name the three principal contributions offered via the Fellowship (the responses were self-reflective in the case of the Fellows). The activities identified as valuable can be categorized in four distinct groupings: (1) visual design; (2) design thinking; (3) documentation; and (4) interpersonal skills, with most responses clustering around the first two groupings. If we analyze these groupings against the characterization of design as a knowledge domain with "four orders," a classification established in the literature by Richard Buchanan,[31] we can note that most contributions by the Fellows in these government settings seem to focus on first order design, with grouping 1 (which is the design of communications through signs and symbols) as well as third and fourth order design with groupings 2 (design thinking/strategy) and grouping 4 (interpersonal skills that lead to the design of interactions and processes addressing system issues). These findings are also reflective of the activities that engaged Fellows in both of our case studies presented. For the Los Angeles i-team, visual design was core to the design outputs for the Rent Stabilization Ordinance campaign. For the Long Beach i-team, the integration of design thinking processes was central to the Fellowship's activities. Table 1 below compares statements from these groups across these four categories.

31 Richard Buchanan, "Design Research and the New Learning," *Design Issues* 17, no. 4 (2001): 3–23.

Table 1. Fellows' principal design contributions to i-teams.

	I-TEAM MEMBERS' ASSESSMENT (REPRESENTATIVE STATEMENTS)	FELLOWS' ASSESSMENT (REPRESENTATIVE STATEMENTS)
1.Visual Design (communication design via symbols and images, through especially graphic design outcomes)	-graphic design -production (deliverables, prototypes, events, media collateral) -excellent graphic designs	-designed logos and identities, web design, presentations and slide decks -offered visual design support as needed -provided clarity and cohesiveness to i-teams visual communication/ promotional material -branded the team -branding and materials for city -visual communication: flyers, web pages, infographics, annual reports, banners, email newsletters, branding/identify development
.Design Thinking/Strategy/ Methods (using design thinking techniques such as design research methods and user journeys, developing toolkits, mentoring other team members on design methods to problem-solve)	-good strategy -putting a physical form to ideas -providing guidance on implementing design-thinking process -project management (framing and implementing the design thinking process) -disseminating the value of design to and through our team and stakeholders	-user-centered design, research, strategy design -user journeys for team initiatives -toolkit to instigate thinking about how to communicate their work outside of the team via a portfolio and transparency -designing a visual map for the team to follow for priorities -designed and facilitated a workshop for youth on design thinking -led design thinking and prototyping workshops -offered design thinking knowledge for all team members -design thinking -represented ArtCenter and what good design can do for the city
Documentation (synthesizing and capturing the i-team workflow processes and initiatives)	-documentation of work process	-documented team's initiatives with photography
Interpersonal Skills (forging connections, bringing unique perspective to weigh on complex problems)	-perspective (providing additional capacity, unique perspective and energy as a team member) -good interpersonal skills -connecting multiple disciplines and stakeholders through design	-making connections with team members and others in Long Beach -an outsider's perspective

Finding 2—Design Attitude: Shifting Perceptions of the Value of Design Capabilities

A key finding of this survey points to the transformative dimension of embedding designers in these innovation practices both from the perspective of the designers (in this case study, Fellows) and from the perspective of the non-designers (in this case study i-teams members).

In no uncertain terms, our survey data indicates a progression that occurs in the recognition and appreciation of design capabilities and skillsets by i-teams as they interact with the Fellows. In addition, the survey presents evidence that Fellows also see a maturation of their own understanding of their capabilities and the potential impact they may be able to exert in these settings. For example, we see that 75% of the i-team members cite the Fellowship experience as changing "the way I imagine the role of designers in the public sector." The perspective shared by Fellows is strikingly similar, 80% of those surveyed agree with the same sentiment, considering their Fellowship experience as greatly reaffirming. Furthermore, the shift in perception manifests at the lexical level—i-team members selected terms aligned with visual design to describe how they viewed designers prior to working with the Fellows, including "Artists," "Creatives," "Graphic Designers," and "Illustrators"; post the Fellows' insertion, they instead selected the words "Researchers," "Problem Solvers," and "Service Designers," as seen in **Figure 8**.

These responses emphasize the shift in perspective that occurs when the teams integrate design capabilities. Not surprisingly, first-order design outcomes such as communication design are anticipated at the outset of collaborative integration, while third- and fourth-order design contributions remain abstract—and thus not necessarily articulated—until after the experience and exposure to the designers.

Finally, the survey responses provide us with new insights about key dimensions of design attitude such as empathy and creativity, as well as established design techniques such as prototyping and visualization that are often identified and valued in innovation contexts **(see Figure 9)**.[32]

32 Amatullo, "Design Attitude and Social Innovation."

Two Sides of the Same Coin—Communication and Collaboration

The last section of the survey asked Fellows and i-team members to identify unexpected challenges and opportunities that arose during the Fellowship experience. A key rationale behind this probing was to surface insights about potential barriers to design adoption, and/or unanticipated opportunities.

The data we gathered indicates that the challenges and opportunities respondents articulated relate to issues around communication and collaboration, both within the i-teams and with other city departments and stakeholders the i-teams work with.(Table 2) We can infer that the close relationship between challenges and opportunities encountered indicates that

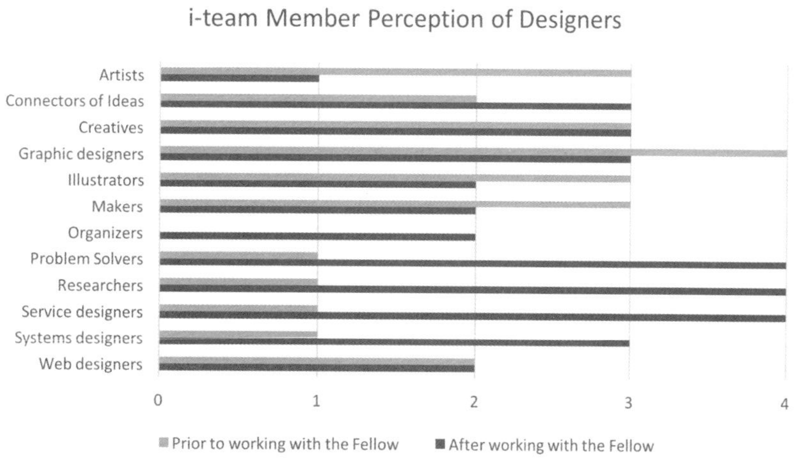

Figure 8 Comparison of i-team members' perceptions of designers prior to and after working with Fellows, drawn from 2016 survey. Copyright © 2017 Designmatters.

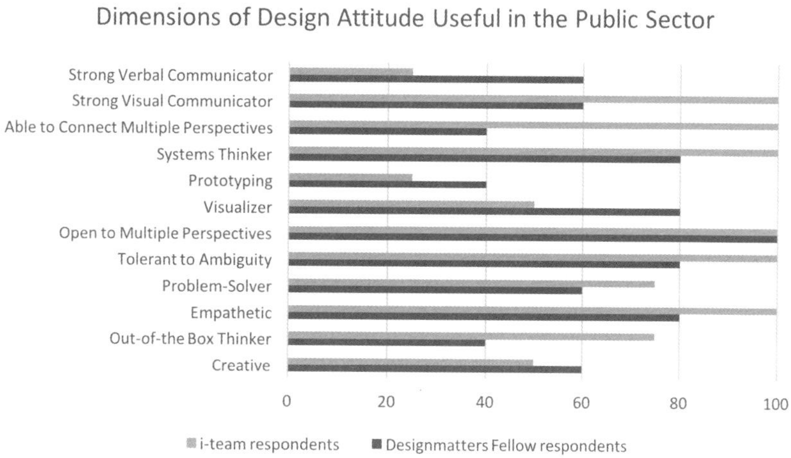

Figure 9 Comparison of i-team Members and Fellows assessments of useful dimensions of Design Attitude in the Public Sector, drawn from 2016 survey. Copyright © 2017 Designmatters.

opportunities often arise from barriers. For example, in the case of the Long Beach i-team, the challenges of integrating the team's methods and initiatives across the more bureaucratic divisions of City Hall became the point of departure for the Fellow to design a toolkit that visualizes and communicates clearly the goals of the i-team initiatives for City employees.

Table 2. Challenges and Opportunities of embedding design Fellows in i-teams.

	COMMUNICATION & COLLABORATION (REPRESENTATIVE STATEMENTS)
Challenges	- I didn't expect to feel anxiety about long-term relationship building.... I felt pressure not to tarnish the i-team's relationship with [external departments]. (Fellow) - The level and nature of communication and collaboration I was accustomed to at ArtCenter was not present in City Hall. It was very challenging to create an atmosphere that was conducive to inspiration and innovative, unconventional lines of thinking. (Fellow) - I talked to a lot of team members about building trust as one of the most important things the team has had to do within and outside of City Hall. For me personally, I was challenged with trusting myself to share ideas in a new space. (Fellow) - [There was a] mismatch in expectations—early Fellows were surprised we wanted their help with design thinking and not just their particular skill. (i-team Member)
Opportunities	- Many agencies we work with are new to design thinking, so being able to provide limite graphic design support—which is also desperately needed in government—was an effective way to get a foot in the door to move the conversation into design thinking. In my mind, the support of the Fellow helped to elevate our conversations from theory and concepts into practical shapes and forms, and helped people to start seeing the art of the possible. This opened up opportunities in terms of partnerships and projects. (i-team member) - I think there are continual opportunities for designers, design thinkers, and design researchers to be embedded in all departments of city government. This is evidenced by short consultations I provided to teams like IT and HR who were trying to think through their interview and on-boarding experiences. While they thought they were bringing me in for an interior design consult, they ended up with a new framework for thinking abou the problem. (Fellow) - We were in a position to meet with a lot of different individuals, departments and organizations. The i-team was in a unique position where it needed to build connections relationships and partnerships with a broad spectrum of populations and demographics. It was really interesting to be a part of some of these meetings and hear a variety of perspectives. (Fellow) - We were really impressed with the ability of some Fellows to inform the Bloomberg Innovation Delivery Approach. Our Fellows were able to help us clarify the design thinking process in ways that benefited Long Beach as well as the entire Bloomberg Innovation Team global network. (i-team member)

Limitations

We use case-study methodology and an exploratory survey to gather insights and triangulate original empirical data against current theory to ad dress a gap in articulation about the experiences of designers in governmen innovation settings as well as the perceived value of their contributions in these organizational environments. Our study's sample is small and limited to the perspectives of a few individuals engaged with two government innovation teams in the cities of Long Beach and Los Angeles who have ha designers embedded through the Designmatters Fellowship program. The size of our sample represents one key limitation of this research. For example, one aim of the survey was to probe the barriers and opportunities of integrating design Fellows into the i-teams, and whether those barriers and opportunities were unique to the public sector. Unfortunately, our instrument did not yield any conclusive insights on these questions, partly due to the lack of data to surface patterns from. Further research is warranted on this issue. More broadly, we recognize that our analytic lens and logic for the research design of this study may have precluded us from interpreting data converging differently, which could well have led to other generalizable insights. We hope that future research might build on the conclusions we offer and continue to elucidate the value designers bring to government innovation practices.

Conclusion

The results of this case reveal a growing orientation toward bringing design understanding to bear on government innovation—an emergent field of practice where designers typically have not been present before[33]—at least not with the level of strategic intent and engagement that we see from the present data. The case also offers generalizable insights about the opportunities and barriers for design that are encountered in this space. Innovating in government can seem like a herculean task to achieve, with designers often needing to overcome cultures that are risk-averse, accountability-prone, and new to a design attitude approach to problem solving.[34] This case presents compelling evidence about the value of integrating upstream designers in these government innovation practices and the importance of incorporating design knowledge, methods and values in order to inform decision-making and catalyze change.

33 Victor Margolin, *Healing the World: A Challenge for Designers* (Chicago: Archeworks, 2004).

34 Joyce Yee, Emma Jefferies, and Kamil Michlewski, *Transformations: Seven Roles to Drive Change by Design* (Amsterdam: BIS Publishers, 2017).

Appendix A: Survey Main Categories and Aims

This appendix offers a summary of the four main categories of survey questions. Full survey results can be found in Appendix B.

1) Primary Contributions

In order to assess the value the Fellows brought to the i-teams, both groups of Fellows/i-team staff were asked to rank how strongly they agreed with the statement "The Designmatters Fellow/I made significant contributions to the i-team." A follow-up question asked each group to list the top three contributions the Fellow made to the i-team.

2) Design Attitude Dimensions

In order to identify the specific skills and abilities the Designmatters Fellows brought to the i-teams, we used the dimensions of design attitude that have been validated in the empirical and theoretical literature (Michlewski, Amatullo, 2015) for the positive significant impact they have to account for innovation results in organizations. Our study respondents were first asked to select any of the dimensions they felt described the skills and abilities of the Designmatters Fellow (Fellows were asked the question in a self-reflective mode, i.e. "please select the terms that best describe your own skills and abilities"). Respondents were then asked to identify whether any of the skills or abilities were especially useful in a public sector setting.

3) Perception of Design Roles: Before and After

Respondents from the i-teams were asked to reflect on their views of designers by selecting from a list of typical "design" roles—artist, graphic designer, illustrator, web designer—mixed with a list of more strategic roles—organizers, problem solvers, researchers—to first reflect on how they viewed designers prior to working with the Designmatters Fellow, and then on how they viewed designers after they worked with the Designmatters Fellow. Respondents were also asked to rate how strongly they agreed with the statement "The Designmatters Fellow changed how I view the role of designers in the public sector."

Respondents who were Fellows were asked to reflect on how they viewed the role of designers prior to the Fellowship, and how that perception changed after. Respondents were also asked to rate how strongly they agreed with the statement "My Fellowship experience changed the way I imagine the role of designers in the public sector."

4) Barriers to Design Adoption

Finally, both sets of respondents were asked to identify unexpected challenges and opportunities encountered during the Fellowship, and whether any of those challenges and opportunities identified was unique to the public sector.

Appendix B: Full Survey Results

Designmatters Public Sector Fellowship Survey—for i-team Members

Your Title (Optional)

- Project Manager
- i-team Director
- Project Manager
- Deputy Director

How did you interact with the Designmatters Fellow?

- 1- Direct Supervisor
- 1- Team Member- assigned tasks to Fellow
- 2- Team Member- worked directly with Fellow

The Designmatters Fellow made significant contributions to our team:

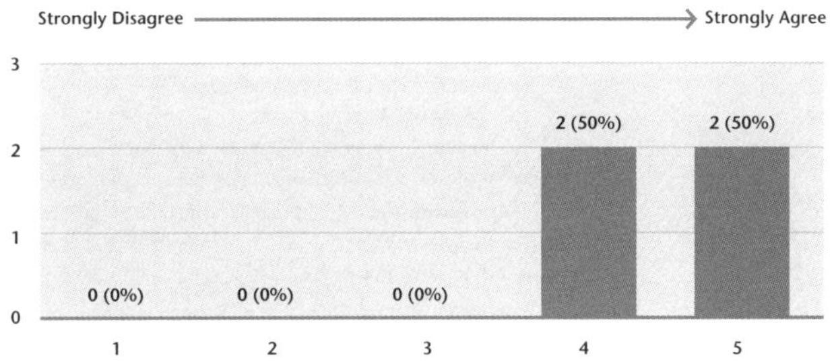

Please list the top three contributions you feel the Designmatters Fellow made to your team:

- Providing guidance on implementing design-thinking process, documentation of work/process, and graphic design.
- (1) Production (deliverables, prototypes, events, media collaterals), (2) Project Management (framing and implementing the design thinking process), (3) Perspective (providing additional capacity, unique perspective, and energy as a team member).
- Excellent graphic designs, good interpersonal skills, good strategy.
- Putting a physical form to ideas; connecting multiple disciplines and stakeholders through design; disseminating the value of design to and through our team and stakeholders, including a youth leadership academy.

The Designmatters Fellow changed how I view the role of designers in the public sector:

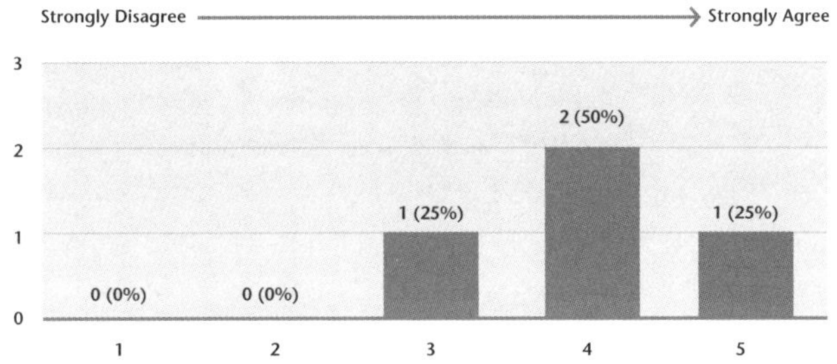

Prior to working with the Designmatters Fellow, I viewed designers as (Please check all that apply):

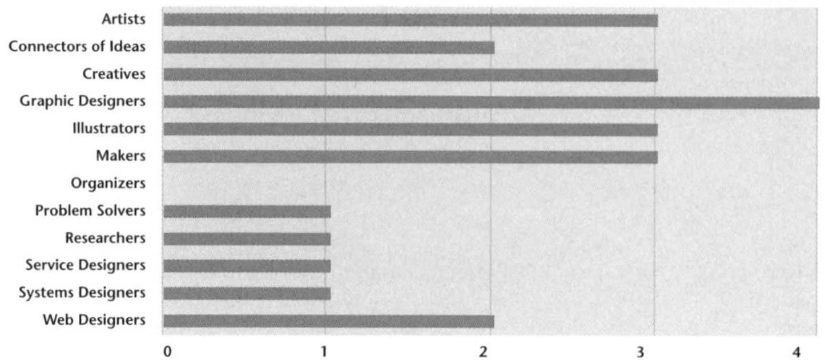

After working with the Designmatters Fellow, I view designers as (Please check all that apply):

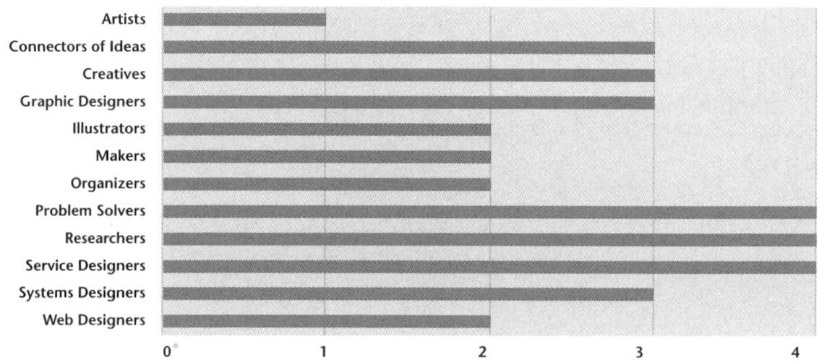

Did you or your team face any unexpected challenges in working with the Designmatters Fellow? If so, please describe those challenges below.

- Initially there was a mismatch in expectations—early Fellows were surprised we wanted their help with design thinking and not just their particular skill.
- We have hosted (4) Fellows at this point and each one is very different. One of the challenges we faced was the level of experience and maturity of some Fellows as compared to others.
- Honestly, he did a great job and was a pleasure to work with.

If you listed challenges above, do you think any of these challenges were unique to the public sector/government setting?

- I do not believe this to be a unique problem, rather something that stems from working with students in a setting that has not previously engaged designers.
- No. These were issues of maturity and experience working in an organizational setting. Working in government means (1) working in an organizational setting with other people, (2) understanding that leadership must respond to lots of internal and external stakeholders, (3) being flexible with the process (understanding that we are not in control), and (4) speed—working quickly and not letting the perfect get in the way of the good.
- N/A.

Did you or your team encounter any unexpected opportunities in working with the Designmatters Fellow? If so, please describe those opportunities below.

- Not that I recall.
- Yes. We were really impressed with the ability of some Fellows to inform the Bloomberg Innovation Delivery Approach. Our Fellows were able to help us clarify the design thinking process in ways that benefited Long Beach as well as the entire Bloomberg Innovation Team global network.

- Yes, he helped us figure out some technical issues related to color matching/printing with the commercial printer.
- We were fortunate that our Fellow was very flexible, and in addition to design thinking, was also willing to do some graphic design work. Many agencies we work with are new to design thinking, and being able to provide limited graphic design support (which is also desperately needed in government) was an effective way to get a foot in the door to move the conversation into design thinking. In my mind, the support of the Fellow helped to elevate our conversations from theory and concepts into practical shapes and forms and helped people to start seeing the art of the possible—this opened up opportunities in terms of partnerships and projects.

If you listed opportunities above, do you think any of these opportunities were unique to the public sector/government setting?

- No. Although government and public service is about participation of all stakeholders, and is much more complex environment than most single-market businesses face. User Centered design can be even more effective in the government space because of the complexity.
- No.

Please check any of the below that you feel describes the skills & abilities of the Designmatters Fellow.

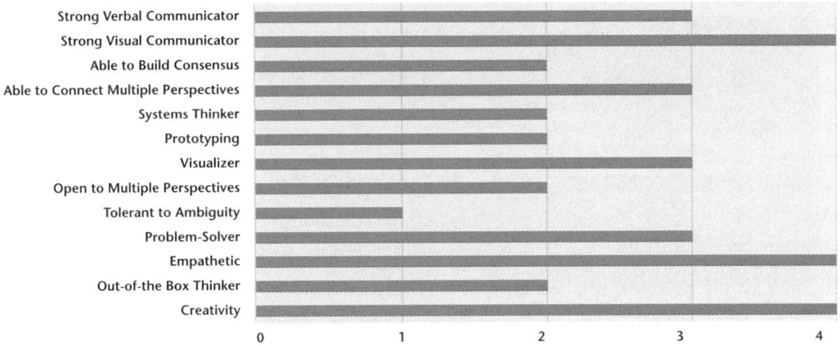

Of the skills you checked above, do you think any skills are especially useful in the public sector/government setting? Check all that apply.

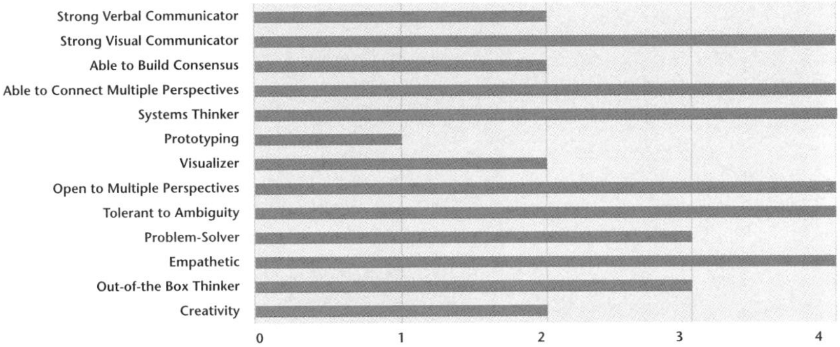

Please use the space below to list any additional comments about your experience as a Designmatters Fellow on a public sector team.

- Very talented young designer, look forward to working with him again.
- It was a pleasure having a Fellow on our team and together we were able to achieve quite a lot in a short amount of time. Given the pace and learning curve of the public sector environment, it would be great to have a longer period of time with the Fellow to go beyond researching and conceptualizing projects together, to focusing on project implementation and really thinking about how to embed some of these design philosophies into the public sector.

Designmatters Public Sector Fellowship Survey- for Fellows

Your Discipline

- 2- Graphic Design
- 1- Graduate Industrial Design
- 2- Graduate Media Design Practices

Did you have any Public Sector (defined as an organization that is owned and operated by a government) experience prior to your Fellowship (including previous degrees, internships, volunteering or jobs)?

- 5- No

Describe some of the activities and tasks you undertook as the Designmatters Fellow.

- Co-led the Welcome to the Neighborhood project with the Highland Park Neighborhood Council, designed logos and identities for city departments, designed presentation narratives and slide decks for the i-team, designed the team's website, did production design for a public awareness campaign around the city's Rent Stabilization Ordinance, designed and facilitated a workshop for youth on design thinking, documented team's initiatives with photography.
- User Centered Design.
- Responsible for designing and managing the visual communication for the i-team and other departments within city government, such as the Mayor's office and the City Manager's office, which included flyers, web pages, infographics, annual reports, banners, emailnewsletters, and branding/identity development.
- Branding of the Long Beach i-team | participated in research | designed materials for the city, city mayor, and Breakthrough Long Beach | Introduced i-team to organizations across LB | Participated in the creation of the LB i-team.
- Strategy design; User journeys for 4 of the team's initiatives; Graphics for Mayor Garcia's 2nd year accomplishments; Design Thinking and prototyping workshops.

I made significant contributions to the team I worked with as a Designmatters Fellow.

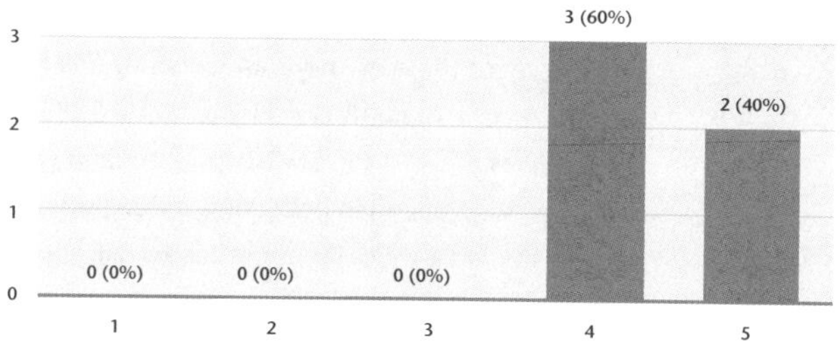

Please list the top three contributions you made to the team during your Fellowship.

- Led an initiative to foster community amongst residents of Highland Park; offered design thinking knowledge for all team members to take advantage of; provided (visual) design support, as needed.
- Branding, Research, Design Thinking.
- Helped to reinforce design thinking and an outsider's perspective. Made a strong argument and push for a dedicated communal space, which would encourage better collaboration, communication, creativity and teamwork. Provided much-needed clarity and cohesiveness to the i-team's visual communication/promotional material.
- Branded the team, represented Art Center and what good design can do for the city, Made connections with the team and people of Long Beach while I served them the best that I could.
- Designing a visual map for the team to follow during the upcoming priority; User journeys for initiatives; a toolkit to help them start thinking about how to communicate their work outside of the team via a portfolio and transparency.

My Fellowship experience provided significant learning and professional growth for me as a designer.

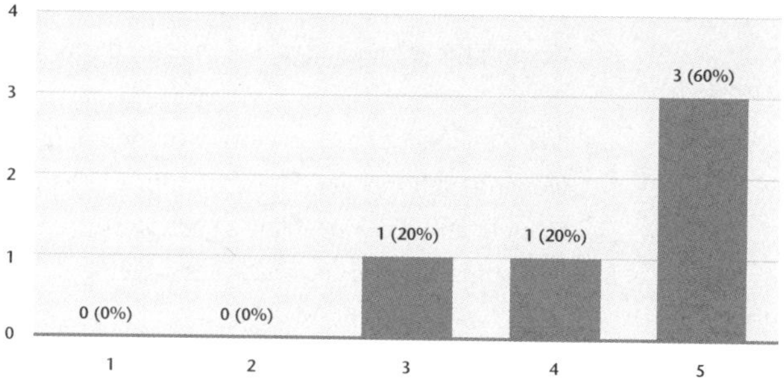

Please list the top three most valuable learnings from your Fellowship.

- That civic sector work is mission-driven work; that the civic sector is beginning to designers as more than just graphic designers, but instead researchers and problem solvers; that I am interested in pursuing a career in government work.
- Improving my skills in human centered design and design thinking, collaborating with non-designers.
- Physical layout and design of a workspace can play a crucial role in a team's ability to function as a cohesive unit. There is a serious lack of inter-departmental communication and collaboration in city government. It would be great if there were a space that allowed for more spontaneous collisions and conversations between people from different floors and departments within city hall itself. Innovation Teams and other government departments should participate in more hands-on workshops to learn

about design thinking as a whole group. Reading about it is not enough. It takes actual practice for these methods and ideas to sink in.

- Working as a multi-disciplinary team for a city government, how to represent design principles, how to serve with optimism and excitement.
- I really like working in politics (as a designer); that designers have the tools to literally sit at the table with city leadership to talk about the future of the city; how to explain design (and design thinking) concepts in a real life scenario to people from other disciplines.

My Fellowship experienced changed the way I imagine the role of designers in the public sector.

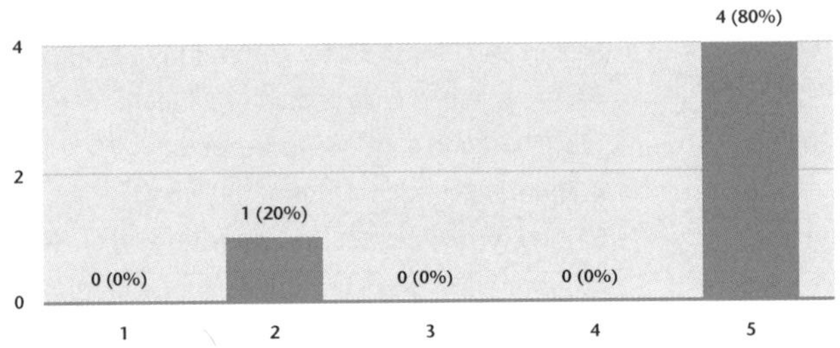

Prior to your Fellowship, what role did you think designers played in the public sector?

- Based on government website design, I never thought designers were employed by the public sector!
- Little.
- More like a traditional contract-based, designer-client relationship, where the designer is simply handed a brief.
- None, really other than as the occasional graphic designer.
- Prior to the Fellowship it was hard to imagine designers being integrated in a role beyond the traditional role of making things look good.

After your Fellowship, do you think about the role of designers in the public sector differently? If so, how?

- I didn't expect to feel anxiety surrounding long-term relationship building. For example, working with the city printer to print a large public awareness campaign and needing to meet ambitious deadlines, I felt pressure to not tarnish the i-team's relationship with him after asking for favors or not meeting delivery deadlines (If this is quoted, I'd prefer it be done anonymously).
- As mentioned earlier, the level and nature of communication and collaboration I was accustomed to at ArtCenter was not present in City Hall. It was very challenging to create an atmosphere that was conducive to inspiration and innovative, unconventiona lines of thinking. Government can also be extremely slow and behind the times in how it gets things done.
- Yes. Politics are political. That probably isn't a surprise, but I talked to a lot of team members about building trust as one of the most important things the team has had to do within and outside of City Hall. For me personally, I was challenged with trusting myself to share ideas in this new space where I was a newbie.

If you described challenges above, do you think any of these challenges were unique to the public sector setting?

- I do think the politics of being is politics is unique to the public sector. When you ask fo favors, when you ask for buy-in, when you ask for support are all choreographed move that strategically help you deliver projects.

- Yes. In the private sector, a company needs to innovate and be streamlined in order for it to survive and thrive. Public sector has no reasons to improve efficiently. There is no competition to drive them or their employees.
- Yes. Getting approval and funding is always more challenging in the public sector. There's a lot of red tape and bureaucracy involved.
- Working in city government has a completely different set of motivations for many of the people; I don't worry about being re-elected at my job.
- No. Imposter syndrome and the need to gain trust of your co-workers and those outside the team is probably not unique to the public sector.

Did you encounter any unexpected opportunities in your Designmatters Fellowship? If yes, please describe those opportunities below.

- I think there are continual opportunities for designers, design thinkers, and design researchers to be embedded in all departments of city government. This is made evidenced by short consultations I provided to teams like IT and HR who were trying to think through their interview and on-boarding experience. While they thought they were bringing me in for an interior design consult, they ended up with a new framework for thinking about the problem.
- To lead because many in the team were too jaded.
- We were in a position to meet with a lot of different individuals, departments and organizations. The i-team was in a unique position where it needed to build connections, relationships and partnerships with a broad spectrum of populations and demographics. It was really interesting to be a part of some of these meetings and hear a variety of perspectives.
- I had a wonderful opportunity to meet some of the people at IDEO.org during my Fellowship and have been so impressed with the role they have been able to play in the philanthropic world.
- The opportunity to dig into my business and strategic thinking background was a surprise. That said, it was an amazing opportunity to weave design and business together to really dig into some of the pain points around the processes and needs of the team going into their next priority.

If you described opportunities above, do you think any of these opportunities were unique to the public sector setting?

- I think the private sector has realized the benefits of having the design perspective, and public sector is a few years behind that.
- Yes. Public sector has people with very little drive/passion and when they do have drive its skewed for their own political/social benefit.
- Not necessarily.
- Perhaps. I think that, particularly now, the public sector asks for people to have a diverse background and experiences. That's similar to design in that designers are asked to have a wide array of skills.

Please check any of the below that you feel describe your skills & abilities as a designer.

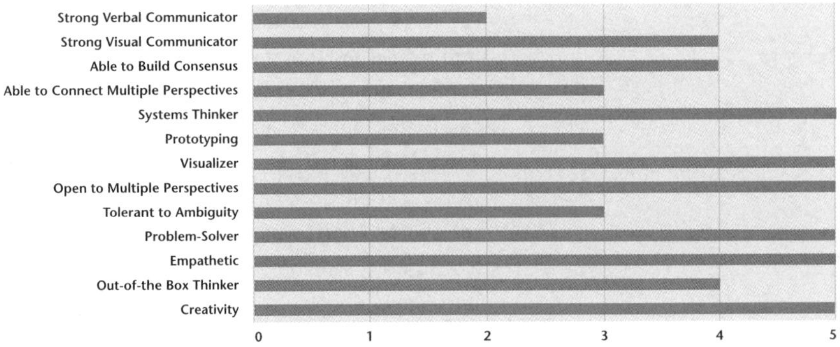

Of the skills you checked above, do you think any skills were especially useful in the public sector setting? Check all that apply.

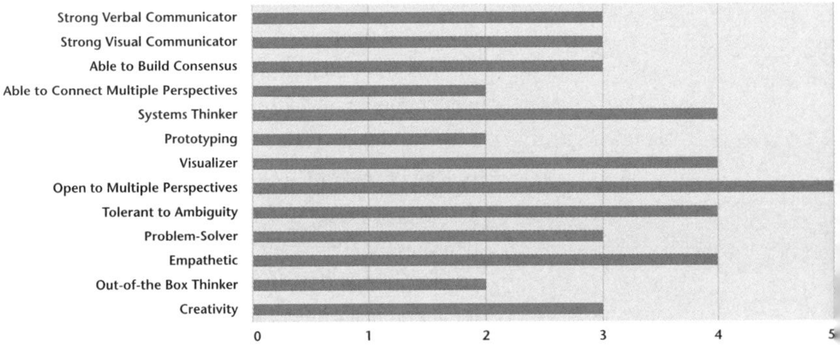

Please use the space below to list any additional comments about your experience as a Designmatters Fellow on a public sector team.

- Overall, a truly eye-opening experience. Even though I was only in City Hall for a short time, I gained valuable insights into how government operates. But there is still so much more that can be learned. Trying to absorb it all was sometimes daunting and overwhelming. But I think the challenges I encountered simply provided opportunities for learning and growth.
- I loved my time working not only with the amazing people in Long Beach but also with the Designmatters team. Designmatters gives students and faculty an amazing opportunity to give and focus on hard problems that don't often get solutions. My life and perspective have changed due to my experience, I hope to work in the public sector again soon.
- Thank you for the amazing opportunity. It has really helped to shape my path as a designer.

Policy Design to Improve the Delivery of Old Age Security in Canada for Vulnerable Seniors

Alexander Keith Eady

Carleton University, Canada

Ryan James Hum

Carleton University and OCAD University, Canada

Canada's Old Age Security (OAS) program provides financial support for persons over the age of 65 (seniors). A multi-disciplinary team was tasked with designing prototypes for an e-service version of the OAS application process. Instead, the team diverged from the requested project and applied design methods to understand how OAS serves its most extreme users—vulnerable seniors. Procedural and cultural problems were identified, leading to designed solutions and triggering a cultural shift towards human-centered perspectives in one branch of the Public Service. The outcomes are discussed in their relation to DesignX complex problems.

Keywords **Vulnerable, seniors, income insecurity, engagement, policy**

Alexander Keith Eady is a design researcher, pursuing a doctorate in Digital Media at Carleton University in Ottawa, Canada. He looks at deformable technologies, including rapid prototyping methods and possible applications; his doctoral thesis will explore the applications of deformable technologies for therapy of the hand and wrist. Alex interned at the Central Innovation Hub of the Government of Canada where he explored and adapted design methods to interesting and complex problems. He holds degrees in Criminology and Information Technology.

alex.eady@carleton.ca

Ryan James Hum is the chief designer and data scientist in the Central Innovation Hub where he leads the design-insights and data-analytics practice to improve policy, program and service delivery in the Government of Canada. Over his career, Ryan has worked on issues regarding social, health, immigration, and natural resources. He was a Special Lecturer in engineering and public policy at the Universities of Toronto, and currently teaches design at Carleton and OCAD Universities, where he is an Adjunct Professor. He has degrees in engineering, biology, product design and is completing his Ph.D. where he studies changes in global health.

ryan.hum@gmail.com

Canadian Seniors and Old Age Security

In Canada, the Old Age Security (OAS) program provides financial support to persons over 65 and is a critical financial support for many low-income seniors, especially given rising poverty among seniors in Canada.[1] In 2014–15, OAS and related financial supports provided CAD$44.1 billion in support to 5.6 million people,[2] making it the single largest program of the Government of Canada.

Eligibility for OAS is simple in concept—a person must be over the age of 65 and have been a Canadian resident for a minimum of 10 years. Payments of the OAS benefit are prorated based on residency, with a maximum contribution available to persons with 40 or more years of residence. Unlike many support programs, the amount of financial support provided by OAS is not contingent on having worked in Canada or paid taxes—it exists to ensure that seniors have a basic pension income. This program can be supplemented with other financial support programs such as the Guaranteed Income Supplement and Allowances, which are income-tested and act as further protections for lower income seniors from poverty, and the Canada Pension Plan (CPP), which is based on contributions made during employment years. These supplemental programs are administered after enrollment in Old Age Security.

E-governance and Modernization

The Government of Canada is undergoing a period of modernization, with many paper-based services and lines of communication transitioning to digital platforms and channels. This approach is akin to that of other national governments, who are pursuing a "digital first" strategy, aiming to give "greater and easier access to government information and resources"[3] to their citizens. This is a multi-year undertaking that affects every department of government.[4] Recognizing that service design is not one-size-fits-all, each department is responsible for the design and implementation of new forms for its services, or altogether new services.[5]

This is not without challenges. Departments, and even sub-units within departments, must grow their competencies in many domains. To successfully modernize, departments must be able to identify the challenges that occur when redesigning a service for a digital medium, to understand the possible impacts such an action will have on a diverse population, and even to identify which technologies best serve their needs. In traditional policy process in Canada, interviewing end-users or their allies is still rare. It is overshadowed by a preference for expert analyses, literature reviews, and international case studies, with an aim to apply a reductionist or theoretical lens and frame the problem in terms of a simplified socio-economic model.

This case study serves as an example of how governments—like the Government of Canada—can utilize design methodologies to create citizen-centric policies, programs and services.

1 Richard Shillington, "An Analysis of the Economic Circumstances of Canadian Seniors," *Broadbentinstitute.ca*, February, 2016, https://d3n8a8pro7vhmx.cloudfront.net/broadbent/pages/4904/attachments/original/1455216659/An_Analysis_of_the_Economic_Circumstances_of_Canadian_Seniors.pdf?1455216659.

2 Government of Canada, "Canada Pension Plan (CPP) and Old Age Security (OAS) Annual Statistics Tables," *Canada.ca*, last modified November 17, 2016, http://open.canada.ca/data/en/dataset/f064a144-b4e0-4e9b-9970-e0fc2f84d1a8.

3 Government of Canada, "Digital Canada 150: 2.0," *Industry Canada Web Services Centre* (Ottawa, 2015), 14.

4 Government of Canada, "Digital Canada 150: 2.0"; Government of Canada, "Destination 2020," *OECD Publishing*, vol. May, 2014.

5 Government of Canada, "Destination 2020."

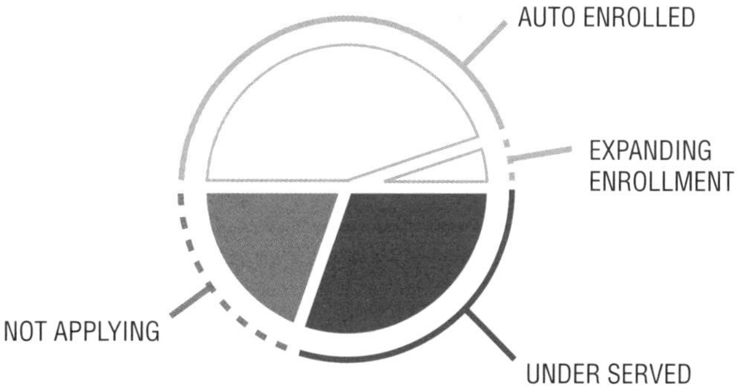

Figure 1 Segmentation of how the Canadian seniors are served by the OAS program. Copyright © 2017 Alexander Keith Eady and Ryan James Hum.

Background on the Old Age Security Program Modernization to Date

The Government of Canada has made significant improvements to streamline the application process for the OAS program. Since 2013, the Government of Canada offers automatic enrollment into the program to eligible seniors identified using data from CPP and Quebec Pension Plan (hereafter, included with CPP) and recent tax filings.[6] By the end of 2016, more than half of newly-eligible Canadian residents will be automatically enrolled in OAS at age 65. **Figure 1** illustrates the segmentation of how the OAS program serves eligible persons.

Persons who are automatically enrolled do not have to initiate any process, they receive a letter in the mail after they turn 64 outlining their eligibility and stating that they can choose to receive their payment at age 65, or defer for a period and increase their benefits. Currently, the automated process emphasizes program integrity, with strict inclusion criteria to ensure only cases certain to be recipients will receive the benefit—for example, non-self-employed, tax-paying Canadians with easily identified 40 years of residency in Canada. In the upcoming years, the government will be expanding their inclusion criteria to identify more nuanced cases.

For those persons 64 years of age who are not automatically enrolled, a manual, paper-based Old Age Security application must be self-initiated and mailed into government. This can be problematic for seniors who did not have a history of paid work in Canada—such as women who were primary care givers to their children—persons who have never filed taxes, or those who have disengaged from their government or from society. With over 6 million seniors in Canada,[7] there are approximately 400,000 seniors not enrolled in OAS. It is problematically unclear how many of these are eligible for the program but unaware of, unable to, or unsuccessful in their application. Though the exact demographics of this population are unclear, this group comprises vulnerable populations like persons with disabilities and mental illnesses, the homeless and economically vulnerable, people in rural areas or otherwise isolated, people not native to Canada, and underserved groups like aboriginal peoples.

6 Government of Canada-ESDC Internal Audit Services Branch, "Audit of Automatic Enrollment for an Old Age Security Pension Phase 1A" (Ottawa, 2014): 3.

7 Government of Canada-ESDC, "Government of Canada: Action for Seniors," *Government of Canada*, 2014.

From a macro-perspective, this becomes an unintended policy realization where those most in need of financial support have a higher application burden than those who are easily identified and may not require the support.

Modernizing OAS Enrollment

Design Brief: Electronic OAS Services for Seniors

Employment and Social Development Canada, and Service Canada—the two departments responsible for the administration of the Old Age Security program—sought advice to improve accessibility of the program. The original project brief requested a prototype, e-service style application to reach those seniors not identified in the automatic enrollment process. The term *prototype* was not defined in the design brief, but storyboards, wireframes or alpha build—a working app prototype—were desired.

Masters of Design Student Team

To embark on a citizen-centered design process, the Government of Canada approached a Carleton University (Canada) design instructor for assistance, and this project became the sole project for a graduate-level studio course. Interdisciplinary Design Development Studio (IDES 5103) is a team-based studio course which draws on interdisciplinary design development methods to achieve a common design objective; knowledge (but not expertise) in design research methods—including journey maps, personas, mental models—is a pre-requisite. It is a one-term (thirteen-week, three-hour per week) design studio mandatory for the Masters of Design graduate students and elective for graduate students enrolled in Human-Computer Interaction. In the winter term of 2016, ten students were enrolled in the course with academic and professional backgrounds in interactive media design, graphic design, human-computer interaction/user experience design, interior design, product design, journalism, criminology, and anthropology. The instructor for the course was the Chief Designer of the Government of Canada's Central Innovation Hub.

Entering this project, the team expanded on the existing research and literature review conducted by the client and conducted user-centered research (on seniors, government employees and existing service workers devoted to helping senior citizens). The goal was to provide artifacts and recommendations for the departments to develop and implement as pilot programs. An exploratory approach was taken to discover and redefine the problems and needs of stakeholders, citizens and employees. User-centered and ideative design methodologies were used to conceptualize and develop policy and service solutions. In this case study, we outline our process, findings, and impacts as well as interpret this experience to provide broader lessons for the practices of policy innovation for DesignX problems.

Challenging the Design Brief

We chose to eschew the proposed project goals in favor of a divergent approach, intentionally rejecting the existing problem definition in favor of allowing new problem definitions to be developed and challenged during the exploration phase. This approach assumes that, behind the perceived need for an e-service platform, there exist unspoken assumptions, undiscovered problems, and unidentified needs. Consequently, we started by trying to understand OAS as it currently exists and how it interacts with and impacts the lives of Canadians.

Describing the Problem

Old Age Security is a large program and to understand the problem of how to approach its modernization, it is helpful to use some of the metrics of social policy theory. This project meets many of the criteria of Rittel and Webber's formulation of Wicked Problems in social policy.[8] It is particularly helpful to draw attention to two of their criteria—the planner cannot risk being wrong,[9] and the problem description begets one specific solution.[10] Indeed, the potential impact a mistake could have on the lives of many seniors is high, and the framing of the brief requests prototyping the migration to an e-services platform. Levin et al. built on these criteria to formulate Super Wicked Problems, and from their discussion we draw the caution that the problem solvers, who formulated the design brief, are also closely entwined with its causes.[11] Echoing this, from a political science/public policy theory perspective, Dunn[12] states that one of the most important challenges facing analysts is reducing the change of a "type III error," defining the wrong problem.

Given the initial client-imposed technological solution, we can also draw from design theory for human-computer interaction. Baumer and Silberman present three central questions for the design of a technological intervention: "Is there an equally viable low-tech or no-tech approach to the situation? Might deploying the technology result in more harm than the situation the technology is meant to address? Does the technology solve a computationally tractable problem rather than address an actual situation?"[13] These are questions not answered, or answerable, through the initial research and design brief. Critical, unanswered questions about the appropriateness of a technological solution therefore serve to further justify a divergent approach.

Modernizing OAS is a Super Wicked Problem, requiring a deep exploration of the problem space, including delivery of the OAS program, identifying the needs and goals of the target users of the service, the priorities of other stakeholders involved, and other factors that might inform the design of a targeted intervention. In public policy theory, this relates to problem structuring—the first stage of the policy development process—however, it is seldom applied in practice.

8 Horst W. J. Rittel and Melvin M. Webber, "Dilemmas in a General Theory of Planning," *Policy Sciences* 4, no. 2 (June 1973): 155–69, DOI: https://doi.org/10.1007/BF01405730.

9 Ibid., 166–67.

10 Ibid., 166.

11 Kelly Levin et al., "Overcoming the Tragedy of Super Wicked Problems: Constraining Our Future Selves to Ameliorate Global Climate Change," *Policy Sciences* 45, no. 2 (June 2012): 127–28, DOI: https://doi.org/10.1007/s11077-012-9151-0.

12 William N. Dunn, *Public Policy Analysis*, 5th ed. (New York: Routledge, 2015).

13 Eric Baumer and M. S. Silberman, "When the Implication Is Not to Design (Technology)," in *Proceeding of the SIGCHI Conference on Human Factors in Computing Systems* (New York: ACM, 2011), 2271, DOI: https://doi.org/10.1145/1978942.1979275.

Critical Assumptions in the Brief

The brief framed a problem that allowed only one solution—the creation of an e-service platform for OAS. This is the central assumption that we set out to challenge. It is founded in implicit assumptions that must be recognized before they can be validated or challenged. Among them are the following:

- People will be willing to shift from a paper-based service to e-service delivery;
- The people meant to use the e-service are the same as those for who the paper application was built;
- An e-service will serve stakeholders' needs better than the current system;
- The current system can be migrated to an e-service platform; and
- The medium of service delivery (paper or digital) is the part of the service most in need of modernization.

Critical analysis of the proposed solution also suggests that the original goals may have been motivated by austerity measures—electronic means will lead to efficiency and subsequently reduce government operation spending—rather than improved accessibility of the Old Age Security program.

How Might We Improve the Adoption of OAS for Vulnerable Seniors?

To maximize the potential positive impact for people, we chose to take an extreme-user design approach and emphasize vulnerable seniors—lower-income persons, rural residents, homeless persons, and persons with disabilities, for example—where auto-enrollment is not a current or likely future option. We inferred that this population could benefit most from access to the financial stability offered through OAS. Through designing solutions for extreme users, it was expected that we could identify gaps and pain points in the service model that were invisible to policy makers and not explicitly obvious for an average citizen or stakeholder. It was with vulnerable seniors in mind that we began our initial divergent exploration and framed three broad exploratory research questions that were revisited throughout the process:

- What are the daily routines of vulnerable seniors?
- What are the barriers and pain-points that slow or prevent people from accessing OAS?
- Is the existing understanding and model of the user valid and sufficient to design interventions that will boost enrollment in OAS?

Approach and Process

The design team employed the United Kingdom Design Council's "double-diamond"[14] user-centered design approach(Figure 2) to design policy or service interventions. Entering this project, the team expanded on the existing

14 United Kingdom Design Council, "The Design Process: What Is the Double Diamond?," accessed March 1, 2017, http://www.designcouncil.org.uk/news-opinion/design-process-what-double-diamond.

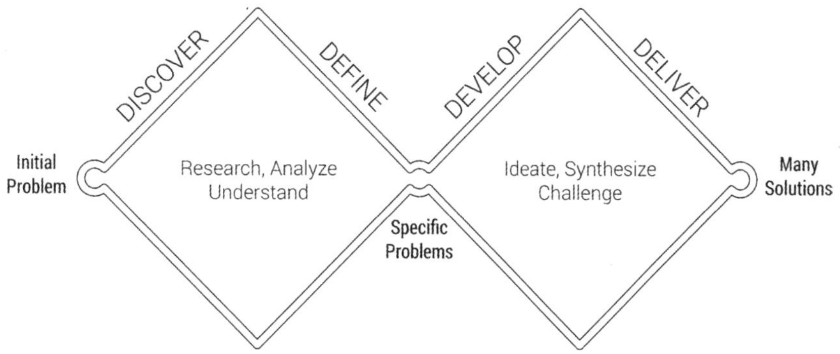

Figure 2 Applying design methods to generate understanding, insight, and solutions for problems in the Old Age Security program. Copyright © 2017 Alexander Keith Eady and Ryan James Hum.

research and literature review conducted by the client and conducted user-centered research (on clients, and on the government employees and existing service workers devoted to helping senior citizens). An exploratory approach was taken to discover and redefine the problems and needs of stakeholders, citizens, and employees. User-centered and ideative design methodologies were used to conceptualize and develop policy and service solutions. In this case study, we outline our process, findings, and impacts as well as interpret this experience to provide broader lessons for the practices of policy innovation for DesignX problems.

In the discovery phase, we used ethnographic research methods—which included expert and opportunistic interviews in public spaces, shelters, crisis centres, and government service centres—to understand the problem space. During these site visits, non-verbal factors were collected and coded via an AEIOU framework (Activities, Environment, Object, Interaction, User). We engaged with seniors, support workers, volunteers, government employees, and domain experts. In this stage, we revealed the heterogeneous nature of the problem space—some findings appeared to contradict what we had learned from the information delivered with the design brief, while others provided validation. We came to realize that much of the personal knowledge of seniors that we brought into the project was, in fact, founded in assumptions of our own about Canadian seniors. For example, the project team (and the client) assumed that vulnerable seniors would be hard to find—how do you find a homeless senior when they do not have an address? In reality, people do not instantaneously become marginalized at the specific age of 65; a paper trail of youth, mental health, social services and other government services likely exists for any given individual.

To make sense of what we learned, in the definition phase we employed journey maps, stakeholder maps, personas, and developed mental models to analyze and synthesize the data. These design artifacts helped to visualize and understand the system, and its actors, plus archetypes of vulnerable seniors and their thought processes and inter-relationships, and the impact of time. We created artifacts that describe the OAS program, its various actors, and vulnerable seniors. These artifacts led to insights into the needs of seniors and the problems inherent in the OAS system. Sample draft artifacts and their resulting insights can be found in Table 1. Three strategic directions—empowering government employees, empowering champions currently assisting vulnerable seniors, and unclogging transitions between government programs—were advanced to the development phase.

In the development phase, we applied different methods to our insights to generate ideas on how to modify policies, services, or the administration of the OAS program. Ideas were generated using Mandal Art, reverse brainstorming, and science fictioning. Afterwards, we used Value Hypotheses and Pugh matrices to sort the ideas generated based on predetermined success criteria. These artifacts allowed us to identify which ideas could be the most impactful and implementable. The use of design artifacts to make these choices was critical. For example, the Pugh matrices were important to dispel personal biases that favoured the novelty of one idea over another, but may not have objectively evaluated or ranked well against desired policy outcomes.

To convey our ideas back to the departments, we used story-telling techniques, fashioning our personas, scenarios, storyboards and science fictioning into video narratives to expose the public servants to our insights and rationales, and prepare them for our proposed solutions.

Table 1. Design methods used in human-centered design for Old Age Security, discussion, and example artifacts.

STAGE	METHOD	DESCRIPTION	EXAMPLE OUTCOMES/ARTIFACTS
Discovery	Observation, Intercept Interviews, Expert Interviews	We engaged seniors, service Canada and ESDC staff, community supports, and crisis intervention experts.	Data dump comprised of written observational notes, interview transcripts, photos, government documents and forms.
Define	Journey Maps	Understanding the experiences of aging in Canada, qualifying for OAS, navigating the OAS application process, communicating with the GOC. We discovered that the journeys of seniors are not well mapped along the chronological age of the applicant. Security and crisis are more useful—people who are in crisis (emotional, physical, or financial) are more likely to experience barriers that prevent access to OAS. The challenges encountered by vulnerable persons do not start at age 65. Many people struggle through adulthood, moving in and out of crisis, and find themselves with diminishing emotional, physical, and financial resources with which to combat new crises as they approach seniority.	 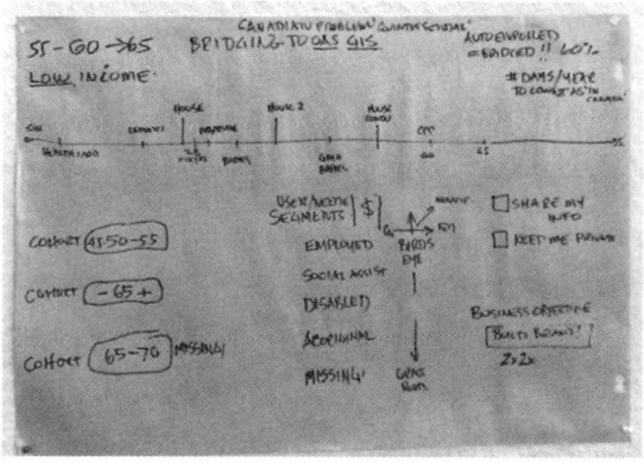
	Stakeholder Maps	Identifying the different interests surrounding OAS. Understanding how different government programs interact with each other, with clients, and with both formal and informal community support organizations. We identified many groups, formal and informal, who have access to and interact with vulnerable seniors; expelling the notion that these seniors are hard to find. We recognized that there are many processes that parallel that of the OAS program, but there are not formal connections between them.	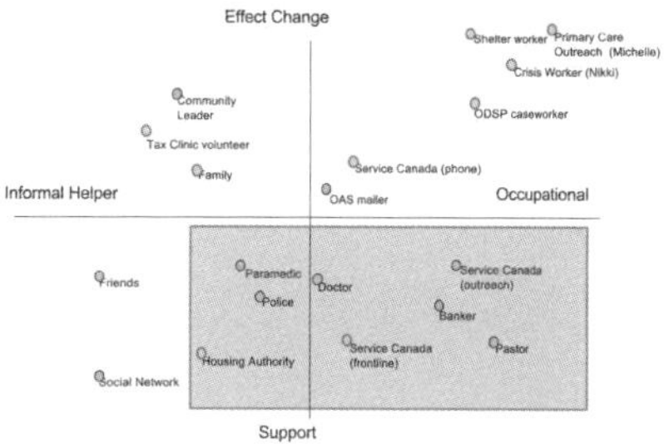 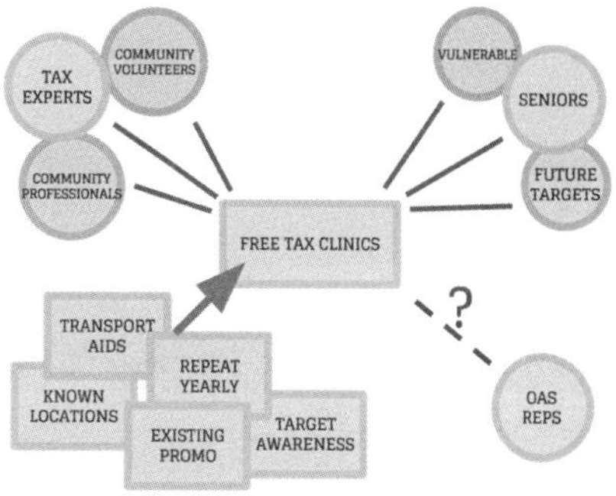

User Position Maps

Position mapping allowed us to understand how our target population distributed along spectrums of crisis, organization, and contact with others.

We came to understand that we were not directly reaching all the people we had aimed to contact, but instead learning about them through others.

We also came to realize that different support systems move individuals out of crisis and that these support workers can be a viable design direction.

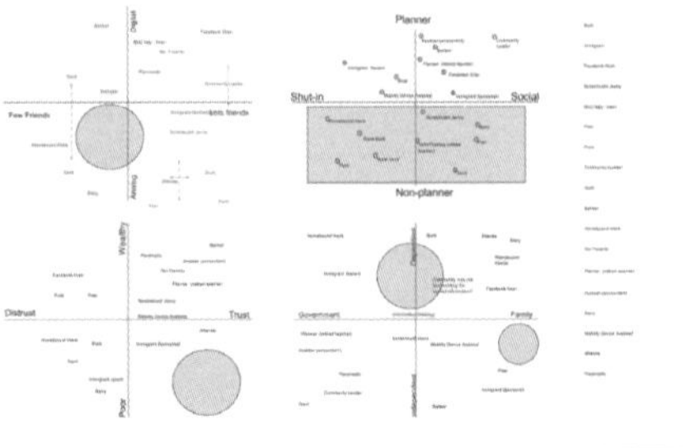

Personas

Representing the archetypes of the people with encountered—their needs, challenges, and goals, as well as typical experiences with the OAS program and systems.

Personas embodied important lessons about vulnerable seniors to inform the design of solutions.

For example, persons whose disabilities impact both their ability to access government services and their motivation to persist through a difficult process.

Develop

Mandal Art

A structured process—a single design direction can generate 64 inter-related ideas.

This led to a multitude of ideas that were based on our observations and learning, along different themes, and which addressed problems and needs in unexpected ways.

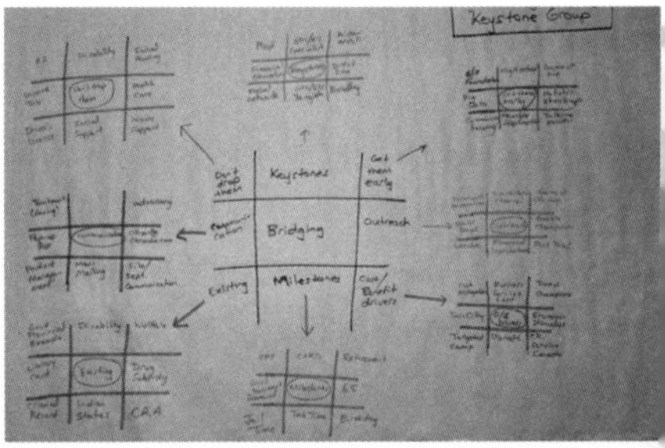

Science Fictioning

By developing an idea as if it were already implemented, we identified potential pitfalls and address oversights, further refining the ideas.

This led to user stories that described the experiences that people could have with a redesigned OAS program.

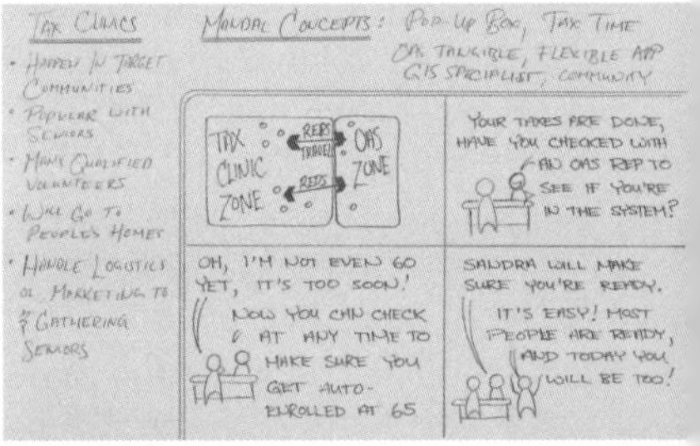

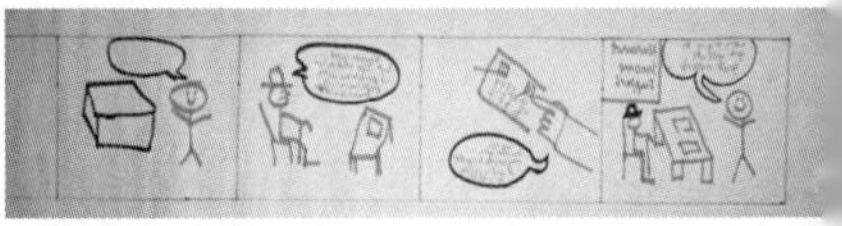

Value Hypotheses

Exploring ideas through value hypothesis allowed us to identify which concepts relate other aspects of the lives of seniors.

Some ideas build up existing systems, or meet needs above and beyond applying for OAS.

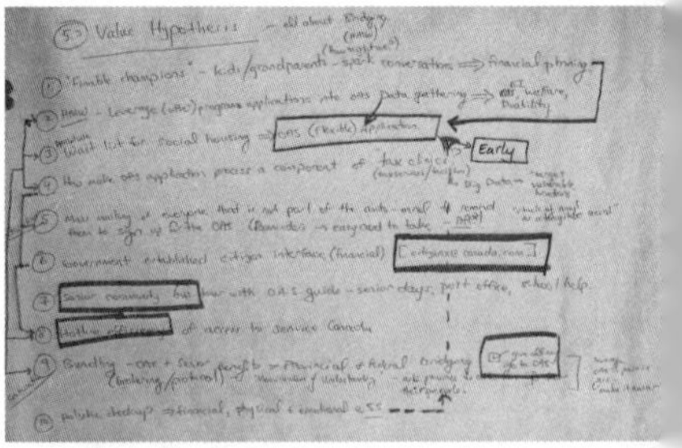

	Pugh Matrices	We identified success criteria for a good concept—for example, addressing problems and meeting the needs of seniors, the GOC, and external stakeholders. Scoring our ideas using specific criteria, we weighed their contribution and found that high scores did not always align with the ideas held passionately by the design team.	
Delivery	Storytelling	Condensing our work into short video presentations for the government client allowed the design team to revisit the process, key findings and create a narrative that was more logical for the client (rather than the chronological progress of the project).	

Findings and Outcomes

We have defined the task of updating OAS as a Super Wicked Problem. The criteria from Rittel and Webber and Levin et al. are useful for pointing out problematic factors in the state of a system. However, in the process of exploring and designing a solution to such a problem, Don Norman and Pieter Jan Stappers's properties of DesignX problems[15] are helpful when discussing how we have come to understand a problem the potential impact of solutions.

Profile of Unenrolled Seniors

In trying to find and understand the needs and perspectives of vulnerable seniors, it is helpful to look through the lens of the first category of DesignX systems, the *Psychology of Human Behaviour and Cognition*.[16] In building a case for an e-service platform for OAS, the departments involved devised a solution to improve upon the existing system, without challenging the assumptions and simplifications it was built upon.[17] This idea—the people meant to be served by the paper-based application are the same as those who will use the e-service—is one of the critical assumptions we challenged and found to be problematic. While Canadian seniors are becoming more technologically literate and more willing to use the internet to engage with government,[18] this is less evident for low-income or low-education[19] seniors and pre-seniors—the very applicants that are likely not to be automatically enrolled in OAS.

15 Donald A. Norman and Pieter Jan Stappers, "DesignX: Complex Socio-technical Systems," *She Ji: The Journal of Design, Economics, and Innovation* 1, no. 2 (2016): 86–90, http://www.sciencedirect.com/science/article/pii/S240587261530037X.

16 Ibid., 86–87.

17 Ibid., 87.

18 Government of Canada—ESDC Strategic and Service Policy Branch, "Profile of Canadians Aged 50 and Over: National and Regional Comparisons," 2015, 17; OECD, *Measuring the Digital Economy:A New Perspective* (Paris: OECD Publishing, 2014), 94–95, https://doi.org/10.1787/9789264221796-en.

19 Government of Canada, "Profile of Canadians Aged 50 and Over," 18.

People in Crisis

We found compelling stories that describe the experience of vulnerable seniors. Many live in crisis, with financial problems compounded by personal, social, medical, or residency issues. Often these issues are cyclical, with problems in one area having repercussions throughout a person's life.

A crisis intervention worker specializing in the needs of seniors described the experiences of many of her clients. One man, who was visually impaired and suffering from depression, throws out his mail because he cannot read it. Throwing out mail, we have learned, is not an atypical behaviour or limited to those with disabilities—many vulnerable seniors have language, literacy, or other issues that make reading mail difficult or impossible. For some, anticipation of more bad news is reason enough to avoid incoming mail. Some support workers regularly make a habit of going through their clients' garbage to rescue unopened mail. In extreme cases—such as after eviction—they may have clients' mail forwarded to their offices, but with individual caseloads often numbering in the hundreds, this is not a scalable solution. While this might appear to support the goal of moving to a digital platform, seniors and their supports both felt poorly about e-services. They worried about access to computers and the Internet, maintaining email accounts, and remembering passwords. When asked how to best respond to this behaviour, one crisis worker responded that the government should persist in sending multiple copies of correspondence until a response is triggered.

Others are overwhelmed by their circumstances to an extent that, even if applying to OAS will solve many of their problems, they do not have the time or capacity to pursue a long-term solution when more immediate needs are pressing. When faced with eviction, starvation, or other crises, the burden of a cognitively-heavy application procedure—which could take months to complete and lead to months of waiting for a potentially uncertain government approval—is perceived to be too onerous. While the application form is only five pages long, applying for OAS for vulnerable seniors is a multi-step process involving real obstacles like determining residential addresses for a forty-year period, tracking down decades-old documents which may no longer exist, opening a bank account, travelling great distances to government offices in areas without public transit, finding someone to read or translate documents, or relinquishing financial autonomy to a third-party representative.

Transition from One Program to Another

Crisis can be both acute (the loss of a spouse, debilitating accident) and chronic (debt, declining health). However, crisis does not begin at the age of 65—it only becomes aggravated at this age because key financial supports for pre-seniors, such as employment and provincial disability support programs, are timed to end when OAS should begin. Importantly, we could not find any formalized transitioning procedures to feed into OAS (a program

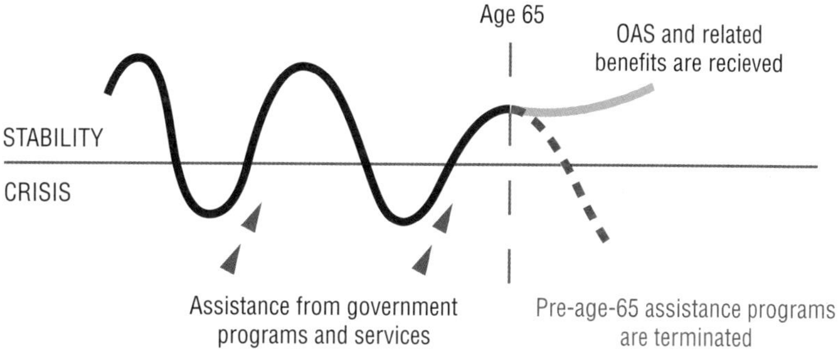

Figure 3 Under current practices, seniors can slide into crisis before OAS and related benefits come into effect. Copyright © 2017 Alexander Keith Eady and Ryan James Hum.

administrated by the federal government) from support programs that end at 65—which are often administered by another level of government such as the provincial, territorial or municipal. Seniors and crisis centre staff report that moving from programs like the province of Ontario's Disability Support Program[20] into OAS is only assisted by caseworkers when they have good relationships with their clients, rather than as a standard operating procedure by the two government administrators. Regardless of the truth of this sentiment, the lack of a formalized protocol presents a large gap that can lead seniors into crisis. Though crisis for seniors is not best described as a temporal event, it is important to note that many factors on instability converge at the age of 65, as shown in **Figure 3**, making this a poor period to require application for OAS.

It is also important to understand the many people in vulnerable populations will not pursue OAS unassisted and that the time and level of assistance needed to complete the application process is beyond the capacity of service and support providers. Policies, systems, and services of OAS have been created for an idealized user—someone who has had steady income, consistently paid taxes, and lived at the same address for most of their life. The initial plan for the modernization of OAS—design an e-service—was formulated with this user in mind; auto-enrollment removes this "ideal" user from the application process. Instead, the design team took an extreme user perspective that would help marginalized communities and likely also a wider demographic. The personas generated by the project team of different vulnerable senior archetypes help illustrate and design for non-idealized users

Holding off OAS Applicants

While 40 years of residency is required to receive the maximum OAS benefit, the *Old Age Security Act* defines a minimum of 10 years of residency in Canada (after having reached 18 years of age) to qualify for the minimum OAS benefit.[21] This minimum requirement is often lost on applicants and

20 "Ontario Disability Support Program," *Ontario Ministry of Community and Social Services*, accessed December 10, 2016, http://www.mcss.gov.on.ca/en/mcss/programs/social/odsp/.

21 *Old Age Security Act Loi Sur La Sécurité de La Vieillesse* (Ottawa, Canada: Minister of Justice, 1985), s. 3, http://laws-lois.justice.gc.ca.

even some community support workers. With the focus on requirements for the maximum benefit, the project design team met community support workers who undertake the time-consuming endeavor to collect a complete 40-year residency history prior to submitting the application. One support worker at a homeless shelter indicated that given the cognitive space and stress of individuals, it takes approximately eight meetings spanning up to a year with a vulnerable senior to hunt down the full residency information necessary for a complete OAS application. Though it appears that most people who begin the application process eventually manage to complete it, many experts recounted stories of long, drawn out applications involving much back and forth communication. One community support worker, advocating on behalf of a person who had lived in Canada all their life, reported spending more than a year proving the legal status of residency for their client in direct contravention of the application guidelines, which state that "If you were born in Canada and have lived in Canada all your life, you do not need to prove your legal status."[22]

22 "Information Sheet for the Old Age Security Pension," (Ottawa: Service Canada, 2015), 2.

While holding an OAS application may not be so troubling for the average applicant, for a more vulnerable senior, delays in OAS also delays access to subsequent government benefit programs for specific seniors such as the Canada Pension Plan Disability Benefit. Evaluating a partial application also does not preclude the senior from submitting a follow-up application.

Potential Solutions

When evaluating solutions, priority was given to ideas that removed pain points, were culturally sensitive to vulnerable seniors, and aligned to cultural norms in government—cost constraints, emphasis on privacy, and require little legislative or regulatory amendments to implement. Four major idea themes emerged, targeting different points in the system—create new interventions that empower external stakeholders or internal stakeholders, improve transition from one government program for vulnerable seniors to OAS, and remove petty administrative "sludge."

Among these ideas, the government client was initially most receptive towards allowing seniors to submit their applications piecemeal, as residency proof becomes available—exploiting the minimum rather than maximum program requirements. While this idea is an incremental mental model change, the benefits are profound to vulnerable seniors. This would allow seniors to receive benefits without delay. In addition, gaining OAS receivership provides access to other government programs for financially insecure seniors.

This flexible application idea can be implemented immediately—without administrative, legislative, regulatory change or negotiation with other levels of government—and only requires some awareness-building among service staff and social workers. We propose changes to the language of the application procedures, the application form, mail outs and other communication products—program FAQs, websites, and so on—to emphasize meeting the minimum residency criteria. This highlights the government client's inclination towards incremental change that does not require high political capital.

Building on this idea of minimum eligibility in combination with the departments' goals of modernization, we propose that the automatic enrollment program be expanded in include persons meeting the minimum requirements of residency and above. This information is already available to the department.

In addition to exploiting minimum residency applications, the project team proposed that the government develop methods to automatically transition seniors from key disability programs (used by vulnerable pre-seniors) into the OAS program. While this solution direction is sound and can address a large percentage of vulnerable seniors that are willing to accept assistance, the project design team was not comprised of legal or public administration experts and could not fully articulate the logistics. More work is being explored by the government client.

By providing evidence that small changes can make a huge difference when they are grounded in an understanding of the needs and actions of all actors in the system, this research sparked the client's willingness to revisit, using a user-centered design perspective, other priority programs like the Canada Pension Plan, and has contributed to an overall greater willingness to engage in design for policy in the Government of Canada.

Ideas were presented to government officials from Employment and Social Development Canada and Service Canada. Presently, external prototyping and implementation are pending. However, the recommendations have triggered one important result in the departments, which is already bearing fruit—culture change.

Paradigm Shift in Culture

While implementations of potential solutions are yet unavailable, we can draw insights on the value of this DesignX project from how the proposed solutions and the research that drives them have been internalized by the departments as evidenced by shifts in departmental culture.

Since presenting the research outcomes, the government client reports a changing understanding of what modernizing the OAS program means. They have adopted the priorities that we identified in our research. First and foremost, they have abandoned the definition of technology as modernization in favour of a human-centered approach and are targeting vulnerable populations as their users. Pursuant to this, they are focusing on facilitating fast and pain-free enrolment, with emphasis on establishing minimum requirements, within both their systems and their organizational culture and are seeking ways to implement supports to connect with and help those who help. For example, the concept of forming partnerships with provincial support programs to transition people into OAS as they become eligible is being explored. These steps are indicative of an internalization of a human-centered perspective in the organizational culture.

We can see further evidence of this shift in organizational mental models in changes to hiring processes and training, and the hiring of design thinking and user experience experts and the training of these skills at all levels of the departmental hierarchy. This is related to a push in the department to apply design research methods to develop pilot programs to redesign other services within their purview.

Within the OAS program, the department has undertaken efforts to understand how seniors' needs can be served without compromising program integrity. We revealed that proving residency is an extended and difficult process for many seniors, but acknowledged that it was a necessary component of the application. The government client is undertaking an analysis of its records of residency against information submitted in OAS applications, to understand the feasibility of an audit system—which would remove the requirement of file uploads, simplifying applications and reducing processing times and effort—versus the current burden-heavy application process. This would have positive ramifications for vulnerable seniors who may struggle to collect a complete residency history, as well as simplify a future e-service platform for OAS.

Foreseeable Challenges

Some questions have arisen from this project that cannot yet be answered. As the Government of Canada and other bodies push towards service modernization and transition to digital platforms, their specific responsibilities regarding education, training, and guidance for groups reluctant to or challenged by the evolution of service platforms is poorly defined.

In this instance, we determined that the most vulnerable, extreme users of the OAS program would be best served by modifications to the existing processes and polices, along with proposing more radical directions for modernization which account for the specific needs of the target population of service users. Given the challenges experienced by vulnerable seniors, we perceived that interventions to help them adapt to the changing systems would present a shift of the burden of effort onto them, a burden that did not seem justified. This may not apply to all populations and all programs.

Similarly, our exploration focused on the departments' goal of enrolling the existing population of un-enrolled eligible seniors. With the changing demographics of seniors and trends towards greater technological literacy, it is not clear if the current proposed interventions are future-proof or for how long.

Lessons for Designing in Complexity

Proponents of experiential learning[23] would likely agree that the best way to learn to identify and tackle DesignX problems is to work on them. The complexity of such problems is only visible through a rigorous pursuit of understanding. Conversely, it is important to note that people working within the system may be experts in domain knowledge, but are not inherently knowledgeable of the complexity and breadth of the problems within the system. We outline here aspects of the OAS project that we felt were successful as well discuss some problems encountered, which may inform future design projects in public policy.

23 David A. Kolb, Richard E. Boyatzis, and Charalampos Mainemelis, "Experiential Learning Theory: Previous Research and New Directions," in *Perspectives on Thinking, Learning, and Cognitive Styles*, ed. Robert J. Sernberg and Li-Fang Zhang (New York: Routledge, 2011), 228.

What Works

Approaching problem definition as an iterative exercise is an important take-away from this project. During a four-month process, we spent more than three months on discovery, looking for and trying to understand the issues within the OAS program. While this might not seem significant to those familiar with design processes, it runs contrary to typical processes of policy and program development, even those that occur under the auspices of innovation. For designers entering a program and policy space, with little direct knowledge of the domain, this was essential to learning, but we would argue that is it also a necessary practice for domain experts to make problem discovery and redefinition a regular part of their work. This observation is also aligned with Norman' and Stappers's assertion that design approaches to problem reveal issues that otherwise remain invisible in the traditionally analyses of policy and programs.[24]

24 Norman and Stappers, "DesignX: Complex Sociotechnical Systems," 90–91.

Challenges and Limitations

Communicating Design Learning and Outcomes to Non-Designers

This project ended with the presentation of findings and recommendations to the client. While the recommendations were received with interest—one public servant observed that we had presented solutions for issues that they knew existed, but had not been able to define or address—it is unclear if the government clients will be able to take the observations and proposals and develop prototypes and pilot programs for further testing. Indeed, our involvement in the modernization of the OAS program ended before the implementation stage, which Norman and Stappers argue presents the most difficulties.[25] Furthermore, our recommended interventions relate strongly to Norman and Stappers' categories of *The Psychology of Human Behaviour and Cognition* and *the Economic Framework of Complex Socio-technical Systems*,[26] suggesting that many hurdles to implementation lie ahead. For a DesignX project of this scale, it would seem wise to follow the recommendation that designers continue through from the initial exploration to the end of implementation.[27] Norman and Stappers make a strong case for doing just that. While it may not always be possible for designers to

25 Ibid., 92.

26 Ibid.

27 Ibid., 91–94.

take an active role in implementation, certain methods can be employed to more effectively communicate the lessons and vision that led to specific recommendations.

More positively, with this government client, we see evidence of effort towards culture change and the acquisition and development of the design and research skills that can aide the organization in building the capacity to tackle implementation.

Encouraging Adoption

Our design recommendations took the form of videos that highlighted specific stories and potential directions for the modernization of the OAS program. As such they were conceptual prototypes that did a good job of making clients aware of the needs of their target population and the convincing them value of following our recommendation. However, it is likely that these conception prototypes did not provide sufficiently concrete or specific examples of how the recommendations might be implemented. This might not present a barrier in a domain where implementation is also an iterative process, but this is not often the case in government.

The methods and teachings of Experience Prototyping[28] provide guidance on how we, as designers, can provide artifacts which server as guides for the implementation stage. Indeed, Buchenau and Suri conceptualize experience prototyping as addressing the design needs presented by the complex interactions present when technology, spaces, and services converge,[29] and description markedly like DesignX.

The prototype examples presented by Buchenau and Suri show how artifacts can become a "living specification," allowing those involved in the implementation process to advocate for the vision of the project and resist external or divergent pressures.[30] It would be interesting to see what form a "living specification" would take in the context of a larger DesignX issue—such an exploration would undoubtedly benefit from the modularization recommended by Norman and Stappers.[31]

28 Marion Buchenau and Jane F. Suri, "Experience Prototyping," in *Proceeding of the 3rd Conference on Designing Interactive Systems: Processes, Practices, Methods, and Techniques* (New York: ACM, 2000), 424–33.

29 Ibid., 425.

30 Ibid., 430.

31 Norman and Stappers, "DesignX: Complex Sociotechnical Systems," 93–94.

Acknowledgments

Improvements to the OAS program are the results of the dedication, effort, and talents of the Carleton University graduate student design team: Arda Aydin, Chen Zhang, Claudie St-Arnaud, Leilla Czunyi, Martin Smith, Natalie Verdon-Chu, Paul Thibaudeau, Rob Watters, and Samantha Lovelace.

Special thanks to the anonymous seniors interviewed in public spaces for this project, the devoted employees of the Government of Canada, the Seaway Valley Community Health Centre, Carling Community Health Centre, and to all who continue to champion the needs of Canadian seniors.

Inovando Juntos: Design Research and Practice for the Public Good*

Sabine Junginger

Competence Center for Design and Management, Lucerne University of Applied Sciences and Arts–Design and Art, Switzerland

Innovation networks are common in the IT industry where such networks are understood to facilitate technological advances. These networks are typically built around a single subject matter and often concern a specific, already known problem. But what is the meaning, relevance, and task for an innovation network intended to foster public sector innovation more broadly? Different government agencies and ministries all have different innovation needs and face varying challenges. What form can an innovation network take that depends on volunteers? What might be its role? Who might be part of it and what might each participant contribute? These are some of the questions addressed in this paper, which reflects on an *Inovando Juntos* project by the Brazilian Ministry of Planning, Development, and Management. It provides an example of design research and design practice at work for the public good when it comes to re-framing problems, engaging people, and identifying actionable problems.

Keywords **Design research, design practice, public sector, civil servants, innovation network**

* A developed version of this paper was published as Sabine Junginger, "Design Research and Practice for the Public Good: A Reflection," *She Ji: The Journal of Design, Econocmis, and Innovation* 3, no. 4 (2017): 290–302, DOI: https://doi org/10.1016/j.sheji.2018.02.005.

Sabine Junginger heads the Competency Center Design and Management at the University of Applied Sciences in Lucerne (Switzerland). She is Fellow of the Hertie School of Governance; Visiting Professor at Macromedia University of Applied Sciences (Germany) and the School of Design at Jiangnan University (China). She serves on several advisory boards, including Mindlab (Denmark); Alpbach Forum Europe (Austria) and Design:transfer (Germany). She has contributed to the EU-Brazil Sectorial Dialogues and "Design for Europe," another EU funded project. She is co-editor of Designing Business and Management (Bloomsbury 2016); Highways and Byways to Radical Innovation (University of Southern Denmark 2014); The Handbook of Design Management (Bloomsbury 2011) and author of Transforming Public Services by Design: Re-Orienting Policies, Organizations and Services around People (forthcoming, Taylor and Francis). Sabine holds a Ph.D. in Design from Carnegie Mellon University (USA) as well as an MDes in Communication Planning and Information Design.

sabine.junginger@hslu.ch

People, Products, Change

Organizational change remains a key issue for management and a challenge for leadership. Richard J. Boland and Fred Collopy[1] position managing as a design practice, while scholars like Richard Buchanan[2] demonstrate why management theories constitute design theories. Their insights do not merely apply to private business, but also to public administration and public management. We are at a point at which design research and design studies offer a new path to organizational change and development by shedding light on organizational design practices, organizational design principles, and organizational design methods across all organizational forms.[3]

Our notion of design and our understanding of its role and relevance to organizational change continue to advance. While researchers approach these issues from different disciplinary perspectives, there is increasing agreement on the need for research into the relationships between people, processes, structures, and purpose. Some are asking what constitutes a resource and what makes a product a product. Others are looking into organizational development methods that will lead to innovation and cultural change, and enable organizations to succeed in the unchartered waters of digital transformation and global and local challenges. The language may differ, and even sound clumsy to the designer's ear. For example, consider the researchers in engineering who seek to integrate "social and technological architectures of socio-technical systems" to overcome

> "the on-going divorce between people who develop and maintain the technological architectures, those who develop and maintain the social architectures, those who make the associated investment decisions, and the social actors that are to play a role in the resulting ActorWebs."[4]

A closer read reveals an urgency for human-centered design and a realization that the success of technological applications and systems, as well as their contribution to a sustainable environment worthy of human living, requires us to begin with an inquiry into human situations and people's life experiences. As one of my colleagues working in the i-homelab at the Lucerne University of Applied Sciences and Arts put it

> "In my work, I am conceiving technological applications for the home, for independent living for other people to use. When I had to care for my elderly mother over the past months, who is living on her own, it was obvious that she should be wearing one of the emergency call buttons around her neck, like the ones we have developed But she won't. It was then that I realized I would never wear one of these things myself and that we need to come up with better ways to develop stuff people can and want to use."[5]

This is in line with Norman and Stappers,[6] who argue that technological

1 Richard Boland Jr. and Fred Collopy, eds., *Managing as Designing* (Standford, CA: Standford University Press, 2004).

2 Richard Buchanan, "Worlds in the Making: Design, Management, and the Reform of Organizational Culture," *She Ji: The Journal of Design, Economics, and Innovation* 1, no. 1 (2015): 5–21.

3 Sabine Junginger, "Organizational Design Legacies and Service Design," *Design Journal* 18, no. 2 (2015): 209–26.

4 Rodrigo Magalhães and Henderik A. Proper, "Model-Enabled Design and Engineering of Organisations," *Organizational Design and Enterprise Engineering* 1, no. 1 (2017): 1–12.

5 Comment made during project team meeting for CaBinet, Case Based research into independent living, March 29, 2017.

6 Donald A. Norman and Pieter J. Stappers, "DesignX: Complex Sociotechnical Systems," *She Ji: The Journal of Design, Economics, and Innovation* 1, no. 2 (2015): 83–106.

failure is too easily dismissed as a shortcoming of the people expected to benefit from technology.

> "There is a tendency to design complex sociotechnical systems around technological requirements, with the technology doing whatever it is capable of, leaving people to do the rest. The real problem is not that people err; it is that they err because the system design asks them to do tasks they are ill suited for. Unfortunately, there is a tendency to blame people for the error rather than to find the root cause and eliminate it. On the whole, complex sociotechnical systems are poorly designed to fit the capabilities and powers of the people who must operate them."[7]

7 Ibid., 87.

The experience of my Lucerne colleague in computer science suggests that designing for human capabilities and empowerment is not enough. Rather, we have to address individual, social, and cultural issues that may deter a person from using a tool from which he or she can benefit—in his example, an emergency button that could save his mother's life.

People, Products, Change, Public

The ability to integrate product, process, and service systems with people's needs, capabilities, powers, and values is of essence to policymakers and public managers who work at all levels of government. It is their responsibility to conceive of, develop, and deliver public services that achieve the desired social outcomes. The availability of digital technology is a significant factor here. For bureaucracies that have been built around paper files, the shift to electronic files and online services, for example, presents both opportunities and challenges. But that shift always involves a reevaluation of existing relationships that institutions and agencies—and governments—have and want with citizens. Each project provides a concrete opportunity—and often exposes the necessity—to revisit the principles, practices, and products an organization pursues. Each project presents an opportunity to realign the organization with its mission and fulfill its mandated purpose to contribute positively to people's lives and society as a whole.[8]

Among civil servants, too, there is a growing recognition that the complexity of the problems they are coping with can no longer be addressed in isolation. Solutions to these problems demand cross-ministerial, cross-governmental, and cross-organizational collaborations, and new methods for these (separate) entities to design and develop together.[9] In line with the notion that management theories and management practices are a matter of design, these government employees have started to inquire into their own design principles and reflect on their own practices to transform how they go about generating and developing the kinds of solutions that lead to desired outcomes. Central to their efforts are the ideas of human-centered

8 This is not the place to expand on the notion of the five Ps in design, but I want to call readers' attention to the fact that "Principles, Practices, Processes, Products, and People" is distinct from the four Ps in marketing, namely "Product, Price, Place and Promotion." For more on this, see Rachel Cooper, "Design and the Customer Experience," *New Product Development and Innovation Marketing* 1, no. 1, (1999): 91–99.

9 The March 2017 report by the *OECD Observatory Platform for Public Sector Innovation* calls for systemic changes and addresses design issues for the first time. Jocelyn Bourgon, former Secretary to the Canadian Cabinet, calls for a new synthesis and has founded the *Public Sector Innovation Group* to promote an integrative approach. For more information, see Jocelyne Bourgon, *Public Innovation and Public Purpose: A Follow Up to the OECD Conference, Innovating the Public Sector: From Ideas to Action* (Ottwa: Public Governance International, 2015); Jocelyne Bourgon, *The New Synthesis of Public Administration* (Copenhagen: Dansk Psykologisk Verlag, 2017).

design, which manifest themselves in interaction pathways into organizational life,[10] but also in the novel recognition that insights into human experience and human interaction can reduce disconnects between civil servants, public managers, and frontline workers.[11] In addition, many are beginning to understand that generative and iterative design processes long employed by product design can aid integration of policymaking and policy implementation, and foster innovation.[12] New forms of design leadership and design management in the public sector are now being called for.[13]

This burgeoning area of design practice and design research challenges us to find out how design research may inform and initiate changes in the practices of people working towards the common good. How and why may a design focus aid public managers in their quest to conceive of, plan, develop, and deliver the kinds of products and services that support their mission and fulfill their mandates? What might design research and design practice look like within a public body? Where are the boundaries for design research and design practice in the public realm? Or in public administration? The list of questions is long. By offering a reflection on my work with the Brazilian Ministry of Planning, Development and Budget in Brasilia from January 2016 to May 2016, I hope to shed some light onto how such work may take place, what such work may involve, and how learnings and insights gathered in this process can find their way back into design research and inform future design practice while pointing to future design education needs.

Project Set-Up, Questions, and Approach

The project was funded by the EU-Brazil Sectorial Dialogues Program. My official role was that of Academic Senior Expert in Design. My broad assignment was to support the ministry's effort to foster public sector innovation, and, in particular, to assist the ministry in setting up an innovation network that would integrate individual innovation efforts by public servants across Brazil's national government—both within and across different departments and ministries.

My work on this project began in January 2016 with a videoconference and ended with the delivery of the final output in May 2016. The formal outputs I agreed to produce and deliver included a report on government lab innovation networks in the EU (Output 1, February 2016); a workshop with forty civil servants working on innovation projects within twenty Brazilian government agencies and ministries (Output 2, April 2016); and a report and reflection on the workshop (Output 3, May 2016). I visited Brasilia twice. My first visit was in February 2016, when I presented Output 1, met the team, and co-developed the first rough concept for the workshop. I returned to Brasilia in April that year to finalize and run the workshop while working with the innovation team at the ministry in two further workshops. All communication between those two visits was by

10 Richard Buchanan, "Human-Centered Design: Changing Perspectives on Design Education in the East and West," *Design Issues* 20, no. 1 (2004): 30–39, DOI: https://doi.org/10.1162/074793604772933748.

11 Omand Adebowale and Ken Starkey, Sunningdale Institute Report for the UK Cabinet: Engagement and Aspiration: Reconnecting Policy-Making with Frontline Professionals (United Kindom, 2009); Jesper Christiansen, "The Irrealities of Public Innovation" (PhD dissertation, Arhus, Denmark: Arhus University, 2013).

12 Sabine Junginger, "Policy-Making as Designing: Policy-Making beyond Problem-Solving and Decision-Making," in *Design for Policy*, ed. Christian Bason (London: Routledge, 2014); B. Guy Peter and Nenad Rava, "Policy Design: From Technocracy to Complexity, and Beyond," published online by the *International Public Policy Association*, see http://www.ippapublicpolicy.org/file/paper/5932fa23369d0.pdf; Matt Andrews, Lant Pritchett, and Michael Woolcock, "Escaping Capability Traps through Problem-Driven Iterative Adaptation (PDIA)" (working Paper, Center for Global Development, 2012).

13 Christian Bason, *Leading Public Design* (Bristol: Policy Press, 2017), see https://policypress.co.uk/leading-public-design - book-detail-tabs-stison-block-content-1-0-tab0 for more information.

e-mail, as the connection was not good enough for videoconferences—an issue we discovered during the first videoconference session, when I met the team.

I pursued the project as a participant-observer so I could capture the challenges and opportunities for design research and design practice in public management, public administration, and policymaking. As participant-observer, I took notes on meetings and conversations, and carefully observed the contexts in which people sought to develop new and innovative practices, processes, products, and services. I conducted this research as part of my ongoing studies into human-centered design in reorienting policies, organizations, and services around people. For this, I have looked into forms of participation in the public sector[14] and design processes in policy-making and implementation.[15] I have also researched policy studies, public administration, design management, and design leadership, and compared and contrasted the literature with insights and experiences gained in seminars, workshops, and discussions with policymakers and public managers over several years.[16]

14 Junginger, "Organizational Design Legacies and Service Design."

15 Junginger, "Policy-Making as Designing."

16 This includes a seminar on participatory government and interaction design at the Offices of the Israeli Prime Minister in 2012 with a group of senior policymakers; an advisory role at the Mexican Centro de Investigación y Docencia Económicas assessing the Mexican President's Office's program "Agentes de Innovaçion" in Mexico City; my work with NESTA, the OECD Observatory Platform for Public Sector Innovation; and my previously mentioned role as advisor to Denmark's Mindlab.

Designing an Innovation Network

Above all, I was—and remain—interested in what designers can contribute to public sector innovation within government organizations. How can we encourage, engage, and enable public managers to use methods that require different forms of engagement and interaction with colleagues, senior managers, and staff from other ministries and departments? What is the value and relevance of design here, and how can we convey and clarify both to people who, traditionally, have not seen themselves in the business of designing, and for whom—according to innovation experts like de Joong[17]—innovation too often is synonymous with implementing new technologies rather than changing organizational structures, processes, and attitudes?

> "For too long, the innovation dialog has been dominated by technical foci. We have to be careful how we approach the topic that for long has been too abstract. We also need to remember that problem solving in situ is more important than innovating. The discourse has been too casual, often technocratic and instrumental. Innovation for public value, this implies value trade-offs and politics as societal choice. We need to embrace 'messy practices,' 'situated problem-solving,' and 'wicked problems' as the context for public sector innovation."[18]

17 Sanderijn Cels, Jorrit de Jong, and Frans Nauta, *Agents of Change: Strategy and Tactics for Social Innovation* (Washington: Brookings Institution Press, 2012).

18 Comment by Professor Jorrit de Jong (Harvard University) at the OECD Conference entitled "From Idea to Impact: Public Sector Innovation," OECD Headquarters, 2014, Paris (via skype).

The desire to establish a cross-ministerial innovation network defied any technical solution—and thus opened the door to messy practices, situated problem solving, and wicked problems. But early conversations with the group at the ministry revealed that they saw a network as a kind of object or thing. With that, the expectations on me were to design this "network

Figure 1 (L) The Frankfurt Kitchen-Vienna (1926). Photo by 8linden Christos Vittoratos, used in line with creative commons.

Figure 2 (R) The B2 Bulthaup Kitchen (2009). Copyright © 2009 Bulthaup.

thing"—a task as simple as identifying the appropriate elements and fitting them together in the right shape and form—et voilà! Understandably, and naturally, the group applied its own design understanding, its own version of design thinking to the task. Yet the group's design approach was deeply rooted in the management thinking and in management practices. Those were good practices for managing operations, but not so much for developin something that depended on people to engage, contribute, and feel part of.

My first challenge was, therefore, to articulate, communicate, and illustrate how the group's design thinking, design practice, and its development process were driven by their understanding of management. My secon challenge was to help the group understand that a network is a dynamic, self-organizing, interactive, and living system. Both issues would be central to achieving the project's objectives: bring people interested and engaged in government innovation together for insights and collaborations.

I decided to challenge both notions visually. I wanted to demonstrate how design thinking links with ideas of management, and show how and why networks are distinct from objects, and what that meant for the ministry's objective to set up an innovation network. To do so, I chose two images

of kitchens in family homes from two different time periods. Using kitchen stories, I sought to illustrate the relationship between design thinking, management practices, and work process. A third image depicted a carnival down the river Danube in my hometown in Germany. Though hardly anyone in Brasilia could be expected to know the German town of Ulm, I knew they could connect to the concept of a carnival—Rio de Janeiro is world famous for its annual event.

Connecting Management Concepts & Practices with Design: Kitchen Stories

The Frankfurt Kitchen,(Figure 1) by Margarethe Schütte-Lithotzky, has its roots in scientific management and the rationalization of workplaces. It was designed to enable effective work practices in the kitchen: a woman—at the time, there was no question that the person in charge of the kitchen would be a female—should be able to find everything in the right place so she could quickly and efficiently prepare and cook meals, and easily preserve and store food for her family and household. The cupboards and shelves where arranged to reduce the steps needed to walk from one end of the kitchen to the other. And the design put as many drawers and shelves within her reach as possible. At the same time, each cupboard and shelf was covered or closed, so that everything remained clean and orderly. The Frankfurt Kitchen design made the woman the kitchen expert—she knew better than anyone else what was behind each cupboard and was in control of its contents. She worked behind a closed door—shut off from the remainder of the house—creating dishes with secret ingredients and using processes she did not wish to share or make public. After all, they were messy; her individual responses to situated problem solving—quickly adding a potato to an overly salty soup, or scraping off the burned side of the toast—remained well out of view of guests and others in the family. When she finally emerged from the Frankfurt Kitchen, it was to show off the perfect dish and be the perfect host.

Cooking is no longer the sole responsibility of women by 2009, and people who cook no longer needed to do so in isolation. The Bulthaup B2 kitchen demonstrates this.(Figure 2) Here, all the cupboards are open. The island in the center allows visitors, guests, kids, and family to watch, observe, and comment on the food preparation. They can join in and even take the lead. The space is open—the area where food is being produced is shared and common. In management terms, this also means that it is no longer clear who the expert is, what expertise the person doing the cooking needs, or even what counts as expertise. In fact, the notion of the expert may change as the host discovers that one of the guests just completed a cooking class about how to cook and carve a chicken, and another person in the room announces an allergy to garlic. The design of the B2 supports participatory and co-designing activities. It embraces messy practices and allows in situ problem solving to become a shared and agreed-on element in

Figure 3 Nabada Ulm, Germany. Photo by author.

an emerging design process. This is different then from the Frankfurt kitchen, where in situ problems—a burned turkey or a vital ingredient dropped on the floor, for example—were challenges solved by the individual and lone expert that called on her to improvise to protect her status as expert by either hiding any mistakes or finding a way to present them as intended outcomes.

These two images serve two key purposes. Each nicely illustrates how the form we give to our work environments already implies and conveys certain kinds of designerly and design thinking. Moreover, the images allow us to see how organizational forms reveal and reflect our values, and suggest or even ascribe how we move and act in a workspace. Broadly speaking, both kitchen images effectively illustrate the changes that are currently happening in the public sector—especially within government agencies. It is here that we find structures that have also been built around the ideas of the nineteenth century that focus on rationalization, scientific management, and a key concern for productivity—just like the Frankfurt kitchen—and it is here that new collaborative practices are calling for new designs.

From Object to Action: Reconceiving an Innovation Network as a Carnival

The second set of images showed a picture of my German hometown, Ulm, and its annual river carnival Nabada, which means "bathing down the river" in the Swabian dialect.(Figure 3) The idea—though on a significantly smaller scale in size and number of participants—echoes that of Brazil's annual Carnival in Rio: organized professional groups (Samba schools, music bands, and other performers) join with everyday citizens to form a jolly parade down the river. The familiarity of the carnival concept allowed me to home in on the aspects that might have relevance for an innovation network. While some carnival groups plan far ahead, and spend their weekends designing and building their themed vessel throughout the year, individual citizens and families may grab rubber boats on the spur of the moment. They may fetch a bucket, a water pistol or something else they can quickly get their hands on to participate in the water ride and the spraying action. There is no barrier to entry. A basic organizational structure is provided. Yet the final form depends on those who participate and engage with it to make every year's carnival unique. It is an example of a network that lives off the people who bring it to life.

Looking at an innovation network through the lens of a carnival offers a different perspective on the concept, structure, and process of an activity-based network. The Ulm carnival was not unlike what this ministry hoped to achieve by setting up an innovation network: people passionate about innovation working together to create something bigger than what they could achieve on their own. A carnival is creative, and allows for new ideas and experimentation. And yet, a carnival still needs structure and some kind of guidelines. If someone falls into the water, an emergency crew has to be there and know what to do. The police must manage traffic and crowds. But these are supporting, background roles that allow people to come together, have fun, and create something together that they value and remember.

Reframing the Innovation Network

Moving from network-as-object to network-as-action immediately challenged the ministry to rethink its own role in a future innovation network. In its original understanding, the ministry would take on a traditional management and leadership role. In the new understanding, the ministry had yet to find its place. The carnival emerged as a vehicle to reframe the notion of a network from one that is static to one that unleashes the energy of all the other innovators and becomes a platform for sharing and generating insight. This was a radically different proposition than their original idea to set up an innovation network—which implied creating something new on top of everything else that already existed. Now, new questions formed, among them: what is the unique contribution of the ministry's innovation group to an innovation network? How can it support the innovation efforts of other, already existing innovation groups across government?[19]

19 Valuable research into reframing problems in the policy context was conducted by Donald Schön and Martin Rein in the 1970s. For example, see Martin Rein and Donald Schön, "Problem Setting in Policy Research," in *Using Social Research in Public Policy Making*, ed. Carol H. Weiss (Lexington, Mass.: Lexington Books, 1977), 235–51; Martin Rein and Donald Schön, "Reframing Policy Discourse," in *The Argumentative Turn in Policy Analysis and Planning*, ed. Frank Fischer and John Forrester (Durham: Duke University Press, 1993), 145–66; as well as Martin Rein and Donald Schön, *Reframing: Controversy and Design in Policy Practice* (New York: Basic Books, 1994). This work is significant for design research—particularly in the public sector. The topic has been picked up in design research more recently, for example in Kees Dorst, *Frame Innovation: Create New Thinking by Design* (Cambridge, Mass.: MIT Press, 2015).

Inquiring into the Need for an Innovation Network

Once there was clarity within the ministry about the kind of network they were looking for, I requested meetings with some of the external innovation teams at other ministries that we hoped would join the future innovation network. I was able to engage in conversations with the innovation group at the Brazilian Ministry of Justice, the Federal Court of Accounting, Caixa Bank—Brazil's second largest bank, and a major actor in the government's social programs—and the Ministry of Education. My aim was to learn as much about their respective motivations, specific projects, aims, resources, and challenges as possible. Once again, here was an opportunity to be amazed about the initiative and inventiveness of public servants who often make do with very little. When I felt I understood what they were doing, how they were going about it, and why they were undertaking their efforts, I asked about their relationship to the Ministry of Planning and how they viewed the role of that ministry in light of their own innovation efforts.

During each of these conversations, I was accompanied by at least two members of the project team from the Ministry of Planning. Knowing that they were already in contact with the innovation groups we were visiting, I worried after each hour-long meeting if I had simply wasted their time. But when I asked, "Did you learn anything new and valuable?" the answer was always "Yes." I learned that, during previous meetings, the Ministry of Planning would simply share their own intentions and plans but failed to inquire what the other teams were working on or concerned about

20 Comment made by senior team member from the Ministry of Planning after visiting an innovation group in February 2016.

"So we would come in and say, 'This is what we want to do, would you like to join us?' We never asked them what they were doing."[20]

It was during a meeting with an external innovation team that the Ministry of Planning learned about its own possible role in the future innovation network. In response to my question about how the Ministry of Planning could support the innovation team's work within their own (separate) ministry, the head of that innovation team turned to the accompanying project team members from the Ministry of Planning with a specific request. "Could you change the way we have to submit our annual reports to your ministry?" It was the first time the Ministry of Planning had heard a concrete suggestion about how they could fill their own role as innovation partner. It also clarified that to foster change, there would have to be some changes within the Ministry of Planning as well. They, too, would have to be willing to join in some of the projects to earn the respect and acceptance of their innovation partners.

The First Innovation Network Meeting: Mapping & Connecting

This research into the needs of those who were supposed to benefit from a new innovation network generated the content and purpose for the first innovation network meeting I was responsible for. We agreed to name this workshop *Inovando Juntos—Innovating together because the sum of government is greater than its parts.*

Co-developed with the team at the Ministry of Planning, this workshop sought to foster new collaborations among people within different ministries and government agencies who were actively working on public sector innovation in one way or another. From my research with the various innovation groups at the ministries, I saw that some people struggled to engage with others they had not been introduced to or met previously. So one of the first stated objectives of the workshop was to ensure that participants would get to know new people from different ministries and departments. Upon entering the room, participants received a card with a handwritten task asking them to engage with another person in the room. For example, one card said, "Find a person in the room who cycled to the event today." During the morning coffee break, this participant had to circulate and ask people she usually did not speak to or engage with about the way they travelled to the meeting. Another person was asked to ask someone "two meters away from you" if he could get him some coffee. This initial round of tasks turned out to be very successful, and shortly thereafter, the room was abuzz with conversation. In the next step, participants were asked to find a seat at one of the tables next to someone they had not spoken to yet. Each participant then shared information about the kinds of networks they engaged with individually, using templates that I had prepared based on the conversations with the ministry's innovation group and all the other innovation groups we had visited and talked to. The template classified networks into four category areas: networks in government, in business, in academia, and in civil society. After this, each table used a second, larger template to collectively represent their respective, existing networks. This activity produced the first finding from the workshop: each of the forty participants reported good connections within government, a few connections to business, but hardly any to academia or civil society. To achieve the kind of public sector innovation they all were striving for and working on, we realized that the engagement and participation of all four sectors was necessary.

For the innovation team at the Ministry of Planning, this insight clarified the need to expand the innovation network. As a consequence, the plan for the follow-up workshop was to include experts from academia and civil society. The workshop reaffirmed that, rather than creating something new on top of everything else that already existed, the task for the ministry was to connect all innovators and enable collective sharing of insights and challenges so these could be addressed conjointly.

On a side note, I should mention that the innovation group at the Ministry of Planning participated hands-on in the preparation for the workshop. We knew early on that, with so many key staff members linked to the highest government offices in an extremely turbulent time in Brazil, many participants would be distracted by their mobile phones. We conceived of mobile phone parking slots attached to a wall, so nervous people could always be close to their phones. To reduce anxiety, "stress reduction bottles" were available at the "parking" area—an idea one of the civil servants had borrowed from his childcare drop off area: To reduce people's anxiety when they had to let go of their mobile phones, the childcare center handed everyone a bottle filled with beautifully colored sand and water to look at, shake or squeeze! During the afternoon portion of the workshop, the innovation team had prepared several topic areas that required the collaboration of the various innovators across the government. The ministry hoped for projects to develop during this part of the day. Participants were encouraged to join any one of the topic areas, explore issues, and develop action plans by the end of the day. In exit video interviews, this second part of the workshop was not received with the same enthusiasm as the morning session. Teams were left to their own devices, and, in retrospect, I realize that more guidance and coaching would have been helpful. In fact, few actionable items emerged from the afternoon session. However, participants did get to know each other better, and the foundations for new relationships among innovators across government ministries and agencies were laid.

Findings and Outcomes

On a project level, this project shows that design research and design methods can contribute to public sector innovation in significant ways—not only by reframing concepts, but also by opening up new avenues for management thinking and practice. In this case, a major ministry reconceived the purpose of its innovation network from that of an object or a thing to be controlled and managed, to one of action and communication, where the ministry became an equal partner and contributor. In this process, several high-level government employees developed new forms of interaction with their colleagues, subordinates, and others across some twenty ministries and government organizations.

Network participants conducted a preliminary analysis of the strengths and weaknesses of their network. The workshop revealed that the network lacked contacts with civil society organizations, business, and academia, and realized that these were needed to accomplish many of the targeted public innovations.

Design leadership and design research played a role from the beginning to the completion of the first innovation workshop. This research demonstrates, among other things, how design research and design practice might tie into public management, and how design research and design methods can support the objectives of ministries and public organizations for integrated innovation. More specifically, I found that

- Visual conversation pieces and storytelling are useful tools for high-level public employees and policy makers.
- Facilitating and enabling real human interactions is a central task and opportunity for designers.
- Sustainable efforts to change design practices have to account for minimal resources—don't introduce anything people cannot recreate on their own. We used brown paper and flip charts. All but one of the templates was handwritten. The phone parking spaces were made of foam, cut by hand, and attached to the wall with tape.
- Small steps and incremental approaches can make a big difference
- Human-centered interaction design principles that invite, engage, and enable are relevant to the public sector.
- The dedication and inventiveness of public staff working with minimal resources cannot be underestimated.

Conclusion

Scholars in policy studies and in public administration are in the process of revisiting design.[21] In many public sector innovation labs, human-centered design receives explicit mention.[22] Methods like design thinking or customer journeys have entered into the vocabulary of civil servants. This project shows that design research and design methods can support the efforts of public officials to identify new ways of working and aid in the implementation of new thinking and doing. There are many questions still to answer in terms of design management and design leadership—both concepts derived in the context of consumer goods and markets. What we are witnessing, increasingly, is a new kind of design leadership emerging within the many

21 Aside from work by Martin Rein and Donald Schön, Michael Howlett, M. Ramesh, and Guy Peters have also written recently on the topic. For example, see Namrata Chindarkar, Michael Howlett, and M. Ramesh, "Introduction to the Special Issue: 'Conceptualizing Effective Social Policy Design: Design Spaces and Capacity Challenges,'" in "Policy Design and Non-design in Social Policy," ed. Namrata Chindarkar, Michael Howlett, and M. Ramesh, special issue, *Public Administration & Development* 37, no. 1, (2017): 3–14; Or Peters and Rava, "Policy Design: From Technocracy to Complexity, and Beyond."

22 For example, in Mexico by CIDE and the President's Office's Project Agentes de Innovaçion, in Chile by the Laboratoria Gobierno or in the US by the US Office of Personnel Management but also within the iLabs by NESTA, UK.

constraints of the public sector. Though not nearly as salient as, say, design leadership at a company like Apple, such leadership is neither silent nor invisible.

In this role, designers are part of a group that achieves significant outcomes for potentially millions of people who will never know their name. But their work will not be in vain—it will be for the common good.

Acknowledgments

This project was funded by the EU-Brazil Dialog Program and in cooperation with CESOS Portugal.

Movable Feasts: An Exploration of the Heritage, Flavors and Possible Futures for Shanghai Street Food

Francesca Valsecchi

College of Design and Innovation, Tongji University, China

Moveable Feasts is an online platform (http://sh-streetfood.org) that aims to research, savor, catalogue, preserve, and engage with Shanghai's rich street food heritage. The platform contains knowledge acquired through urban observation and exploration. By disseminating this knowledge, the platform contributes to a local model of urban growth in Shanghai that aims to honor and promote its culinary heritage, provide safe and nutritious snacks, and preserve and expand Shanghai's richly diverse street life and culture. This essay comments on the project evolution and offer some reflections for future development.

Keywords **Cultural heritage, urban sociability, urban diversity, informal economies, future cities, public space**

Francesca Valsecchi is an Italian communication designer and researcher. After graduation at Politecnico di Milano as a fellow of Density Design Research Lab, she moved to China for a post-doctoral research about sustainable heritages. She currently serves as Assistant Professor at College of Design & Innovation, Tongji University; her research interests cover the area of information and data visualization, digital social innovation, open design, design and culture. Since 2010 she is based in Shanghai, enjoying the Asian trans-cultural lifestyle, and the thrilling mix of international environment with traditional heritage. She is currently mainly active on a project to document and map Shanghai street-food culture and places, and within the community of interest of Chinese opendata using analytics to produce cultural services.

francesca@tongji.edu.cn

Figure 1 A fragment of the painting "Along the River during the Qingming Festival", by the Song Dynasty artist Zhang Zeduan (1805–1145).

Figure 2 Photograph of an alleyway in Shanghai in 1990s, by Yuanmin Lu (陆元敏). Used with permission.

Project Context and Framing

Moveable Feasts is an online platform (http://sh-streetfood.org) that aims to research, savor, catalogue, preserve, and engage with Shanghai's rich street food heritage. The platform shares knowledge acquired through urban observations and explorations. By disseminating this information, the platform contributes to a local model of urban growth in Shanghai that aims to honor and enjoy its culinary heritage, situate places offering safe and nutritious snacks, and preserve and expand the richly diverse life and culture of the street.

Although the website looks like a typical design project outcome, *Movable Feasts* was not originally a design project. It was developed outside—and beyond—the traditional boundaries of academic and design practice. The simple platform is able to leverage input from academics and practitioners from any number of disciplines in addition to contributions from citizens, city-dwellers and urban planners.

Let us begin by looking at three historical images that convey the relevance of street food as a topic for urban studies, and which represent the profound importance of street food in Chinese society. **Figure 1** shows a painting that is quite familiar to all Chinese people—a scene of a village during Qingming Festival;[1] **Figure 2** is a photo from the twentieth century, taken in Shanghai, of people sitting near a traditional *lilong*, or alleyway; and **Figure 3** is a much more recent image (from 2013) of what was once called the "Pengpu Market" in north Shanghai, which has since been shuttered.

1 Digital version available at http://www.comuseum.com/wp-content/uploads/2016/01/zhang-zeduan_qing-ming-shanghe-tu.jpg.

These images take us on a trip through Chinese urban cultural history. Each represents an urban space where food plays the central role, and offers insights into the history of Chinese social habits and activities that revolve around food.

Qingming is the largest family festival in China. This painting (Figure 1) —which dates from the Song Dynasty, around the eleventh century CE—is so iconic to traditional Chinese culture that it was chosen as the centerpiece for the Chinese Pavilion at Expo 2010 Shanghai and brought to life in an animated digital tapestry. By looking closely at the scenes and settings represented, we notice that many of the activities and interactions the artist depicts are centered on food preparation, consumption, exchange, and so on.

The second photograph (Figure 2) is from a more modern urban setting—possibly in early 1990s. It is a perfect street food still life, depicting materials, equipment, prepared dishes, and, of course, people, in an ordinary and characteristic Shanghai street landscape.

Figure 3 was taken a few years ago. It is an aerial shot of a crossroads—a bus stop in Pengpu district, in fact—where one of the more vivid street markets in town was held. The food experience in this street market was so engaging for the residents that the market grew to the point of occupying the entire roadway and blocking the bus routes, impeding the regular flow

Figure 3 A bird's eye view of Pengpu Night Market in 2013, before closure. Copyright © 2013 by Yi Yang.

of people and vehicle traffic on a nightly basis. Eventually, the night police had to shut down the market and clear the streets, in an effort to restore order, but by doing so, one of the most amazing informal public spaces within Shanghai was lost. This episode provoked a considerable reaction on social media, where the contradiction between a city that needs to be functional and a city that wants to be social fiercely emerged.

These images of the past point to a number of questions. How might these beautiful forms of social life be cultivated in the future? How can their existence be guaranteed in ways that respect urban regulations and public safety concerns? How might the discourse around street life become a conversation about urban public space—more than one about safety? Finding answers to these questions is increasingly challenging, given the wave of digitization pervading urban development, and that the hype around smart cities has shifted the focus away from analogue and low-tech forms of urban identity. Citizen engagement has become crucial to the survival of these important urban social spaces.

A Platform Built by Citizens for Citizens Who Want to Share Their Culinary Heritage

Initially, this project was not really a design initiative. Everything started a few years ago, in a rather underground fashion. One day a flyer was distributed at Xinchejian—the first Shanghai hackerspace—calling all the food lovers in town to meet and participate in a conversation about local street food and its future. I went—there were twenty people from different countries, of varying ages and professions. Our conversation principally revolved around a deep appreciation of the street markets, although awareness and concerns about how much space they were given in the city of the future were very diverse. We knew that there are ways to keep food stalls on the streets, and that food markets could be clean, safe, and healthy, as they are in other cities around the world—like Bangkok, Singapore, Kuala Lumpur, Taipei, Vancouver, and New York, to name a few places. At the same time, we were sure that any intervention should respect and preserve the social nature of the markets—as an alternative to the commodification of the food courts found on the top floor of every mall in the city. We recognized that the nourishment locals were getting from street food was not only about the dishes they were eating, it was also about what they were experiencing in terms of culture, values, inspiration, desires, fantasies, and so on.

That meeting sparked a small wave of activity. We conducted grassroots search and exploration activities that we documented, uploading our findings to a single location on the web. This method of research was very different than having a clear plan—it was more a combination of individual, spontaneous initiatives that we decided we wanted to share publicly. We coded a web platform at night and on weekends, where we eventually uploaded our data.(Figure 4)

The platform provides three main types of information:

- A locator map—developed and augmented with input from students over the course of several years—depicting the best street food spots in town.(Figure 5)
- An encyclopedia listing over seventy local dishes available in the streets of Shanghai, including details about how they are cooked, their region of origin, which traditions they are associated with, and how they have evolved over time.(Figure 6)
- Stories about what makes the Shanghai street food experience a richly social one—short pieces about the history of street food and sellers, local trends, and current street food topics—written by visiting students and locals.

Content selection was driven by our passion for street food and our desire to share it with others.

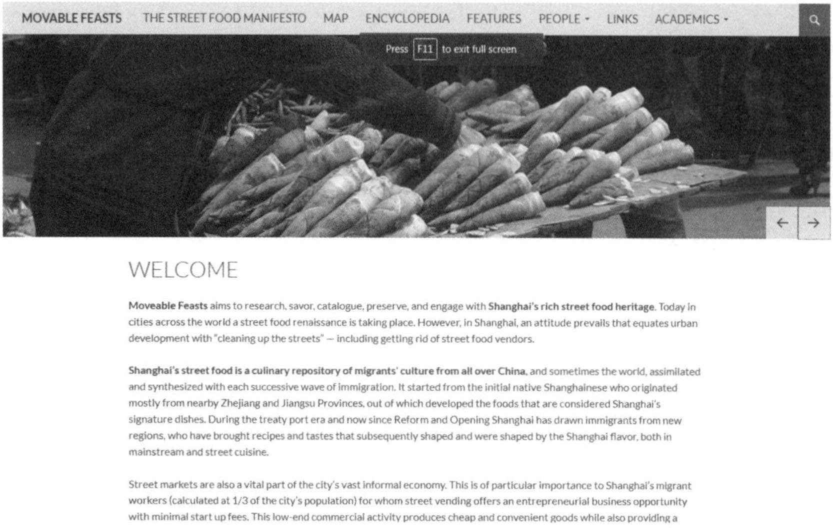

Figure 4 The *Movable Feasts* homepage. Copyright © 2016 Movable Feasts.

Figure 5 Visitors at the Shanghai Movable Feasts exhibition held during Milano Design Week 2016. Copyright © 2016 Movable Feasts.

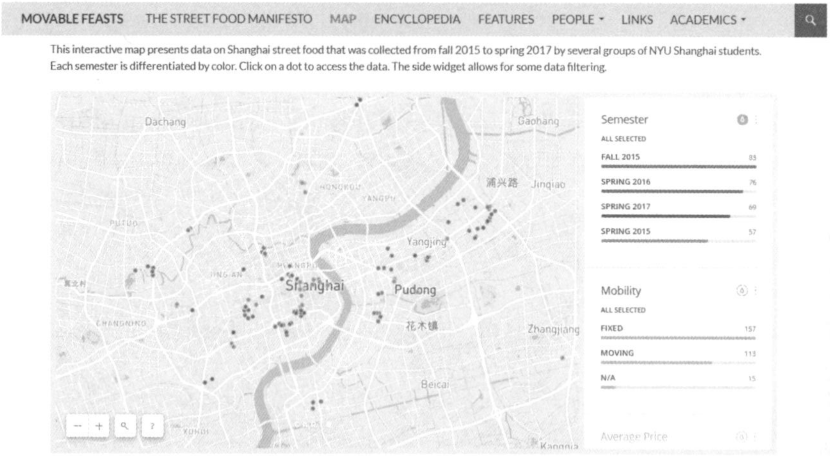

Figure 6 The street food locator map produced by NYU students (2015–2017). Copyright © 2016 Movable Feasts.

On the Social Relevance of Street Food, and Future Research

Social values around food practice represent the heritage of the city, and as such deserve to be preserved in inhabitants' active memories. Shanghai, not too many decades ago, was not an urban settlement—it was a fishing village experiencing waves of migration due to Western occupation and economic trading, which made it a unique gathering point for the cultures coming from every corner of the globe. And despite the prevalence of univocally sweet flavors from this part of China, Shanghai is a city where you can sample the food from everywhere. Cities throughout history seem to be intrinsically built on diversity and variety, and this might contradict with the tendency and the aspiration of contemporary metropolises to become clean and international in a way that looks fairly uniform.

Shanghai's street food is a culinary repository of migrant culture from all over China, assimilated and synthesized with each successive wave of immigration. In its rich variety, Shanghai's street food is a real testament to the hybrid culture of this migrant metropolis. Street markets are a vital part of the city's vast informal economy. This is of particular importance to Shanghai's migrant workers, for whom street vending offers an entrepreneurial business opportunity with minimal start up fees. Such low-end commercial activity produces cheap and convenient goods while also providing a crucial contribution to the culture of the street, which is so critical to the vibrancy of urban life. We often witness a prevailing attitude that equates urban development with cleaning up the streets—including getting rid of street food vendors, and grounding city identity with uniformity. As creative practitioners, researchers, and citizens, we believe a sustainable approach to urban development should appreciate and better support the values represented by street food, including an engaged public space, the resilience of informal economies, and cultural diversity.

People thrive off the intensity of street markets, which give cities life and counter the sterility of shopping malls with their fast food courts and restaurant chains. We believe that this approach cannot be top-down—it requires active citizen engagement. How can academic disciplines and researchers contribute to and interact with governance to produce and implement different models for future cities? We want to learn from cities across Asia, Europe, and the Americas that have found ways to preserve and celebrate their street food heritage, and include it in their future visions. More specific questions are being developed within a multi-disciplinary approach where design interventions are connected with speculative and analytical reflection from social and urban studies. In particular, how can communication devices and services support and ease public participation in contemporary city development? How can citizens' participation be valued as an urban resource? Can inclusive models of alternative economies support and enhance bottom-up social benefits?

Even though the website began as an interface to support background field research and inquiries, it has eventually become a springboard for student projects and assignments, involving the students in a wider project connecting classroom exercises with real, existing issues. In the past two years, we have involved students from several courses from both Tongji D&I and NYU Shanghai. These classes are based on experiments with field research, digital mapping, communications, and service design, and contribute to a variety of open projects about street food and its role in social infrastructure in the city of the future.

This approach describes the food system as a complex system, considering the stakeholders involved, the informal character of the markets, the regulatory constraints, and the material and immaterial issues related to social equity and health safety. This gave the students access to a complexity frame on a real world scale. Street food, as a topic, garners immense interest, and creates connections and bonds within citizens and community. On the other hand, documenting efforts are time-consuming and slow, so we have not been able to get far beyond creating a platform that is a continual work-in-progress, despite it being a repository of fascinating content. The ultimate goal of informing governmental decision making has yet to be achieved, and this might be read as a drawback of the design—meaning a limited capacity to bring insightful intellectual offerings to bear on actual policy.

The Limitations of Design's Influence on Social Innovation

Despite design's capacity to competently frame the street food discourse as a systemic reflection on urban development, and its more than adequate ability to use the existing digital architecture to visualize the nature and the composition of the system itself, the project is still lacking in overall impact.

Making the Conversation Public

Even though the topic of food—and in particular the reference to social forms of food in public spaces—effortlessly captures people's attention and inspires conversations with the wider public, it is also true that the project still lacks a public forum for discussion. I realised that often we express values and meaning in a form that makes them understandable only for those who are already engaged. I define our street food exchanges as *private*, because although they happen within circles with no constraints of access, a public discussion—where, for example, governance would be involved—has yet to emerge. The difficulties of engaging the government in participatory or citizen-informed initiatives are probably less a question of "they don't want to talk" and more an issue of "we don't know how to approach them," which means our call is poorly oriented. We are aware that our ideas and concerns have value, but that fact itself does not guarantee that we are delivering and sharing them in the appropriate way. One comment we received is that when referring to sustainable development policy, there is increasing discussion of the "triangle of polarity" that includes government civil society and citizens, and business. We have also been told that this triangle is regulated by the "I will if you will" principle—meaning that each stakeholder needs to see that the other two are already engaged, before taking the risk of engaging as well. This might seem paradoxical, but in fact it is a condition that should facilitate collaboration between stakeholders. We have not, in fact, done much in the way of organizing something that would bring the governance and the citizens together—we always have thought of them as two separate and, to a certain extent, conflicting entities, and we have limited ourselves to involving people that already love the markets in the belief that they would be inspiring to others. In fact, this might be a limit of design thinking too—we have not resolved, in any way, the paradox of the value of cultural heritage versus the idea of a modern urban environment as it is conceived in development and planning, since bridges between different these different perspectives have not yet been built.

A Lack of Interventional Continuity

As positive as it is to work on breadth, a lack of depth and consistency does not help. This is particularly true when we look at the projects produced by the students—some of them are trying to improve the service offered by the markets, others wish to boost food hygiene practices, still others want to make food transportation efficient, innovate food safety and product traceability, or improve the workload of cooks and enhance their social bonds. Multiplying services, boosting quality, and improving job conditions are all keywords that significantly address the complexity of the urban system, and they are all relevant domains for design interventions, thus working systemically across them might not have been meaningful as working systematically on few.

Reality is Even More Complex Than the Notion of Complex Systems

By design's limitations, I am mainly referring to the limited progress we have made in changing the system. Many things have been proposed—we prototyped new trash bins, designed new carts, and involved the cooks by asking for their feedback, and we have been doing a lot of co-design and engagement activities—but none of this has been pushed to a level where a transformation could actually take place. And this is not because our knowledge of how the system works is limited, it is because, very often, despite knowing how the system works it is not easy to jump into a particular issue and, from there, re-design the overall system of relationships.

I think there is a problem of scale here. This project did not begin with a design perspective; it was a choice motivated by activism that had a specific connection with reality—a response to a top-down intervention to clean up the streets. Activism has the risk of sometimes drowning in loops, though: it is not the focus point of the projects to convince the government that it's not beneficial for the city to send the police—but this involuntary often became the main way in which we were telling the story. In fact, this story of the police is not such a valid argument: policy is applied in very different ways across different neighborhoods, gray areas of interventions occur largely outside downtown areas, and because there is, in fact, an enormous mainstream profit-driven interest in street food. The problem was that the situation did not look the way we wanted it to.

One significant part of the research involved going out to observe the phenomenon, as well as question our hypotheses and make sure smaller realities do match larger realities, so then the focus of our intervention would be consistent. For instance, I still have a very confused opinion about initiatives such as the "Love Food" trucks—a collaboration between city administration and a private company. Love Food trucks are parked at metro stations, and are part of a distributed system that sells centralized food products. According to the wording on the permit, whoever works in these trucks is no longer a cook but only a vendor, and only food produced and delivered by the company should be sold. In reality, we see a hybrid situation in place most of the time—people are still cooking in the trucks, and it is hard to understand the role of these private businesses in relation to the larger street food public discourse. The trucks might create employment, but also represent a grey area of legality that put informal vendors under an even stronger threat.

The Issue of Scale

I believe that when the information platform is up and running smoothly, there are only a few moves to make for the projects to evolve toward some impact.

On the one hand, our projects should scale up, and shift away from representing the activist vision—something we are protecting—towards the design vision of what we could enable. Scaling up means, therefore, moving from our bottom line perspective—an interest—to a top-line perspective, which is where impact might happen. The idea of design activism runs the risk of leading to an attitude of resistance that is misleading. Resistance does not efficiently create collaboration where no common ground exists. A design initiative would be future oriented, would indeed cope with the different forces at play, and be creative within existing constraints, eventually pushing them from the inside instead that breaking them. Design activism is perhaps a delicate balance between conflict and coping, and in this sense we might need to scale up from resistance to collaboration.

On the other hand, it is even more important for us to scale out. What does that mean? Whenever we talk about food, whenever we present the project, everyone is immediately engaged, everybody has a story to tell—an opinion, a memory, an experience—and everybody smiles while they are talking. This seems a bit superficial—yes, it is beautiful, but it is really nothing beyond idle social chitchat. People talk about food because they like it, and because it is nice to have pleasant conversations, but if those conversations do not get into something deeper, if they just remain idle, then we have not made progress toward real citizen involvement.

Right now, most of the project's participants look at the problem from an outside perspective, as something that they might or might not like. In future, design interventions should move to activate engagement and make locals feel they are primary characters in the story. Otherwise, the risk is to be not only the foreigner in China carrying typical foreigner interests but also the foreigners within our own inner system (or maybe just saying "foreigners to our own selves"), and this is ultimately a limit to our creativity. In this sense we should work more on what the primary users of the system want, what is at stake in the system; scaling out means reflecting on the actors and what they really want—which might be something different from what we would like—and finding out what trends can help forecast the future and help the workers improve their conditions within the new paradigm set.

We have often considered creating a street food brand—something that could convey the cultural identity through a formal business setup that would also respect the informality of the practice. We thought about proposing a seal of quality, including ways to evaluate and assess quality, and ensure its reproducibility by new vendors and when new practices emerge. But at the same time, our primary interest is to research the food system, not organize a new food service. Our main goal is to have governance recognize the cultural value of street food for society. Even though the connection between food and business would be relatively easy to design, the link between government and citizens is still missing, which would make the scaling out process difficult. For the moment, we recognize that creating a public space where knowledge can be collected, and cultural consumption is possible, is the first step. But the central open question we are facing is how to make this knowledge incremental and dynamic in its evolution.

Acknowledgments

The work and contents published on the Movable Feast website are the results of work with Professor Anna Greenspan (NYU Shanghai, IMA program), who was the main instigator and promoter of the project. The work of the students from IMA program (producing the maps) and the students from D&I (prototyping design experiments) are the primary results we can share so far. For a broader intellectual perspective about Shanghai and its development paradox, you are welcome to refer to Anna Greenspa *Shanghai Future. Modernity Remade* (London: Hurst, 2014).

Design for Human-Robot Acceptability: The Case of Edutainment Robotics for Children

Maria Luce Lupetti

Department of Architecture and Design, Politecnico di Torino, Italy

This article reflects on the current concept of acceptability and its role in the field of human-robot interaction. Two main aspects emerge from an analysis of multiple acceptability models and case studies. On the one hand, key acceptability factors are typically addressed separately. On the other hand, acceptability is generally addressed during the evaluation stage of a project. However, developing acceptable robotic solutions implies incorporating these factors as drivers of the design process. Thus an acceptability-driven approach was proposed and applied during the Robot & Gaming project, in which edutainment robots were used to design play experiences for children.

Keywords **Edutainment robotics, robotic toys, design for acceptability, child-robot play**

Maria Luce Lupetti is Ph.D. candidate at Politecnico di Torino (Italy), Department of Architecture and Design, and visiting Ph.D. candidate at X-Studio, Academy of Art and Design of Tsinghua University (China). Her research, focused on Playful HRI, is founded by TIM, a major Italian telco company. She is currently involved as Publicity Chair for the next edition of the Pioneers of HRI workshop (Vienna, March 2017) and as Program Committee for the 1st International Workshop on Robotic Computing for Cultural Heritage (Taichung, 2017).

maria.lupetti@polito.it

Introduction

Nowadays, alongside other technologies, robotics are shaking the pillars of our society. Moral issues,[1] economic drawbacks,[2] and social impact[3] are just a few of the effects emerging from the spread of robotic products. These issues become even more relevant if we focus on vulnerable subject populations such as children. Edutainment Robotics are increasingly present in children's everyday lives. Kids can build robots, drive them, program them, and even empathize with them. Empathy, in fact, raises concerns related to the possible consequences of the bond that forms between a child and a robot.[4] And children's exposure to any technology not only worries their parents, it worries their teachers. Designers need to understand when and how robotic toys can be useful, desirable, and safe—which places the concept of acceptability squarely at the center of our concerns. As explained by Šabanović,[5] people frequently perceive technological changes as inevitable and tend to adapt to them unwittingly. However, a robotic solution should meet expectations and needs through its implicit and explicit qualities. Acceptability at every level—from functionality to ethical implications—should be considered. Although this topic is present in the literature, it has been largely addressed as part of the evaluation stage of project development, rather than during the definition of needs and the design phases. Moreover, most acceptance models portray robot acceptability as a framework of separate aspects rather than a system of interrelated factors. It is precisely here that design could play a strategic role. These considerations are at the foundation of the "Robot & Gaming" project developed at Jol CRAB lab—supported by TIM, an Italian telco—in which a design process focused on acceptability factors supported exploration of the the company's domain and technological potential.

The Concept of Acceptability

Acceptability has been defined by Dillon[6] as "the demonstrable willingness within a user group to employ information technology for the task it is designed to support." Often recurring in human-robot interaction (HRI) studies, researchers address this concept from two different perspectives—*accepting* (or *rejecting*) *users* and *accepted* (or *rejected*) *technology*.[7] Accepting users means taking into account all the human characteristics that might influence acceptability—like cognitive style, personality, demographics, and user-situational variables.[8] Such aspects are often addressed via cross-cultural study, which can reveal how the same robot behavior or characteristic can elicit different feedback from within different cultural contexts. For example, Choi et al.[9] conducted a questionnaire-based study about educational robots involving both parents and children from Europe and Korea. They observed a general difference between the two groups of parents—the Europeans appeared to have a more negative view of the robots and were reluctant to consider robots as friends for their children.

1 Mark Coeckelbergh, "Moral Appearances: Emotions, Robots, and Human Morality," *Ethics and Information Technology* 12 no.3 (2010): 235–41.

2 Michael Nagenborg, Rafael Capurro, Jutta Weber, and Christoph Pinget, "Ethical Regulations on Robotics in Europe," *AI & Society* 22, no.3 (2008): 349–66.

3 Selma Šabanovic´, "Robots in Society, Society in Robots," *International Journal of Social Robotics* 2, no. 4 (2010): 439–50.

4 Wolmet Barendregt, Ana Paiva, Arvid Kappas, and Asimina Vasalou, "Child-Robot Interaction: Social Bonding, Learning and Ethics," in *Workshop proceedings of Interaction Design and Children Conference* (New York: ACM, 2014), 1–3.

5 Šabanovic´, "Robots in Society, Society in Robots."

6 Andrew Dillon, "User Acceptance of Information Technology," in *Encyclopedia of Human Factors and Ergonomics*, ed. W. Karwowski (London: Taylor & Francis, 2001).

7 Ibid.

8 Maryam Alavi and Erich A. Joachimsthaler, "Revisiting DSS Implementation Research: A Meta-Analysis of the Literature and Suggestions for Researchers," *MIS Quarterly* 16, no. 1 (1992): 95–116.

9 Jong-Hong Choi, Jong-Yun Lee, and Jeong-Hye Han, "Comparison of Cultural Acceptability for Educational Robots Between Europe and Korea," *Journal of Information Processing Systems* 4, no.3 (2008): 97–102.

10 Marcel Heerink, Ben Kröse, Vanessa Evers, and Bob Wielinga, "Assessing Acceptance of Assistive Social Agent Technology by Older Adults: the Almere Model," *International Journal of Social Robotics* 2, no. 4 (2010): 361–75.

11 Shiri Azenkot, Catherine Feng, and Maya Cakmak, "Enabling Building Service Robots to Guide Blind People: A Participatory Design Approach," in *Proceedings of the 11th ACM/IEEE International Conference on Human-Robot Interaction* (Christchurch, New Zealand: IEEE Press, 2016), 3–10. Also available at http://ieeexplore.ieee.org/document/7451727/.

12 Everett M. Rogers, *Diffusion of*

Similarly, acceptability factors have also been investigated in relation to other categories of users, such as the elderly[10] or people with disabilities.[11]

Referring to a robot as acceptable means addressing the aspects that characterize them, such as relative advantage, compatibility, complexity, trialability, and observability.[12] To this end, many studies deal with the issue of acceptability by focusing on preferred robot behaviors[13] or characteristics, such as voice[14] or typology.[15]

These examples show how the theme of acceptability is not a novelty in HRI studies, but also how it is usually addressed by focusing on a specific determining factor or set of factors. A broader view of as quality of life and education with the theme, instead, is provided by acceptance models largely inherited from the field of Human-Computer Interaction (HCI). These acceptance models—typically used during the design evaluation stage—take on the issue of acceptability from different perspectives. In 1989, Davis[16] proposed a Technology Acceptance Model (TAM) in which two main characteristics affect acceptance—perceived usefulness and perceived ease of use. This was followed by a series of other models that attempted to describe the complexity of acceptability across different variables. The Technology-to-Performance Chain model (TPC)[17] introduced individual characteristics as influencing factors, together with task-oriented and technological characteristics. A further contribution in this regard was introduced by the Unified Theory of Acceptance and Use of Technology (UTAUT),[18] which shows how technological characteristics—*performance expectancy* and *effort expectancy*, for example—and human characteristics—*attitude* and *social influence*, for example—are impacted by user-specific factors such as age, gender, experience, and intention for use. This model was widely used and adapted in a number of HRI studies. For instance, Heerink[19] adapted and extended the UTAUT model by explaining the intention for use not only in terms of functionality but also in terms of social interaction concerns including trust and anxiety.

Another model developed specifically for robot acceptance is the USUS,[20] an acronym that stands for the key aspects it tracks—*usability*, *social acceptance*, *user experience*, and *societal impact*. According to this model, a robot's acceptability can be evaluated by taking into account these four aspects and the key factors that illustrate them. Compared to the UTAUT, this model addresses human characteristics more deeply. For instance, it associates such factors as *quality of life* and *education* with societal impact, and certain kinds of social *grouping* and *attachment* with social acceptance. These aspects appear to be particularly relevant to HRI—rather than HCI—because of the embodied interactions that robots enable and the social presence that they represent.

From the Acceptability Evaluation to a Design Approach

Most case studies and models reveal that the concept of a robot's

Innovations, 4th ed. (New York: Free Press, 1995), 1002–1037.

13 Grégoire Milliez, Raphaël Lallement, Michelangelo Fiore, and Rachid Alami, "Using Human Knowledge Awareness to Adapt Collaborative Plan Generation, Explanation and Monitoring," in *Proceedings of the 11th ACM/IEEE International Conference on Human-Robot Interaction* (IEEE Press, 2016), 43–50. Also available at http://ieeexplore.ieee.org/document/7451732/.

14 Friederike Eyssel et al., "'If You Sound Like Me, You Must be More Human': On the Interplay of Robot and User Features on Human-Robot Acceptance and Anthropomorphism," in *Proceedings of the 12th annual ACM/IEEE international conference on Human-Robot Interaction* (New York: ACM, 2012), 125–26. Also available at http://dl.acm.org/citation.cfm?doid=2157689.2157717.

15 Sonya S. Kwak, Jun San Kim, and Jung Ju Choi. "Can Robots be Sold?: The Effects of Robot Designs on the Consumers' Acceptance of Robots," in *Proceedings of the 2014 ACM/IEEE international conference on Human-robot interaction* (New York: ACM, 2014), 226–27. Also available at http://dl.acm.org/citation.cfm?id=2563684&CFID=727472242&CFTOKEN=29759404.

16 Fred D. Davis, "Perceived Usefulness, Perceived Ease of Use, and User Acceptance of Information Technology," *MIS Quarterly* 13, no. 3 (1989): 319–40.

17 Dale L. Goodhue and Ronald L. Thompson, "Task-Technology Fit and Individual Performance," *MIS Quarterly* 19, no. 2 (1995): 213–36.

18 Viswanath Venkatesh, Michael G. Morris, Gordon B. Davis, and Fred D. Davis, "User Acceptance of Information Technology: Toward a Unified View," *MIS Quarterly* 27, no. 3 (2003): 425–78.

19 Heerink et al., "Assessing Acceptance of Assistive Social Agent Technology."

20 Astrid Weiss, Regina Bernhaupt, Manfred Tscheligi, and Eiichi Yoshida, "Addressing User Experience and Societal Impact in a User Study with a Humanoid Robot," in *Proceedings of the Symposium on New Frontiers in Human-Robot Interaction* (Edinburgh, SSAISB, 2009) 150–57.

acceptability is usually considered during design outcome evaluation—after conceptualization development, and designing are complete. In the case of projects involving the design of novel systems, acceptability is largely determined during the test phase. However, as mentioned by Dillion,[21] the main aim of understanding robot acceptability is to influence the design process to ensure that the resulting solutions are likely to be accepted. In fact, the knowledge about acceptance factors and the application of these as design drivers should lead to an adaptation of the technology to people's needs. As the models demonstrate, these factors relate to different aspects within human-robot interaction scenarios that have a range of dimensions from the physical to the societal. Vincente highlights the importance of "high level" factors, whose scope includes the organizational level beyond the (social) individual.[22] He stresses that the adaptation of technology to human needs implies reflections also at organizational and political level, since technology design, use, and implementation has moral, legal and ethical implications.

Šabanović[23] goes one step further, suggesting that there is a need to design robots that can co-create society with their users, which can occur through iterations that include social analysis and technology design.

So—What does Designing Acceptable Robotic Solutions Mean?

Scholars and practitioners alike have already recognized the importance of acceptability, and even begun using acceptability to guide the design process. Many projects seeking to design acceptable robotic solutions conduct preliminary studies to identify acceptability factors that are then used as design drivers. For instance, Azenkot et al.[24] applied a participatory design approach to identify blind users' preferred behavior and assistance features in a guide robot. However, even though acceptability issues have been considered during the whole process, designers are usually concerned with the acceptability of specific features rather than the complex system represented by the machines. In fact, acceptance of robotic systems cannot be achieved by analyzing functional aspects in isolation, because even a minor design feature can have unexpected impact. For this reason, taking users' perceptions and psychology into account becomes crucial not only for the robot's overall acceptability but also for the prevention of negative effects. Because robots' affordances are often not compatible with real-world contexts, or their use competes with accepted practices, they have to be designed within the context of use—where psychological implications arise. Designers need to design for the unpredictability of real-world environments, to better enable the robots' continuous adaptation to real life situations. The long-term societal consequences of the relationship between humans and robots are equally unpredictable.

Norman and Stappers'[25] define the multitude of socio-technical challenges characterizing complex systems as "DesignX problems." DesignX

21 Dillon, "User Acceptance of Informationchnology."

22 Kim Vicente, *The Human Factor: Revolutionizing the Way We Live with Technology* (Toronto: Vintage Canada, 2010).

23 Šabanović, "Robots in Society, Society in Robots."

24 Azenkot, Feng, and Cakmak, "Enabling Building Service Robots to Guide Blind People."

25 Donald A. Norman and Pieter Jan Stappers, "DesignX: Complex Socio-technical Systems," *She Ji: The Journal of Design, Economics, and Innovation* (2016): 83–106.

problems relate to the psychology of human behavior and cognition; to social, political, and economic frameworks used to organize complex socio-technical systems; and to the technical issues that contribute to the complexity of design problems. Therefore, designing for robot acceptability means embracing complexity and dealing with these problems on multiple levels.

Designers' awareness of non-linearity, impossibility, and other factors contributing to unpredictability will enable them to better control the systems they create. Even though models may appear simplistic—by using rigid structures with highly defined boundaries to describe acceptability, for example—the variety of factors that they highlight can be used as design drivers. In fact, by taking into account some of the most frequently recurring factors affecting robot acceptance, it is possible to identify four main categories of acceptability—*functionality, social ability, appearance*[26] and *ethics*.[27] Functionality largely refers to how a proposed solution works and the scope of its operation, and includes such factors as perceived usefulness,[28] compatibility, trialability,[29] and perceived ease of use.[30] Social ability refers to the robot's particular character, in particular its ability to provide and react to social cues.[31] Salvini et al.[32] highlight the crucial role played by appearance factors such as affordance, friendliness, beauty and perceived safety.

As mentioned before, however, these factors have to be addressed as interrelated parts of a complex system, rather than as a set of individual elements, since every factor interacts and affects the others. To this end, the four main categories of factors can be included in a single framework, as shown in **Figure 1**. To the right, the intersection between the two circles representing functionality and appearance stands for the inescapable relationship of their mutual influence, recalling the traditional form-function dichotomy.[33] The function of a robotic artifact does contribute to the shaping of its appearance, at least in its constitutive parts. And appearance not only boosts attractiveness—it can affect the perceived usefulness of an artifact by determining the way it communicates its function.

The social ability that a robot may have lies at the intersection of these two categories. Sociability is located in this hybrid space because it is impossible to distinguish a robot's appearance from its functional role. The social abilities and their manifestation in terms of appearance determines whether a robot is part of one typology or another, as each enables different functionalities and usage scenarios. For instance, Dautenhahn[34] suggests that non-humanoid mobile robots are more suitable for autism therapy than humanoid or zoomorphic robots, since overly complex appearances and behaviors can overwhelm autistic children.

These three categories—functionality, appearance and social ability—are then included in a larger circle representing ethics. Ethics can affect acceptability at the personal, social, and environmental level. Ethics are implicit in every design choice from the definition of its function—which

26 Jenay M. Beer, Akanksha Prakash, Tracy L. Mitzner, and Wendy A. Rogers, *Understanding Robot Acceptance: Techincal Report HFA-TR-1103* (Atalanta, GA: Georgia Institute of Technology, 2011).

27 Coeckelbergh, "Moral Appearances."

28 Davis, "Perceived Usefulness."

29 Rogers, *Diffusion of Innovations*.

30 Davis, "Perceived Usefulness."

31 Beer et.al., "Understanding Robot Acceptance."

32 Pericle Salvini, Cecilia Laschi, and Paolo Dario, "Design for Acceptability: Improving Robots' Coexistence in Human Society," *International Journal of Social Robotics* 2, no. 4 (2010): 451–60.

33 Eric Landowski and Gianfranco Marrone, *La società degli oggetti: problemi di interoggettività* [The Society of the Objects: Problems of Inter-Objectivity] (Rome: Meltemi Editore, 2002).

34 Kerstin Dautenhahn, "Design Spaces and Niche Spaces of Believable Social Robots," in *Proceedings of the 11th IEEE International Workshop on Robot and Human Interactive Communication* (IEEE, 2002), 192–97.

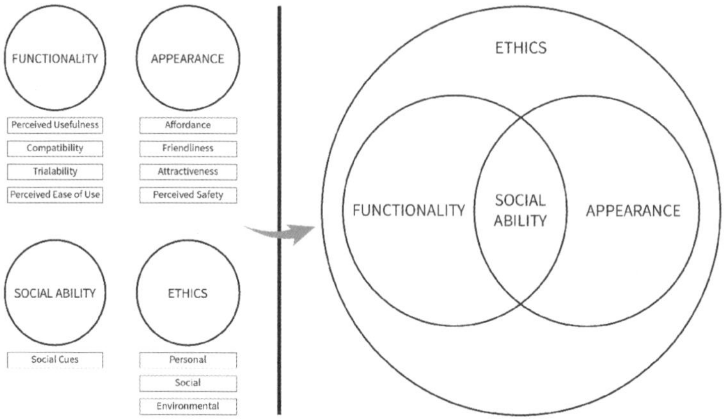

Figure 1 The image illustrates the shift from an idea of acceptability resulting from the sum of independent factors, to an idea of interrelated factors that generate complexity. Copyright © 2016 Maria Luce Lupetti.

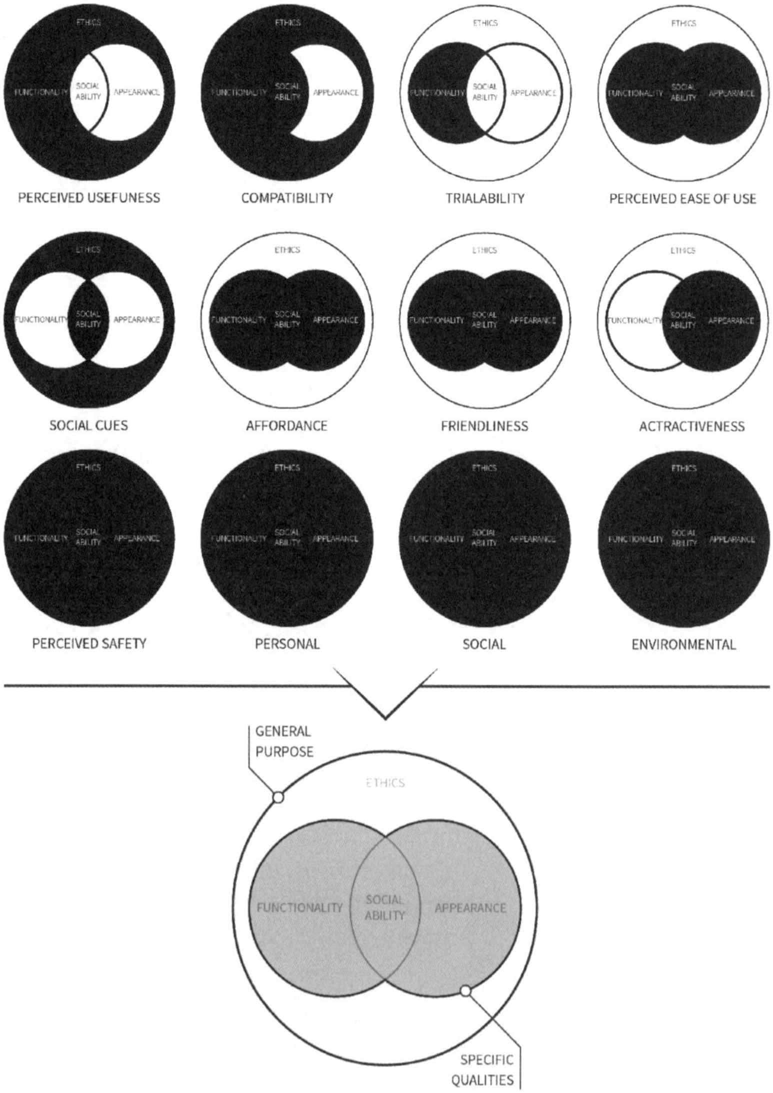

Figure 2 Overview of the relations between the factors and the identification of the two dimensions of the projects: general purpose and specific qualities. Copyright © 2016 Maria Luce Lupetti.

might conflict with human activities and alter human relationships—to the choice itself to adopt robotic technologies rather than alternatives that might be less economically and ecologically burdensome. Ethical implications usually entail reflection about the cost-benefit relationship implied by the adoption of a new technology.

The relationship of between the four categories can be further understood by focusing on the single factors summarized in **Figure 2**. Every circle shows how every factor affects the main categories of the framework.

Consider perceived usefulness in the context of cultural heritage. Telepresence robotics might be used to attract the wider public to historical sites by offering an innovative service to explore hidden areas, as in the case of the Italian project Virgil[35] in Italy, which has the potential to be highly useful due to the existing issue of inaccessibility of heritage sites in the country.[36] It might also be considered ethical, according to how it increases accessibility, affects human-human relationships and enhances its environment. On the contrary, in a different context like Australia, this solution might be unnecessary and provide few benefits when compared, for instance, to allowing remote exploration of a museum for children from rural areas, as in the case of the National Museum of Australia.[37]

In terms of compatibility, and despite a function's usefulness, a solution might be considered acceptable on the basis of the value system of the cultural context. For instance, robot companionship for children has been shown to be acceptable for Korean parents while is strongly rejected by European parents,[38] despite the robots' educational purpose. This phenomenon could be the result of differing educational systems in the two contexts, which could affect perceived usefulness and ethics; and whether or not social abilities and life-like characteristics exist in other tools, which might determine the acceptance or rejection of the robots' social cues.

A robot's ability to demonstrate social cues raises a host of ethical and moral issues related to the unpredictable consequences of fostering emotional bonds with robots.[39] Thus, even if enabling natural communication can increase the efficacy of human-robot interactions,[40] the presence of social cues necessarily calls for attention to psychological, social, and, of course, ethical issues.

Conversely, other factors belonging to the appearance category, such as affordance or friendliness, do not raise great ethical issues. However, these can play a crucial role in overall acceptability because of their great influence on how people perceive and engage with robots. In particular, affordances help people to understand the potential functions offered by a system and thus to behave accordingly. A robot that fails to provide affordances of its functions might be underestimated, misinterpreted, and considered unsafe. Similarly, the familiar appearance or behavior of a robot can recall existing artifacts or functions, helping people understand it and establish positive interaction.

These few examples show how the various acceptability factors

35 Claudio Germak, Maria Luce Lupetti, Luca Giuliano, and Miguel Kaouk Ng, "Robots and Cultural Heritage: New Museum Experiences," *Journal of Science and Technology of the Arts* 7, no. 2 (2015): 47–57.

36 "Museums, Archeological Areas and Monuments in Italy," *Istat*, December 5, 2013, http://www.istat.it/en/archive/106183.

37 "Visiting the National Museum," *csiro.au*, last modified January 19, 2016, http://data61.csiro.au/en/Our-expertise/Expertise-Decision-sciences/Visiting-the-National-Museum.

38 Choi, Lee, and Han, "Comparison of Cultural Acceptability."

39 Matthias Scheutz, "The Inherent Dangers of Unidirectional Emotional Bonds between Humans and Social Robots," in *Robot Ethics: The Ethical and Social Implications of Robotics*, ed. Patrick Lin, Keith Abney, and Geogre A. Bekey (Cambridge, Mass.: The MIT Press, 2011), 205.

40 Cynthia Breazeal, "Emotion and Sociable Humanoid Robots," *International Journal of Human-Computer Studies* 59, no. 1–2 (2003): 119–55.

shown in Figure 2 are related, and how they influence each other. By observing the main relationships between factors it is possible to identify the two main levels of the framework—some factors refer more to the general purpose of a project, while others to its specific qualities. The general purpose represents the aim of a project—the issue that is being addressed, and the value it may generate. The specific qualities are the particular strategies used to achieve the purpose. So, designing for acceptability requires continuous reflection about both the specific qualities and the general purpose of a project, by referring to the related factors.

Addressing the complexity of these emerging systems—in both their macro and micro characteristics—also means reflecting on the tools and design methods that are most appropriate for their development. Weiss et al.[41] suggest that designers combine qualitative and quantitative methods to investigate and evaluate acceptability factors. Expert evaluation, user studies, and interviews are thus more appropriate for usability studies, while questionnaires, physiological measures, and focus groups more suitably measure social acceptance, user experience, and societal impact. This is also confirmed by Norman and Stappers,[42] according to whom traditional design methods—such as observation—are still fruitful. However, they highlight the fact that even if these methods are appropriate, they are not exhaustive because the design process does not end once the outcome is delivered. Designers must work collaboratively with other experts, and pay particular attention to human psychology throughout a project's evolution. They also suggest that designers develop new ways to take into account the interrelationships among the elements of complex systems. Thereafter, design methods for acceptability have to make reference to existing human-centered methods, and be defined for and adapted to the specific context of a project. Every project has peculiarities and constraints that have to be addressed in different ways. In fact, there is no exact, eternally valid perspective from which complex systems can be analyzed, since it is impossible to define their boundaries without losing of some aspects of the system.[43]

Given that it is impossible to control the various dynamics of these systems, it is not possible to define an acceptability-driven design approach that will guarantee a specific outcome, or ensure the success of a novel robotic solution. Nevertheless, designing for acceptability will likely impact complex systems on three (macro) levels—the human, the organizational, and the global. From the human point of view, designing for acceptability could reverse the trend that forces people to adapt to technological innovation, and lead to technologies shaped for and by people. The shift in perspective provided by acceptability data could also spur the development of research and organizational solutions that respond to actual needs in existing socio-cultural contexts. This is particularly relevant for the youngest generations, who are typically exposed to new technologies without appropriate precautions. Organizationally, this approach may help to increase the chances that a project will succeed, and reduce the occurrence of

41 Weiss et al., "Addressing User Experience and Societal Impact."

42 Norman and Stappers, "DesignX: Complex Sociotechnical Systems."

43 Kurt A. Richardson, Paul Cilliers, and Michael Lissack, "Complexity Science: A 'Gray' Science for the 'Stuff in Between'," *Emergence* 3, no. 2 (2001): 6–18.

undesirable consequences. Finally, acceptability could drive the more conscious diffusion of technologies that offer benefits on a global scale.

Robot & Gaming Project

The Robot & Gaming (R&G) project is our first case study focusing on the concept of acceptability. Figure 3 provides an overview of the project flow and the main actors involved.

As it often happens, this project began at the behest of a telecommunications company who funded the research to investigate the potential of commercial edutainment robots that could interact with their latest asset: a cloud robotics platform. Service robots would interact with the cloud computing platform to share the computational workload and access networked data storage, and the platform would also enable remote control. The project involved input from an interdisciplinary team of researchers, including engineers, designers, and a psychologist. The technology push drove the team on two levels. On the one hand, the engineers focused more on technical and functional aspects; while on the other hand, the designers and the psychologist focused more on human factors and user experience. At the same time, the entire team participated in overall project development and execution. As a result, both technology-driven and human-centered approaches were applied in an attempt to mutually shape the robotic solution and society, as mentioned by Šabanović.[44]

44 Šabanović, "Robots in Society, Society in Robots."

The aim was to shift the research focus away from technology and towards humans, even if the project was strongly constrained to developing a technological component. Because the technology-driven and the human-centered are typically mutually exclusive and unrelated, a significant challenge for this research would lie in meeting complex human needs with predetermined technologies.

Methodology

The project was developed by applying an iterative design process (shown in Figure 4), consisting of five main stages—*analyse*, *define*, *design*, *evaluate*, and *refine*—each characterized by a particular activity and outcome. As mentioned before, acceptability is usually assessed at the evaluation stage, while this project intended to assess acceptability throughout the entire process. To this end, every phase included consideration of the dimensions that contribute to determining project acceptability—both for the project's general purpose (GP) and its specific qualities (SQ).

GP mainly concerned human aspects, including the current scenario of children's play, emerging issues, and related assumptions, each of which contributed to defining the aim of the project. The SQ level was more focused on technological functionality, constraints, and potential, and thus on the solutions applied during the project.

Figure 3 The primary actors involved in the project and the general process. Copyright © 2016 Maria Luce Lupetti.

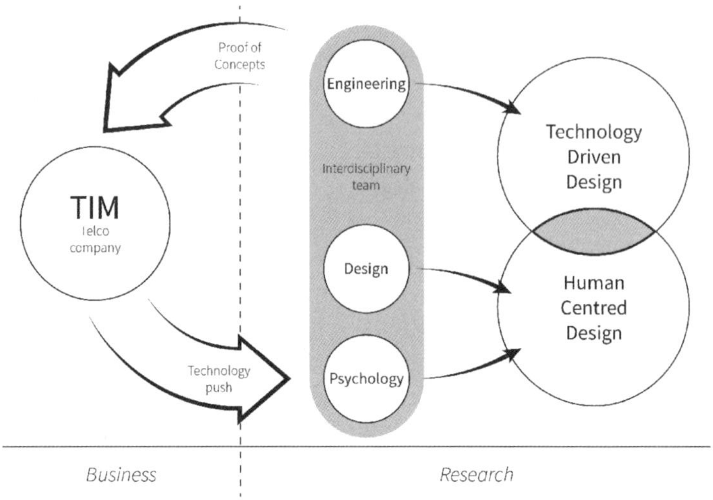

Figure 4 Schema of the methodology applied during the Robot & Gaming project. Copyright © 2016 Maria Luce Lupetti.

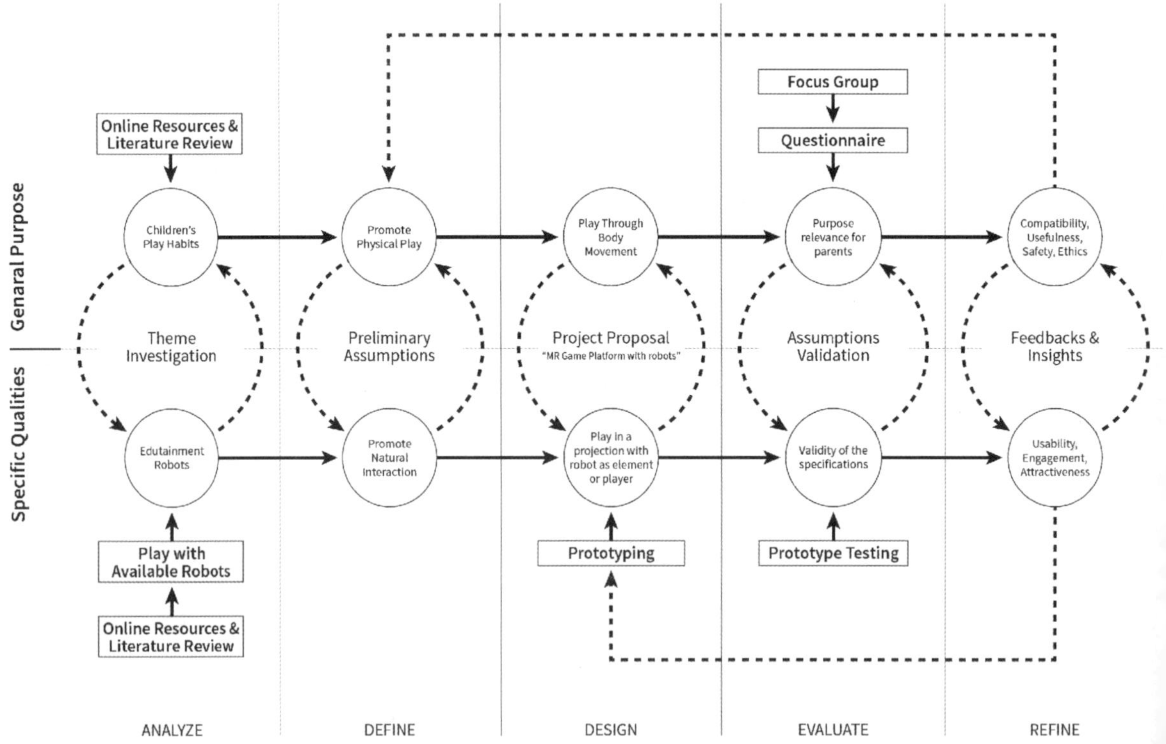

Figure 4 shows how every stage of the project corresponds to a principal activity characterized by two different sets of content (in the circles)—one for the GP level and the other for the SQ level. Both are related by curved dotted lines which stand for the mutual influence that the contents have at both levels.

The rectangles represent key actions carried out to support the main process. In particular, the initial analysis stage consisted of an investigation into the theme supported by a literature review and online research at both levels; however, the nature of the resources chosen was different. We investigated children's play scenarios by referring mostly to scientific literature about developmental psychology, health, medicine, and education, and to statistical reports about children's lifestyles from national (Italian) studies. Technology literature resources consisted mostly of robotics, human-computer interaction, and games research. We supplemented technology research with a more hands-on activity—actual play. Since understanding the experience afforded by robots requires direct interaction, the commercial robotic toys available at the lab were tested using their conventional mobile apps.

The main activities of the design stage were prototyping, platform use and games.

During the evaluation stage, key activity was totally different for the two levels. At the GP level, we proposed a questionnaire and a focus group. Both were meant to get a deeper understanding of the children's play scenario and validate our preliminary assumptions by addressing acceptability factors such as compatibility, usefulness, safety, and ethics. We should note that despite our showing that this action took place at the evaluative stage—alongside prototype testing—acceptability assessment occurred before, and those results informed the assumptions we then made at the GP level. Thus, acceptability evaluation did not occur simultaneously at the two levels, since one depends on the other.

At the SQ level, in fact, prototype testing represents a key action—we evaluated the SQ of the project mainly from the usability, engagement, and attractiveness points of view. The feedback and insights resulting from this action drove the iterations and the refinement of the prototype.

Preliminary Assumptions

The analytic phase of the project allowed us to identify emerging issues and trends both regarding children's play habits and the state of the art of edutainment robots.

Statistics show that children in Italy spend most of their free time at home,[45] have access to more and more devices,[46] the vast majority of them do not do sport regularly, and 15% of them are overweight.[47] These different aspects are in line with an overall increase in sedentary behaviors—defined as the amount of time spent with minimal body movement[48] at the

45 Lo stile di vita dei bambini e ragazzi [The Lifestyle of Children and Teenagers], *Save the Children*, June 15, 2016, https://www.savethechildren.it/cosa-facciamo/pubblicazioni/lo-stile-di-vita-dei-bambini-e-dei-ragazzi-1.

46 Dipartmento per le statistiche sociali ed ambientali, Infanzia e vita quotidiana [Childhood and Daily Life], *Istat*, November 18, 2011, http://www.istat.it/it/archivio/45646.

47 Il benessere dei bambini nei paesi ricchi [The Wellness of Children in Wealthy Countries], UNICEF, Centro di Ricerca, Innocenti Report Card 11, 2013.

48 Aviva Must and D. J. Tybor, "Physical Activity and Sedentary Behaviour: A Review of Longitudinal Studies of Weight and Adiposity in Youth," *International Journal of Obesity* 29, (2005): S84–S96. Also available at: http://www.nature.com/ijo/journal/v29/n2s/full/0803064a.html?message=remove&WT.mc_id=LP_IJO_1401_anniversary.

expense of physical activity—which favors the development of health issues such as obesity or metabolic syndrome.[49]

Edutainment robots can be grouped into three main categories—building and programming robots, driving robots, and conversing and empathizing robots. The use of building and programming robots is constantly increasing. Such high adoption is probably due to their clear function and related benefits, together with the strong potential they have to engage users.[50] Driving robots have also proven very successful. In the last few years, the availability of products like mini-drones has multiplied. One of the reasons they are easily adopted is likely their similarity with remote-controlled cars and other toys, which enables them to circumvent concerns about moral or psychological issues that playing with a robot may raise. In fact, these robots, like programming robots, tend to be perceived mostly as tools. Conversing and empathizing robots are still less popular than other commercial products. These kinds of robots usually take the form of pets or humanoid robots. They can perform a variety of functions, from educating to conversing, giving therapy to children with special needs, or mere entertaining. However, a robot's ability to express emotional states and assume social roles brings up some issues from an acceptability point of view. There is often reluctance to accept robots as social agents, due to the concern about the possibility that a regular interaction with social robots could lead people to become less prone to engaging in social interaction with other people,[51] leading to alterations in human-human relationships.[52]

However, despite the issues related to the social role that robots might assume, empathizing robots have positive key feature—they allow more direct and natural interaction. Programming and driving robots, in fact, usually require additional devices—such as a smartphone or a computer—to enable interaction with them.

According to these preliminary findings, two main assumptions were defined—on the one hand, there is a need to promote physical play for children; on the other hand, commercial edutainment robots can be enhanced by promoting natural interactions.

As a consequence, the question emerges: can a robot's physical form and potential to engage users be used to leverage a reduction of sedentary behaviors through natural interactions?

Project Proposal

The project proposal (Figure 5) consists of a mixed-reality playground in which children can play games with or against a robot. The general purpose of this playground is to promote active behaviors through the use of the body as the game controller. In fact, a combination of projection and tracking systems allows the robot to detect the position of the player and use it as input. The robot is tracked by the system and can be controlled by the player, depending on the role that it is assuming—opponent, partner or

49 Amy E. Mark and Ian Janssen, "Relationship Between Screen Time and Metabolic Syndrome in Adolescents," *Journal of Public Health* 30, no. 2 (2008): 153–60.

50 André Pereira, Carlos Martinho, Iolanda Leite, and Ana Paiva, "iCat, the Chess Player: The Influence of Embodiment in the Enjoyment of a Game," in *Proceedings of the 7th International Joint Conference on Autonomous Agents and Multiagent Systems*,Vol. 3 (Estoril: International Foundation for Autonomous Agents and Multiagent Systems, 2008) 1253–56, Also available at http://dl.acm.org/citation.cfm?id=1402844.

51 Gail F. Melson et al., "Robots as Dogs?: Children's Interactions with the Robotic Dog AIBO and a Live Australian Shepherd," in *Proceedings of the CHI'05 Extended Abstracts on Human Factors in Computing Systems* (New York: ACM, 2005), 1649–52. Also available at http://dl.acm.org/citation.cfm?id=1056988&CFID=727472242&CFTOKEN=29759404.

52 Jason Borenstein and Ronald C. Arkin, "Robots, Ethics, and Intimacy: The Need for Scientific Research," in *Proceedings of the Conference of the International Association of Computer and Philosophy* (Ferrara, Italy, 2016).

tool. Using commercially available driving robots, such as mini-drones, allowed us to leverage available resources and, above all, avoid unpleasant feelings and reluctance from parents or other actors that may be involved. Thus, integrating commercial robots allowed us to develop different games based on their specific features, such as type of motion. The first robot we looked at was *Sphero*, a robotic ball.

The combination of Sphero's features, its role, and the type of control mechanism it uses (body movement) afforded us with a variety of play modalities. Figure 6 shows the three main game concepts we have defined so far. The first, a Pong-like game, consists of a projected game screen were the player and the robot are opponents. The aim is to make projected figures bounce from side to side, without missing the figure. The traditional version of Pong was adapted by adding different geometrical figures, instead of a single square figure, that differ in speed. The second game is more based on the physical characteristics of the robot. It consists of a virtual balance-board that tilts in response to bodily movements, and the robot rolls according to the inclination of the playing surface, simulating three-dimensional space. In the third game, the player controls the robot with body movement, and the robot follows the positon of the player. The aim is to play with the robot, by catching elements—such as fish—that are projected around the play space.

Purpose Validation

Once the main concept was defined, the general purpose of the project was validated through two key actions: a questionnaire and a focus group. These activities were carried out to gain a deeper understanding of the children's play scenario and validate the preliminary assumptions about the need to promote active play for children.

The relevance of sedentary behavior as an issue was evaluated together with people's attitude towards using edutainment robotics to address that issue.

The questionnaire of 35 questions was given to a sample of 511 individuals, aged between 19 and 60 years, of which 60% had children. The questions were organized in sections about children's habits, the issue of sedentary behaviors, the adults' preferences for children's play, and their opinions about edutainment robots.

The focus group involved a group of six parents who were invited to discuss their children's habits, play preferences, opinions about the issue of sedentary behaviors, any perceptions about edutainment robotics and the project concept.

These two activities highlighted a mismatch between the statistical data and scientific knowledge about how children's habits are changing, and the current desires and concerns of the parents involved in the study. According to the parents involved in the study, there is a general

Figure 5 Concept of the Robot & Gaming project: a mixed-reality game platform that allows a child to play with or against a robot. Copyright © 2016 Maria Luce Lupetti.

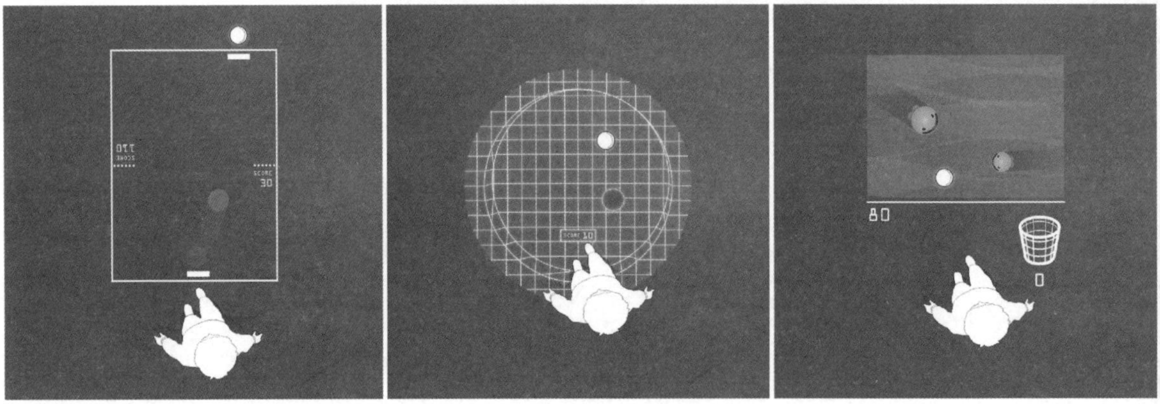

Figure 6 Some examples of the game proposals. From left: a pong-like game in which the robot plays as opponent; a game that simulates a balance-board, in which the robot plays as tool and the child controls the projection with bodily motion; and a catching game where the child catches fish by controlling the robot through body motion. Copyright © 2016 Maria Luce Lupetti.

encouragement for outdoor play and sports activities. They appeared to be aware and worried about children's sedentariness and, especially in the questionnaire, they agreed that sedentary behaviors might increase health issues in children. Regarding technology, they appeared to prefer traditional games compared to technological games and some of the focus group parents, of devices for their children.

Therefore, on one hand, the literature and statistical data report an increase of sedentary behaviors, while on the other hand, parents want to promote active behaviors and are concerned about their children's exposure to technology. Thus, this mismatch enabled us to validate the relevance of the issue addressed and comments from the focus group allowed us to get positive feedback about the project concept. However, the parents involved in the focus group also pointed out that the validity of the concept is strongly related to the context of application, for instance that it should not replace outdoor play.

Preliminary Prototype Testing

The first and the third games showed in **Figure 6** were developed, tested, and improved through multiple iterations. The preliminary tests, carried out in the lab, were particularly useful to get feedback and insights about the specific qualities of the project. In particular, the Pong-like game was the first tested, and the one with the most iterations. Through the various test and iteration cycles, it was possible to identify some limitations determining the quality of the gameplay. First of all, the size of the projected playground was initially to small, enabling only a small amount of movement. Secondly, specific characteristics of the game design were influencing platform usability. Low visibility was mainly caused by the overly-complex game graphic design. Thus, the game was redesigned with fewer elements, higher contrast, and primary and secondary colors. Playability issues were mainly caused by the rhythm of the game. Thus, the game was improved by reducing downtime length, simplifying game logic, and increasing the game's overall fluidity. The various iterations were also highlighted the unsuitability of the robot that was initially chosen for the pong-game—Sphero. As Sphero was unable to perform constrained movements along a specific axis, the robot was changed. Each of these iterations was, then, fundamental to obtaining a solution providing engaging gameplay for children. However, running tests in lab with non-representative samples of participants (lab staff) did not allow us to fully evaluate the usability, engagement, and attractiveness of the platform.

Our need to run tests with children and compare results in conjunction with parental feedback led to our investigations into where and when this kind of solution could be introduced and actually generate value.

Usage Scenarios

Our investigation into the possible usage scenarios could be considered as an iteration of the design stage during which we refined the the project proposal and the related prototype. Our reflections about potential usage scenarios were largely based users' willingness to promote active behaviors in those contexts where children usually have less opportunity for physical stimulation or where the platform could support specific needs. Play context analysis revealed two specific kinds of context—places of physical play such as parks and gardens, and places of "mind" play such as schools, museums, and toy libraries. In places of physical play—mostly characterized by sports and free play—the platform would be less able to add significant value. However, in the context of mind play, it could assume different roles and offer a variety of value. Its role changes according to the context settings—home, school/educational, and healthcare. In the home environment, a virtual playground could be useful not just as an entertainment system, but also as a platform that supports both educational and diversional games. Moreover, it would enable a remote play scenario in which two children (or even adults) could play together from remote locations using the robots as avatars. This concept of robot as avatar is not new. Lee et al.[53] proposed a remote interaction scenario where a semi-autonomous, huggable robot allows two people to interact from remote locations. The same concept of remote play could assume particular value in healthcare contexts, such as hospitals, where in some cases children have to spend long periods without social interaction. Moreover, in this kind of context, the platform could be used to alleviate the strains of hospitalization, since play may act as a diversion, refocusing attention away from stressors.[54] The platform could also support rehabilitation. In fact, human motion tracking for rehabilitation is already a widely addressed topic.[55] Although education is often separated from play, the benefits of their associations are well known.[56] Thus, in the educational contexts of schools, toy libraries, and museums, the platform could be customized to support educational activities featuring playful and active interaction. Museums, in particular, museums appear to be particularly suitable since the platform can be used as an interactive installation.

Additionally, in terms of testing, despite the prototypal nature of the platform it could be perceived as a real-world experience rather than as a research setup, increasing the environmental validity of our study.

Conducting a study using an experimental application engages a representative sample of participants, and establishes a credible environment. As mentioned by Baxter et al., the environment where an evaluation takes place can exert a large influence on the results, and thus tests require experimental authenticity related to the phenomenon under observation.[57] However, real public contexts also present limitations. For instance, introducing the platform as tool among others in a museum context may make it impossible to record users' experiences, since obtaining consent would be

53 Jun-Ki Lee, Robert Toscano, Walter Stiehl, and Cynthia Breazeal, "The Design of a Semi-Autonomous Robot Avatar for Family Communication and Education," in *Proceedings of the 17th IEEE International Symposium on Robot and Human Interactive Communication* (IEEE, 2008), 166–73, Also available at http://ieeexplore.ieee.org/document/4600661/.

54 Mary Kaminski, Teresa Pellino, and Joel Wish, "Play and Pets: The Physical and Emotional Impact of Child-Life and Pet Therapy on Hospitalized Children," *Children's Health Care* 31, no. 4 (2002): 321–35.

55 Hui-Yu Zhou and Huo-Sheng Hu. "Human Motion Tracking for Rehabilitation—A Survey," *Biomedical Signal Processing and Control* 3, no. 1 (2008): 1–18.

56 Ingrid Pramling Samuelsson and Eva Johansson, "Play and Learning—Inseparable Dimensions in Preschool Practice," *Early Child Development and Care* 176, no. 1 (2006): 47–65.

57 Paul Baxter et al., "From Characterising Three Years of HRI to Methodology and Reporting Recommendations," in *Proceedings of the 11th ACM/IEEE International Conference on Human Robot Interaction* (New Jersey: IEEE Press, 2016), 391–98, also available at: http://dl.acm.org/citation.cfm?id=2906897&CFID=727472242&CFTOKEN=29759404.

problematic. Limitations multiply in the case of healthcare contexts, especially hospitals, where privacy and confidentiality are key issues, as does the difficulty of finding neutral spaces.[58] Therefore, even though conducting studies in real environments is crucial to understanding which contexts and scenarios a project may generate value, the complexity of these contexts requires the development of alternatives to recording and measurement observational strategies.

Therefore, the platform has yet to be tested as an experimental application in a real context to get feedback both regarding the specific aspects of gameplay and about how the solution provides an answer to the main issues addressed by the project. This feedback will be crucial for future improvement and iteration of the project.

Project Questioning

The assessment of this project's acceptability is dependent on its contextualization and adaptation to a real environment, which will not only improve the specific aspects of the project but also enable us to reflect on the general impact that the platform can achieve. To this end, the project proposal will be thoroughly examined after tests in real contexts of use with specific attention paid to the acceptability factors that emerged from the literature review. The following questions, then, are perhaps only a few out of a myriad that may arise. Further research would enrich this debate—we welcome the contribution of interdisciplinary and multicultural actors representing different perspectives and values.

For practical reasons, the acceptability factors mentioned earlier will be taken into account sequentially. However, we wish to reiterate that none of the factors is independent.

Regarding the specific qualities of the project, for instance, it will be important to answer questions referring to trialability, and perceived ease of use, such as: *is the platform easy to use? Is it easy to understand how it works? Is its complexity acceptable in relation to the experience it provides? Can people try it before being asked to adopt it?*

Understanding how the proposed solution functions depends on what it affords. Thus, a further question would be: *does the solution communicate its function? How?*

The perceived ease of use is also strongly related to the the friendliness and attractiveness of the solution. Attractive products are perceived as easier to use,[59] and familiarity with a technology or a kind of product can increase its perceived usefulness.[60] In this regard, it is important to answer to the following questions: *is the proposed solution appealing (both for primary and secondary users)? What are the main characteristics that make it appealing? Is it able to elicit familiar feelings in the users? Can users recall familiar interaction modalities or experiences?*

In terms of usefulness, we need to understand what kind of value/

58 Raquel Ros, et al., "Child-Robot Interaction in the Wild: Advice to the Aspiring Experimenter," in *ICMI '11 Proceedings of the 13th International Conference on Mutimodal Interfaces* (New York: ACM, 2011), 335–42.

59 Masaaki Kurosu and Kaori Kashimura, "Apparent Usability vs. Inherent Usability: Experimental Analysis on the Determinants of theAapparent Usability," in *Proceedings of the Conference Companion on Human Factors in Computing Systems* (New York: ACM, 1995), 292–93, Also available at: http://dl.acm.org/citation.cfm?id=223680.

60 Il Im Yongbeom Kim, and Hyo-Joo Han, "The Effects of Perceived Risk and Technology Type on Users' Acceptance of Technologies," *Information & Management* 45, no. 1 (2008): 1–9.

benefit the solution provides to the people it is designed for, how it provides that value, and if it is preferable compared to other solutions. The preference of this solution over others, as well as its adoption or rejection, also requires that we answer two more important questions: *is the solution compatible with cultural norms and existing practices within the specific contexts? Is the solution safe and not create additional concerns?*

The proposal also needs to be questioned from the social point of view. In fact, this is particularly relevant in the case of robotic solutions. A robot's ability to display social intelligence and emotions can increase human-robot understanding and adaptation.[61] Nevertheless, there are possible psychological and social consequences. Thus, it is important to reflect on *whether or not—and if so, how—the robotic solution shows forms of social intelligence.*

61 Beer et al., "Understanding Robot Acceptance."

Any psychological and social consequences of the proposed solution would lead to questions at the ethical level. Thus, three final fundamental questions need to be answered: *could the solution cause psychological, moral, or safety issues for individuals? Could it negatively interfere with human-human relationships? Are the benefits of this solution worth its societal costs?*

As mentioned before, asking these questions would largely be predicated on testing the platform in a real environment. Nevertheless, some questions can already be answered. For instance, programming the robot and projections to interact with the user's bodily movements is a familiar modality that most children and parents have experienced or have seen at least once. Body tracking is already used by existing gaming consoles, and in some cases, interactive projections can be found in commercial play areas or exhibition contexts like children's museums. The choice to use commercial robots also makes the solution friendly. Familiarity and friendliness can have a positive impact on project perception since people will have been able to try the technology before accepting it, and the solution would help them recall previous experiences. Despite this, it is still necessary to understand if and how the games and the general functioning of the platform are easy to understand and control.

The choice to promote active play through body tracking can also have a positive impact on the perceived usefulness of the solution and the value that people can obtain from it. This was also confirmed by the parents involved in the focus group, who were asked to give a preliminary evaluation of the game platform. However, performing a cost-benefit analysis that determines the overall acceptance or rejection of the solution has not yet been possible. Such analysis, in fact, is related to the specific characteristics of each context and to the actions and relationships that take place in it.

The choice to use commercial "driving-robots," has allowed us to avoid concerns about the possible psychological and emotional implications that can arise from a bond with a social robot. In this case, the expectation is that the engaging potential of the robot is enhanced by the child's animistic intuition. Tests in real contexts are still needed to understand if the robots chosen are appropriate. Thus, contextualizing the project is crucial to answer all these questions—this will allow us to understand the project's weaknesses and strengths, and increase the project's acceptability. Finally, the practice of questioning—although still unstructured and mostly driven by gut feeling—represents a design opportunity that is worthy of embracing. In fact, it could be turned into a proper methodology, whose main challenge of will consist in giving structure to the dialogic evolution.

Conclusions and Future Work

This work explored the theme of robot acceptability and its influencing factors. In particular, it appears evident that contextual and solution factors are interrelated, and their variety highlights the complex nature of a robot's acceptability. Introducing a robotic solution, in fact, may generate impact on multiple levels, from individual to societal.

In this regard, the literature provides a wide spectrum of studies and models that describe this theme and the determining factors. This body of knowledge should be used to inform and guide the design process in the development of novel robotic solutions. However, most studies address acceptability issues only during the evaluation stages. In rare cases, acceptability factors are addressed in studies aimed to inform and drive the design process in the subsequent stages of the projects. But even in these cases, only one or a group of acceptability factors are taken into account. Typically, this approach is appropriate when fostering technical advances and improvements in robotics research. Nevertheless, when the research involves real contexts and wants to move from laboratories to real-world environments, further reflection on acceptability is necessary. Thus, designing acceptable robotic solutions requires addressing the multiplicity of factors that influence acceptability and using these as design drivers. Moreover, addressing the complexity of a robot's acceptability means that a solution must first be developed and subsequently questioned at both the general purpose and specific feature levels. These reflections informed the acceptability-driven approach the Robot & Gaming project described in this paper. The project focused on edutainment robotics for children. The general purpose of the project—promoting active play—and its specificities—using the body as controller, interacting with the robot—were constantly addressed, questioned, and iterated upon. Furthermore, during the project two key actions emerged that could help to develop any acceptable solution—exploring and adapting the project to possible usage scenarios, and ongoing questioning of the project. Situating the project in a real context, in fact, allows researchers to deal with existing activities, social relations, behaviors, and the unpredictable factors that models and representations are not able to describe and predict completely. A real context is both fundamental to understanding the issues of a possible usage scenario and evaluating the projects in believable situations. In both cases, designers can contribute to this understanding and evaluation by observing, immersing themselves, and empathizing with primary and secondary users and with all the other actors that may affect or be affected by the project. However, together with the investigation of human factors, designers are also required to familiarize themselves with and play with technologies that—especially in robotics—may be hard to understand. For this reason, interdisciplinary teams become crucial. Traditional design methods, then, appear to be partially appropriate, mostly in the exploratory stages. However, designing for acceptability and evaluating the consequent results might require additional tools.

Regarding these aspects, however, the project is still ongoing. We will focus our future efforts on applying and adapting the platform to real contexts, where different game modalities will be tested, which will also make it possible to assess how the presence of the robot affects users' perception of the experience. We will also develop specific observation tools for these tests in real environments. Finally, we will further articulate the questioning process from a mostly dialogic practice into a more structured methodology, or design tool.

Acknowledgments

This research project is being developed at Jol CRAB lab, by TIM, and carried out by a multidisciplinary team that includes designers, engineers, and a psychologist.

DREAM Complexity: An Approach to Ambulance Design

José Augusto Rodrigues de Sousa Coelho

School of Design, Management and Production Technologies Northern Aveiro (ESAN), University of Aveiro, Portugal

Vasco Afonso da Silva Branco

Research Institute for Design, Media and Culture [ID+]; Communication and Art Department, University of Aveiro, Portugal

A surprising number of health-related challenges, including medical emergencies, may also be design challenges. The medical ambulance is an important touchpoint for the complex pre-hospital healthcare system, yet its design is often the sole responsibility of its manufacturers. To explore a new design for the sanitary compartment of a medical emergency ambulance, we developed a new type of design approach called DREAM (Discovery + Research + Engage + Approve + Make). After preliminary and participatory design research, we involve the Portuguese National Institute of Emergency Medicine, and ambulance coachbuilder Auto Ribeiro Lda. as our design partners. Together, we developed a framework we could use to navigate the manifold aspects of ambulance design, construction, and manufacturing; created a special design "laboratory;" and designed a new sanitary compartment model that is now widely available. Design researchers acted as the conductors orchestrating the process. We learned that without the participation and support of our industry partners, the project would never have made it past the concept development stage.

Keywords **Medical emergency, ambulance, project-based research, product design**

José Augusto Rodrigues de Sousa Coelho is Assistant Professor from the University of Aveiro, and he works as a design professional at School of Design Management and Production Technologies Northern Aveiro (ESAN). He majored in Product Design (undergraduate) and Materials and Product Management and Advanced Studies in Design and Product Development (postgraduate). He is a researcher of the Research Institute for Design, Media and Culture [ID+]— a research unit supported by the University of Aveiro and University of Porto. Currently, he is doing his PhD at the University of Porto. His work experience consists of teaching and professional design practice. His areas of interest include design for health and well-being, design for growth and prosperity, and participatory design.

augustodesousacoelho@ua.pt

Vasco Afonso da Silva Branco is Director of the Research Institute for Design, Media and Culture [ID+]— a research unit supported by the University of Aveiro and University of Porto; and Associate Professor of the University of Aveiro Communication and Art Department (one of the founders of design programs there). He obtained the PhD degree in Electrical and Computer Engineering (Interaction Design), FEUP in 1997. He is a member of the Executive Committee of the European Academy of Design and member of the Editorial Advisory board of some international design journals and magazines, for example, *The Design Journal, The "Radical" Designist, Journal of Design Culture,* and *I+DISEÑO*. His areas of interest include interaction design and ontology of design.

vasco.branco@ua.pt

Introduction

When we think of ambulances, we think of accidents and pain, and experiences filled with anguish, anxiety, and despair. We hope that aid arrives quickly. We hope for the best doctors, nurses, and technicians, and for the most advanced technology and equipment. But we usually do not hope that the designer responsible for the design of the equipment has done his or her job correctly. It is nevertheless a designer's job to provide the optimum technical conditions, in the tightest of spaces, that will enable those doctors, nurses, and technicians to put everything they know into practice.

Emergency medical care is probably as old as human existence, but its character began to formalize as early as the eleventh century, when the Knights Templar established field hospitals to assist both soldiers and pilgrims traveling to Jerusalem. Several centuries later, Queen Isabella of Spain would use the word "*ambulancia*" to define the mobile hospital services she deployed to ensure that troops fighting in the GRANADA War received the urgent care they needed.[1]

French surgeon Dominique Jean Larrey, chief surgeon to Napoleon Bonaparte, changed the concept of ambulance from a mere transport vehicle into a vehicle that brought doctors and their instruments onto the battlefield, in what he called a "flying ambulance."

Larrey's innovative eighteenth-century design signaled a revolution in mobile emergency medical services that would continue well into the middle of the twentieth century,[2] with further advances impelled by wartime efforts and developments in social infrastructures creating the conditions for generalized pre-hospital medical care practices that would take root in most (technologically developed) countries.

Nowadays, although an ambulance can take many forms, it is always inseparable from concepts of service, technical equipment and staff, medical professionalism and care, waiting times, and more. It is easy to see how complex the job of designing an ambulance might be, given the critical nature of its performance and the support it provides to the various members of its crew.

Pre-Hospital Emergency Medicine (PHEM) "deals with endless variety of critical accidents which, by their nature, are unpredictable regarding to place, time, and occasion."[3] PHEM's wicked problems are critical and expensive ones. Any academic "investigations undertaken in medical emergency have privileged primarily the patient guidance centers,"[4] service response times, and clinical and medical practices—bypassing the ambulance as a major factor affecting overall response. There have been no significant changes to sanitary compartment configurations for the last 20 years. The ambulance, as such, is functionally and semantically obsolete, which has caused "a very negative impact on both patient and clinical body."[5] In the last two decades, incremental changes—largely customizations—to ambulance designs have mostly been made on the factory floor, giving rise to a separate set of issues related to functionality in the field.

1 Ryan C. Bell, *The Ambulance: A History* (Jefferson: McFarland, 2009), 21–23.

2 Mariusz Goniewicz, "Effect of Military Conflicts on the Formation of Emergency Medical Services Systems Worldwide," *Academic Emergency Medicine* 20, no. 5 (2013): 511, also available at: http://onlinelibrary.wiley.com/doi/10.1111/acem.12129/full.

3 Anantharaman Venkataraman etal., "Prehospital Research: An Introduction," *Falck Foundation*, accessed March 17, 2015, http://www.falckfoundation.com/doc/Booklet-prehospitalresearch-an-introduction.pdf.

4 Monika Büscher, "Interaction in Motion: Embodied Conduct in Emergency Teamwork," in *Proceedings of the 2nd Congress of the International Society for Gesture Studies*, ISGS (2005), the published version is "Embodied Conduct and Movement in Emergency Teamwork," accessed June 17, 2013, http://www.istpalcom.org/publications/files/Buscher_IiM_final.pdf/.

5 Gianpaolo Fusari, "Redesigning the Ambulance: Improving Mobile Emergency Healthcare," a Report from CenterHelen Hamlyn Center for Design, Royal College of Art, accessed March, 10, 2012, https://www.rca.ac.uk/research-innovation/helen-hamlyn-center/research-projects/2011-projects/redesigning-ambulance/.

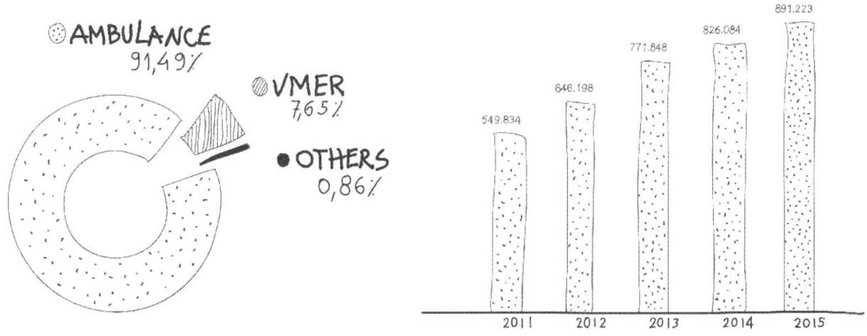

Figure 1 Percentage of each type of vehicle used per total number of emergency calls; evolution in the number of ambulance calls in the period between 2011-2015. Copyright © 2016 INEM.

According to the 2015 annual report published by Portugal's National Institute of Medical Emergencies (INEM), "ambulances accounted for 91, 49% of total emergency calls, and more than 81% of these ambulances are EMA Emergency Medical Ambulances." [6] That year's 891,223 annual calls represent, on average, 1.7 ambulances deployed per minute.(Figure 1)

Providing this level of emergency care for an aging population and other changing demographics requires ambulances that can facilitate up-to-the-minute advances in PHEM practices, including new kinds of equipment and technologies.

6 Instituto Nacional de Emergência Médica I.P. (INEM). Report of Gabinete de Planeamento e Controlo de Gestão, Relatório de Atividades e Contas 2015 (April 2016), 61–62, accessed June 2, 2016, http://www.inem.pt/files/2/documentos/20160519174524546969.pdf.

Design Research Framework

Designing an ambulance's sanitary compartment(Figure 2, left) is a complex project that must reconcile a wide range of human, technical, legislative, medical, financial, and functional concerns. To create a framework that we could use to design and develop a new sanitary compartment for INEM's EMA Emergency Medical Ambulances, Type B (EMA),(Figure 2) we needed a comprehensive and accurate picture of the elements we would have to include.

Our literature review revealed that medical emergency design research is practically non-existent. It was clear from the examples we did find—especially "Redesigning the Emergency Ambulance—Improving Mobile Emergency Healthcare" by The Helen Hamlyn Center for Design at the Royal College of Art[7]—that for design work in this area to have a

7 Fusari, "Redesigning the Ambulance."

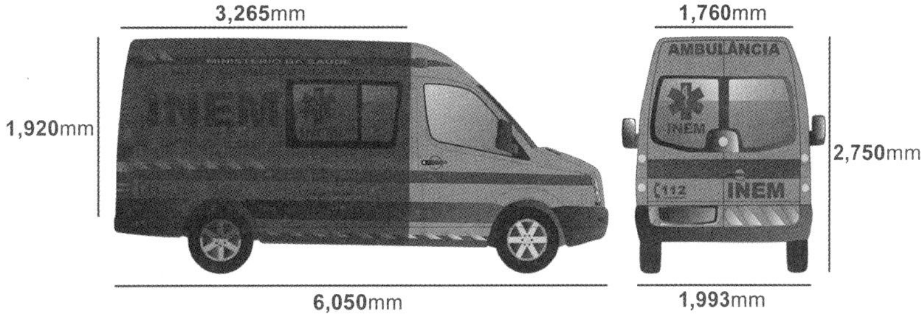

Figure 2 INEM Medical Emergency Ambulance Type B; grey area is ambulance's sanitary compartment. Copyright © 2012 Augusto de Sousa Coelho.

tangible impact on people's lives, we would have to involve stakeholders from across the emergency medical system, including medical experts (upstream and downstream) and ambulance manufacturers.

As a system, PHEM is both intricate and high-stakes. Its effectiveness is often hampered by spatial and temporal constraints. It is influenced by its environment, defined by its structure and purpose, and expressed through its operation.[8] Of course, emergency care system components, such as the ambulance, must strictly comply with technical and safety requirements. However, up to now, designers have not heeded care providers' and recipients' expectations for support in the real world.[9] This failure may be due in part to designers applying a techno-centered approach, and not properly considering the factors, people, machines, and contexts that make up healthcare organizations, systems, and implementation.

8 Gordon Baxter and Ian Sommerville, "Socio-Technical Systems: From Design Methods to Systems Engineering," *Interact Comput* 23, no. 1 (2011): 4–17, DOI: https://doi.org/10.1016/j.intcom.2010.07.003.

9 Pascale Carayon et al., "Socio-Technical Systems Analysis in Health Care: A Research Agenda," *IIE Transactions on Healthcare Systems Engineering* 1, no. 3 (2011): 145–160, accessed July 17, 2017, DOI: https://doi.org/10.1080/19488300.2011.619158.

The Research Phase

Conceiving and designing a new ambulance seems like a near-impossible task. Our aim was to take as many contributing factors, situations, machines, contexts, medical staff members, and patients into consideration as possible. Our approach, which came to be known as DREAM, is a two-stage model we designed to help us establish partnerships among the stakeholders involved in pre-hospital emergency.

The analytical portion of the model, called DRE—Discovery + Research + Engage—enabled us to work in tandem with INEM, our health sector partner. In the second phase of our research, we expanded that model to include a practical element, creating DREAM—Discovery + Research + Engage + Approve + Make—alongside our industrial partner, Auto Ribeiro. Our research had three phases:

1. Analysis. This dimension included a literature review and a characterization of INEM and Emergency Medical Ambulances. We conducted ethnographic research via direct/participatory observation, held a working group with INEM Experts, and made a national questionnaire to INEM experts to evaluate the ambulances that they operated.
2. Interpretation. We took our analytical results and used them to develop a Conceptual Framework of Reference for the design and development of an INEM Emergency Medical Ambulances.
3. Project definition and implementation. We designed and developed new solutions for mobile medical emergency units by integrating the information we had gathered during the two previous phases. We developed technical specifications and built mockups and prototypes to test our findings. For instance, during the collaborative project with industry and INEM, an opportunity arose to develop an Ambulance Type A1—an ambulance that transports individual patient and thus is less complex. We used it as a prototype to apply, test, and validate the results achieved through the earlier investigation.

The Analytical Phase

Our preliminary work began with a literature review. We refined our characterization of INEM and the services it provides and the medical model of care used in Portugal, and we researched Emergency Medical ambulances at the national level in Europe and the United States.

We carried out this research through direct/participative observation, as per our methodology, which allowed us to obtain a qualitative dataset. This dataset helped us design a survey questionnaire, and enabled us to shape and define input for our work group with specialists from the INEM. Our intention was to obtain a set of guidelines we could use to direct and support the interpretive phase.

The INEM

The INEM is the Portuguese Ministry of Health organization responsible for coordinating and delivering integrated medical emergency services in mainland Portugal, by ensuring the rapid and appropriate delivery of emergency health care.[10] INEM's main tasks include providing medical aid on the scene, facilitating patient transport to appropriate hospitals, and ensuring coordination among the system's actors. The INEM has at its disposal a number of ways to respond rapidly and efficiently to emergency care situations.

10 Pedro Pita Barros, Sara Ribeirinho Machado, and Jorge de Almeida Simões, "Portugal: Health System Review," *Health Systems in Transition* 13, no. 4 (2011): 1–156, accessed November 14, 2012, http://www.euro.who.int/__data/assets/pdf_file/0019/150463/e95712.pdf.

PLAY and RUN—The Portuguese Pre-hospital Emergency Assistance Model

Two distinct models for pre-hospital and retrieval medicine exist: *stay and play* (Franco-German approach) and *scoop and run* (Anglo-Saxon approach). The first aims to bring quality emergency care to victims on site, while the second transports emergency patients to an appropriate care facility. These two models presently govern emergency medical care as we know it. It is important to remember that neither approach is appropriate one hundred percent of the time—emergency medical response units adapt to each emergency depending on type, geographic location and features, and pre-hospital emergency team experience, among other factors.[11]

While transporting victims to appropriate healthcare facilities is necessary, it is not always possible or desirable. The Portuguese *play and run* model unites the advantages of both models described above. In the play and run model, depending on the victim's clinical presentation and other mitigating factors—transport times exceeding one hour, for example—there are two possible responses. If the appropriate means and facilities are available, a pre-hospital emergency team carries out victim stabilization and preparation efforts before transportation to hospital; and when local hospitalization is not possible or appropriate, the INEM ensures immediate transportation to an appropriate health facility using a medical rendezvous (medical retrieval) process—the transshipment coordinated process of the victim from one vehicle to a more differentiated one. For this to be possible, the INEM has a set of service delivery means and methods adapted to each need.

11 José Fernando da Silva Monteiro Oliveira Magalhães, "Competências na Intervenção de Enfermagem em Contexto Extra-Hospitalar: Cuidados de Emergência e Gestão de Situações de Exceção," (Master's thesis, Escola Superior de Saúde do Instituto Politécnico de Viana do Castelo, 2015), retrieved from http://hdl.handle.net/20.500.11960/1298.

INEM Emergency Medical Ambulance (EMA)

INEM's current Emergency Medical Ambulance (Type B; EMA) has the silhouette of a light-goods vehicle or van.(Figure 4) It has an original, factory-built chassis and body with a high roof, specially adapted interior equipment and fittings, and two rear doors, plus a side opening via sliding door. The medical and rescue equipment used in the vehicle is designed to meet European legal specifications.[12]

12 See Portuguese legislation, https://dre.pt/web/guest/pesquisa/-/search/64797338/details/maximized; European Standard CEN 1789:2007+A1:2010, changed and replaced BS EN 1789:2007+A2: 2014.

Ambulances in Europe and the US

Ambulance coachbuilders and secondary stage manufacturers construct vehicle interiors using a wide variety of materials. To identify benchmarks for the materials that builders use most frequently, and to gain a better grasp of the criteria they use for materials selection and application, we conducted a survey among notable manufacturers. Although our survey sought to preserve differences between van and box ambulance types, not all of the 38 companies we surveyed—20 European and 18 North American—had information pertaining to both models. Also, the data they did provide did not always relate to the entire vehicle.

Of the 38 companies we surveyed, 9 provided data about materials they used in Type B (van) ambulances, and 15 gave us information about materials used in box models. We created schematic images of each ambulance type interior to help identification of interior parts, and proposed a survey with several sections relating the material-location-choice criteria (wall, ceiling, left and right panel, cabin division, floor, etc.) to the construction of the interior of a sanitary cell. The survey also featured criteria for materials selection and technologies used to assemble them during vehicle manufacture.

Very few of the companies we surveyed were willing to give us detailed information about the materials and methods they used to construct their vehicles; most did not wish to reveal trade secrets. From the resources we did obtain, we noticed that companies on the same continent tended to use similar materials and construction or assembly techniques. The most pronounced differences between makers lay in the configuration and functionality of the interior cabinets—the number and placement of drawers, for example—rather than in the materials used. Visits to two of the sector's key trade fairs—*RETTMOBIL* 2012 and 2014, and *AMBULEX* 2013—reinforced our conviction that, at the European level, manufacturers share similar design, development, and construction strategies and processes.

Participant Observation

Our observation of INEM health professionals in action lasted about 150 hours. We divided our efforts between Emergency Medical Ambulances (EMA) and Emergency and Resuscitation Medical Vehicles (VMER).

To observe the performance capacity and requirements to which the Emergency Medical Ambulances is put to the test, we decided to accompany the VMER ambulance team. This allowed us to access to very serious emergency situations, which always require intervention. In those situations, the crew, at the time of stabilization of the patient, going from two to four people also received more medical equipment from the VMER team.

Emergency Medical Ambulances work with their base crew, emergency medical technicians and the vehicles that assist the VMER. Their job is to get to the location of accident victims or critically ill patients as quickly as possible, stabilize their conditions, and swiftly transport them to the most appropriate healthcare facility.

The VMER (*flying car*) is a vehicle that is intended for the rapid transport of a doctor and a nurse to the place where the patient is. It is equipped with Advanced Life Support and has the function of stabilizing the victim of an accident or sudden illness, and accompanying his/her transport to the hospital. The transport of the victim is always carried out in a Emergency Medical Ambulances which is conducted by one of the two technicians, with the other one accompanying the doctor.

The VMER that accompanies the EMA movement is operated by the nurse. If necessary, during transport the vehicles stop so that the two teams can carry out necessary maneuvers or rescue procedures.

EMAs have a crew of two INEM Emergency Ambulance Technicians (TAE, paramedics). Their job is to get to accident victims or critically ill patients as quickly as possible, stabilize their condition, and swiftly transport them to the most appropriate healthcare facility. VMERs are pre-hospital intervention vehicles with advanced life support equipment. They facilitate patient resuscitation, stabilization, and transport. VMERs are crewed by an emergency medical physician and a nurse, rather than medical technicians.

We participated in 30 rescue missions, enabling us to familiarize ourselves with common medical emergency contexts and the interactions that take place between medical staff, patients, and equipment. The patients suffered from stroke, (iron, volume, pressure) overload, overdose, or respiratory/renal insufficiency, or were victims of drowning or falls from high-rise buildings, among other scenarios.[Figures 3, 4]

The INEM Specialists Working Group

We established a working group alongside emergency ambulance specialists to get their qualitative input regarding the INEM ambulances they use now and would like to use in the future. The INEM selected group members whose skills and experience would comprehensively represent the range of pre-hospital emergency expertise it provides. The majority of these participants each had over twenty years of experience nationally, and sometimes internationally in places such as East Timor.

We first asked the group to rearrange the sanitary compartment of an EMA without changing the size of either the compartment or the vehicle—only the position and location of interior furniture, equipment, and

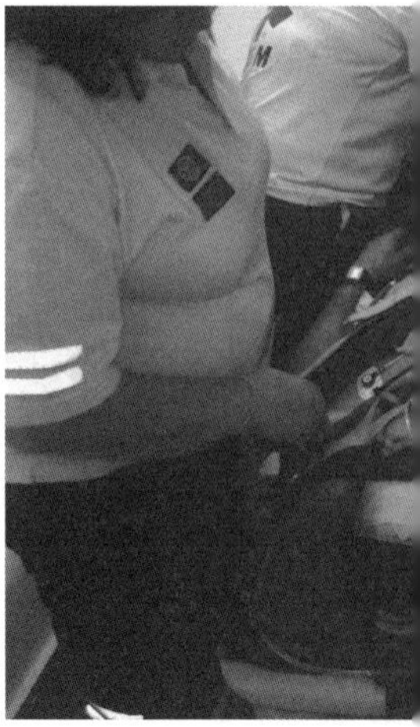

Figure 3 (L) An example of data recording—an EMA patient sketch. Copyright © 2012 Augusto de Sousa Coelho.

Figure 4 (R) Observing the doctor and nurse in Emergency Medical Ambulance, Type B. Copyright © 2012 Augusto de Sousa Coelho.

Figure 5 Scale model of the current sanitary compartment layout of a Type B EMA. Copyright © 2012 Augusto de Sousa Coelho.

Figure 6 Scale model proposal for a new configuration of the sanitary compartment in a Type B EMA. Copyright © 2012 Augusto de Sousa Coelho.

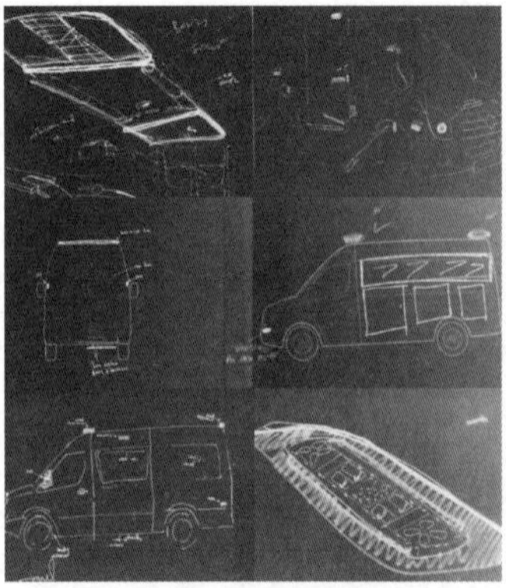

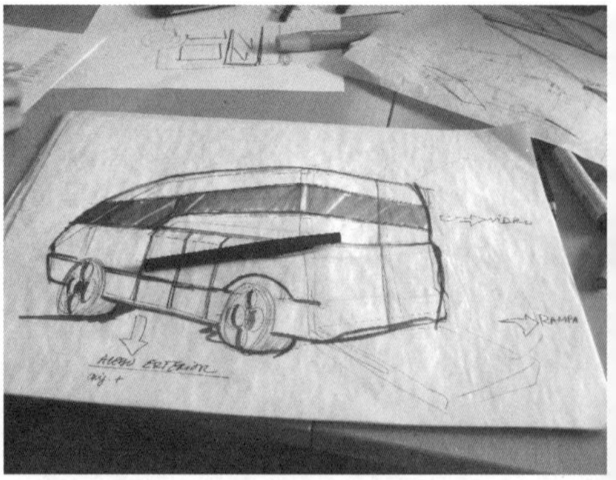

Figure 7 (L) Visual aid materials used during the second exercise alongside INEM specialists. Copyright © 2012 Augusto de Sousa Coelho.

Figure 8 (R) Example of futuristic equipment concepts created by and with INEM specialists. Copyright © 2012 Augusto de Sousa Coelho.

components. Based on their recommendations, we developed new configurations for the interior that best fit their needs. (Figures 5, 6)

In our second exercise, we asked the experts to creatively identify and characterize their requirements, needs, ambitions, and desires for the ambulance of the future. We offered them a variety of printed visuals to inspire their idea. (Figure 7)

We also challenged them to create designs and write-ups of future equipment. (Figure 8) Using scaled down outlines of ambulance vehicles printed on sheets of A3 paper, the experts explored and speculated about interacting with novel concepts for future designs.

The Nationwide INEM Survey

We used the information we had gathered during the previous two research stages to build a user satisfaction questionnaire. In it, we asked INEM medical specialists—doctors, nurses, and medical technicians—to evaluate the equipment inside EMA ambulances at the time.

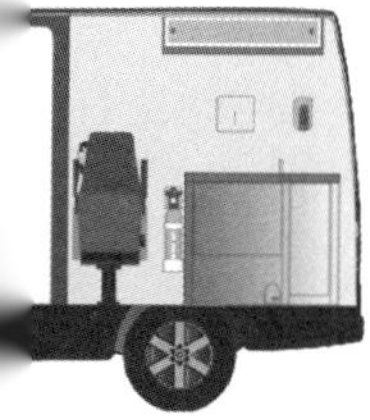

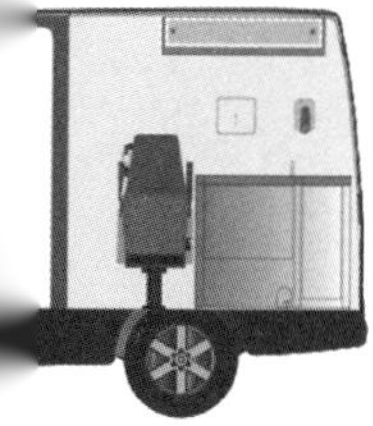

The questionnaire was developed in tandem with the INEM, who also took responsibility for its dispatch to 1011 ambulance technicians and approximately 630 VMER doctors and nurses. The questionnaire had a response period of 3 weeks. A total of 128 valid responses were obtained, corresponding to 7.8% of the target population. We asked respondents to rate the Emergency Medical Ambulance on a five-point scale:

- Very negative—does not have adequate conditions to perform the service;
- Not enough—does not have the necessary conditions to perform the service;
- Enough—have the minimum conditions to carry out the service;
- Good—has the right conditions to perform the service;
- Very good—it has good conditions to carry out the service.

We grouped the survey questions around the following themes:

- the sanitary compartment (dimensions, geometry, volume);
- the mobile medical and emergency equipment (used inside and outside the ambulance);
- equipment usability and ergonomics (fixed and mobile);
- vehicle exterior (location and number of doors, access ladders);
- electrical and communications infrastructure (quantity and location of light points and electrical outlets, intercom); and
- ambulance construction materials (robustness, texture, color, cleaning).

We intended for the survey results to aid our design of a viable new solution that would be recognized as advantageous in terms of its construction, maintenance, and use. Figure 9 shows the results of this portion of our research, expressed as percentages.

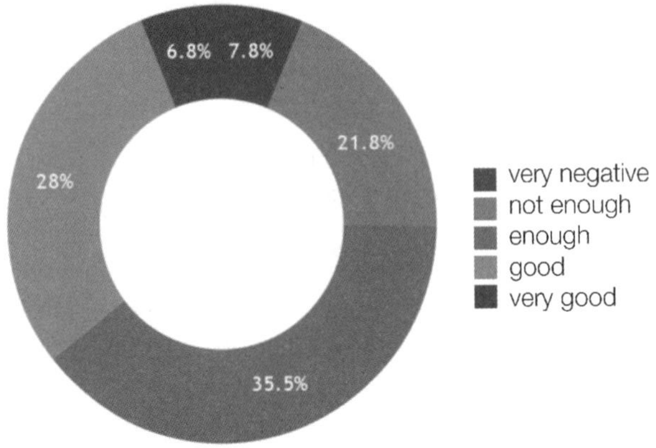

Figure 9 Graph depicting respondents' evaluations of the INEM Emergency Medical Ambulance. Copyright © 2012 Augusto de Sousa Coelho.

The questionnaire results gave us not only quantitative data, but also a set of important suggestions for the future ambulance design:

- 220V connections on the outside, to help the assistance inside out;
- entry system with three steps, with one close to the ground;
- natural light inside the ambulance;
- aesthetic/functional harmony in the design;
- increased sanitary compartment footprint;
- external access to some of the ambulance's internal elements;
- a mechanism allowing several cabinets to be opened simultaneously;
- an in-floor housing for an access ramp to the rear doors;
- an x-belt on the stretcher, similar to those of pilots, to increase patient safety;
- cab and compartment control of electrical and electronic components and appliances; and
- a workbench, drawer, or tray for everyday tasks.

The specialists' input was crucial—we were able to identify the aspects of the sanitary compartment that were in need of a redesign and flesh out our design strategy thanks to them.

Engaging our Medical and Business Partners

A Collaborative Project—the ARBOX

The literature[13] shows that when designing within a complex socio-technical system—in this case, the pre-hospital medical emergency system—without the involvement of key stakeholders, the project will likely not move beyond the theoretical stage.

As our research progressed, we at the University of Aveiro created a number of opportunities to involve sector and industry partners. The INEM

13 See, for example, Ernesto Arias et al., "Transcending the Individual Human Mind—Creating Shared Understanding Through Collaborative Design," *ACM Transactions on Computer-Human Interaction* (*TOCHI*) 7, no. 1 (2000): 84–113; Sharon S. Dawes, Anthony M. Cresswell, and Theresa A. Pardo, "From 'Need to Know' to 'Need to Share': Tangled Problems, Information Boundaries, and the Building of Public Sector Knowledge Networks," *Public Administration Review* 69, no. 3 (2009): 392–402; Helen P. N. Hughes, Chris W. Clegg, Lucy E. Bolton, and Lauren C. Machon, "Systems Scenarios: A Tool for Facilitating the Socio-Technical Design of Work Systems," *Ergonomics* (2017): 1–17, accessed July 17, 2017, http://www.tandfonline.com/doi/full/10.1080/00140139.2017.1288272; Lawrence J. Hettinger, Alex Kirlik, Yang Miang Goh, and Peter Buckle, "Modelling and Simulation of Complex Sociotechnical Systems: Envisioning and Analysing Work Environments," *Ergonomics* 58, no. 4, (2015): 600–614, accessed July 17, 2017, DOI: https://doi.org/10.1080/00140139.2015.1008586.

who had already been involved from the beginning, expressed their desire to contribute to the design of the EMA's new sanitary compartment. We also invited the participation of Auto Ribeiro Lda., a national ambulance manufacturer, who immediately confirmed their interest. We called our collaborative project the ARBOX Project.

We conducted a series of meetings to establish the principal guidelines for the project and create plans for strategic asset allocation. It became clear that the project's complexity was essentially due to its organizational, financial, and legislative implications, all of which depended on existing service and business models.

We worked together to create a project definition. By establishing project parameters and scope, and explicitly stating the limits to each party's responsibilities, we created a context that would guide our future collaboration.

Interpretive Dimension

We developed a Conceptual Reference Framework (CRF) to guide our design and development of a new ambulance sanitary compartment. We needed the framework to help us keep ambulance functionality, ergonomics, safety, and usability in mind, together with complex legal, professional, and manufacturing constraints.

We designed the CRF to be a collaborative mapping tool with a dual purpose: support the development of a novel product and service platform for INEM and the diversification of Auto Ribeiro's range of products. We wanted the CRF to guide an approach composed of overlapping, iterative design spaces informed by interrelated sets of technical, logistical, financial and legislative concerns—rather than a sequence of design steps—so we could more comprehensively reflect on, define, and understand our challenges as the design developed.

Our first task was to create a flow chart that articulated how ambulances are made, and what (or who) influences their design.(Figure 10)

Below are some of the most salient constraints associated with the design of an ambulance's sanitary compartment:

- The INEM is responsible for defining, coordinating, providing, and overseeing Portugal's emergency medical services, and thus its actions are determined by its stated objectives, mission, values, territory/scope, and the resources it has at its disposal (human, financial, and otherwise). Its actions are also governed by current Portuguese legislation, and its purchases regulated by the European Committee for Standardization (CEN). It also conforms to international norms related to emergency clinical procedures and practices.
- INEM staff members are simultaneously healthcare professionals, users, and tax payers of a government service that seeks to provide the highest level of service at the lowest cost; staff must carry out

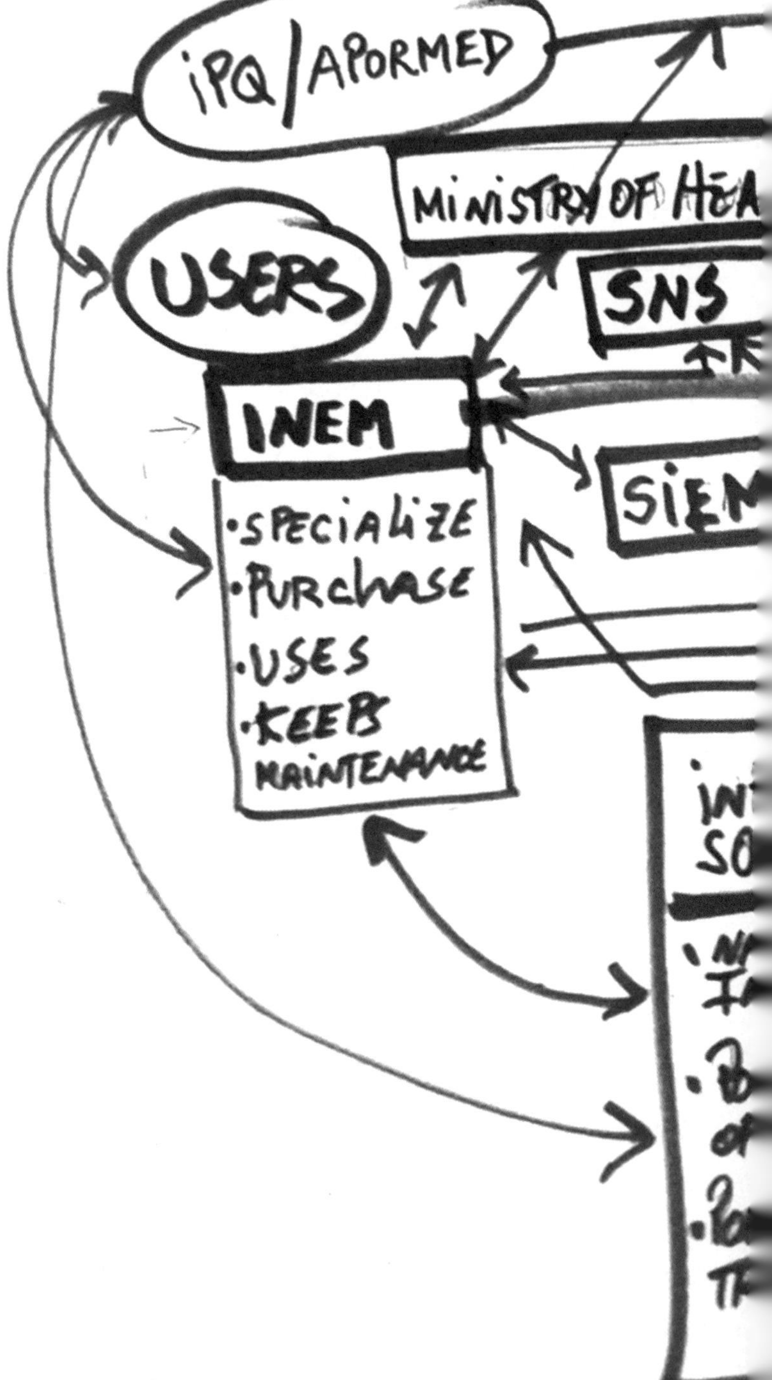

Figure 10 Ambulance manufacturing and use flow chart. Copyright © 2013 Augusto de Sousa Coelho.

CEN
VEHICLE BRANDS
AMBULANCE
STANDARDS
COMPETITIVE
PRODUCTS
PRICE
AUTORIBEIRO Lda.
OBSERVATION
INTERVIEWS
WORKGROUPS
TRENDS IN HEALTH CARE
FUTURE SKILLS
TECHNOLOGIES
MATERIALS
PROCESSES
statistics

their mission to the best of their abilities while also dealing with budget cuts related to the policies and practices established by the government.
- Medical and diagnostic equipment companies do more than design and develop equipment—they sponsor clinical research, determine procedures, and influence legislation.
- Vehicle manufacturers make models whose shapes suit their business strategies, and upgrade their models as and when they decide it is necessary.
- Ambulance coachbuilders have to reconcile all the above constraints, and supply interiors and equipment that can be adapted to evolving requirements.

It is almost impossible for the INEM or Auto Ribeiro to have the authority to impose design guidelines on vehicle manufacturers. On the other hand, manufacturers of medical and diagnostic equipment have been focusing more on the development of static equipment, dedicated to hospitals, medical centers, clinics, etc. From the informal contacts resulting from the investigation, it was inferred that although the size of the "business" associated with the medical emergency is considerable, it is not yet sufficiently attractive to generate its own business area.

The CEN website shows the existence of several working groups and the proliferation of regulations, which are not indexed and associated with similar thematic or business areas.

This reality allows for the proliferation of norms and documents, which refer to other norms and documents, contributing to the dispersion of legislation, increasing the difficulty of identification, understanding, and systematization of information and thus increasing the level of complexity associated with the transformation of vehicles into Ambulances.

INEM technicians in the field can only influence what goes into the brief of a new ambulance. Using the available budget, the INEM then must identify and select vehicle(s) according to geographic requirements and the highest guarantees of performance and reliability throughout the vehicle's life cycle. They must also identify and select medical, diagnostic, and support equipment—stretchers, wheelchairs, oxygen bullets, storage cabinets, thermal and acoustic insulation, and so on—that conforms to European standards. Auto Ribeiro has to accept the order and propose equipment that meets those specifications and still remains within the budget.

The CRF emerged from a literature review, hands-on fieldwork, and critical analysis of the current ambulance service and equipment landscape from a professional, material, financial, and legislative perspective. By co-creating this frame of reference, together we were able to identify and characterize shortcomings and expectations related to present-day ambulances and ambulance services. We were also able to rethink the *symbolic* nature of the ambulance and its components—users' (including medical staff and patients) base their actions on the physical qualities of things *and* on the meanings they ascribe to those things.

The CRF fostered a set of guidelines we could use to address certain practical questions: Is it easy to clean, and easy to monitor stock levels? Is it comfortable? Is it safe in traffic? Are all materials and equipment up to code? Does the technology and equipment match users' needs and expertise? Specifically, the design would have to

- support the complex interplay of product with practice;
- ensure safe and effective patient entry/exit;
- improve the sanitary compartment layout and ergonomics;
- facilitate routine sterilization and sanitation;
- maximize equipment use and compatibility;
- improve vehicle engineering, reduce weight;
- reduce production and control costs; and
- facilitate the eventual dismantling, monetization, and recycling of materials.

The Conceptual Reference Framework also provided INEM and Auto Ribeiro with qualitative information about ways that ambulance components reflect user needs, including what the product's interior design conveys about modern medical emergency practices and the competency of its medical staff. It provided guidelines for a new design that would improve the overall patient and technical staff experience. The design would have to

- ensure patient and staff safety and comfort;
- establish appropriate interactions between people, equipment and context; and
- contribute to improved performance of routine sanitation and administrative tasks.

The CRF revealed incompatible possibilities, and pointed us toward feasible variations and solutions we could explore during the design and development process. It sped up the entire project definition process, and increased our chances of finding a more effective and efficient solution. Based on these findings, we opted to organize our design activities around three dimensions of ambulance quality: the pragmatic (function), the syntactic (technology), and the symbolic (meaning).

Project Dimensions and Implementation

Our development process went from a contextualization phase, in which we identified the main market and technological constraints, through to concept development, and into three-dimensional CAD modeling, including photo-realistic images. We also created mock-ups and prototypes to support our ideas.

Figure 11 Functional identification of physical elements in the sanitary compartment of Ambulance Type B and Type C. Copyright © 2015 ARBOX Project.

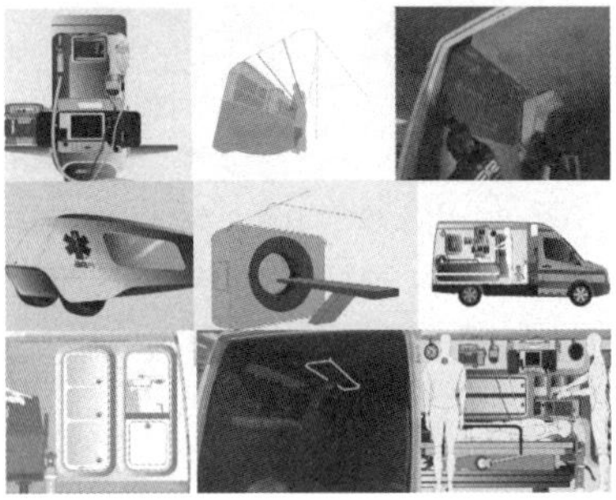

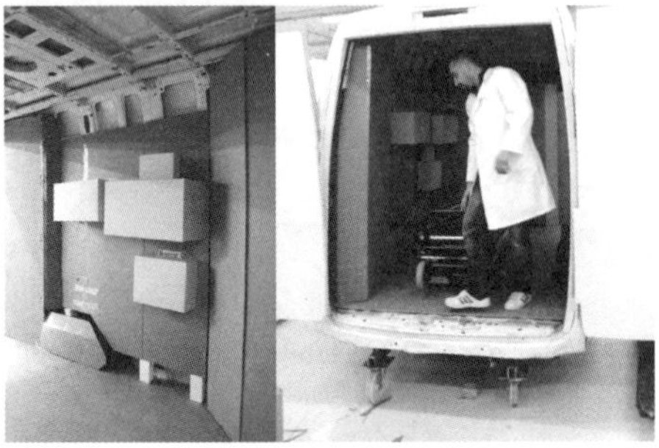

Figure 12 (L) New ambulance concept ideas. Copyright © 2015 ARBOX Project.

Figure 13 (R) Testing concepts at 1 to 1 scale inside a Mercedes Sprinter van. Copyright © 2015 ARBOX Project.

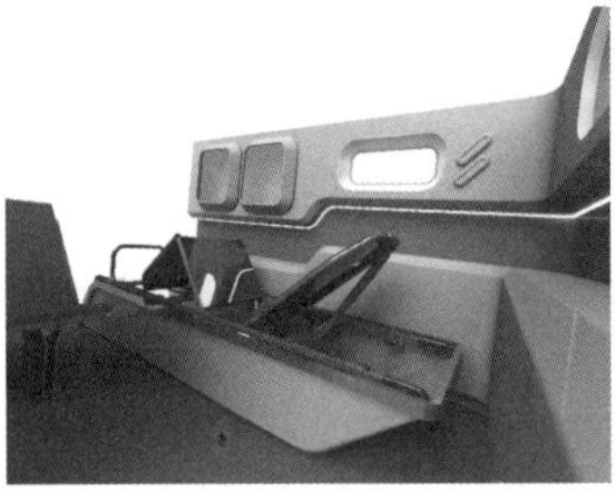

Figure 14 (L) Our concept for the new Type A1 ambulance—the AR.TECH. Copyright © 2015 ARBOX Project.

Figure 15 (R) The AR.TECH Type A1 ambulance prototype. Copyright © 2015 ARBOX Project.

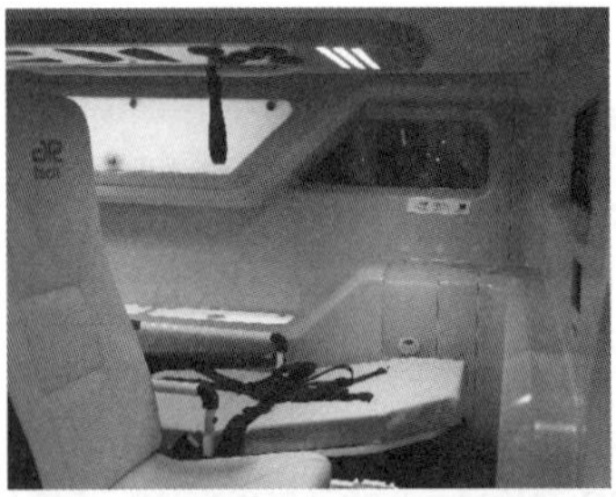

Figure 16 (L) The new Type A1 Ambulance. Copyright © 2015 ARBOX Project.

Figure 17 (R) The AR.TECH Type A1 ambulance prototype at the Segurex 2015 trade show. Copyright © 2015 ARBOX Project.

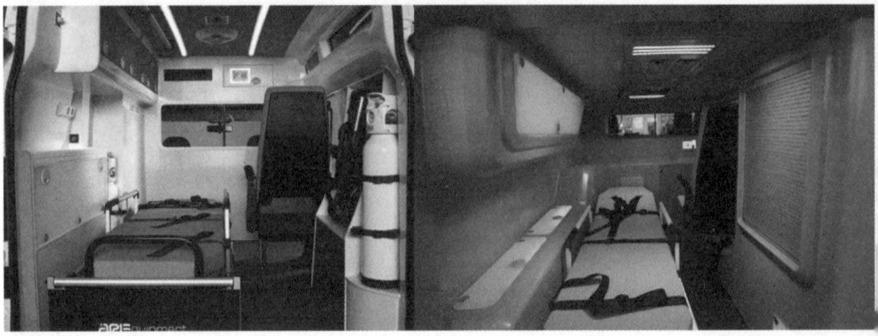

Figure 18 The then-current Type A1ambulance interior (left), and the new AR.TECH ambulance interior (right). Copyright © 2016 ARBOX Project.

Sanitary Compartment Architecture and Proposals for Design Concepts

We generated schematics for the sanitary compartment of Type B and Type C Ambulances, and identified and indexed their physical elements and their functions. This enabled us to generate architectural proposals for each.(Figure 11)

Using a Mercedes Sprinter van, we designed general product architecture solutions for a new sanitary compartment that we could adapt to suit different ambulance types, vehicle models, and user needs. These general solutions served as design guidelines for our new concepts and models.(Figure 12)

To evaluate our general solutions and choose the most appropriate among them, we tested them at different scales. Resizing helped us gain a more realistic perspective of how the space would be affected by each component. We eventually tested our final selections at life size 1 to 1 scale, to identify the most viable solutions with increased precision.(Figure 13)

At this juncture, our industry partner Auto Ribeiro identified a need in the (French) market for a new Type A1 ambulance. The A1 is a patient transport ambulance designed to transport one or two patients on stretchers or in transport chairs. This emerging commercial opportunity led us to created a "laboratory" to conduct further research. We were able to put the CRF through its paces and use our findings to design a less complicated product.

Using our previous research, we developed concepts for a Type A1 ambulance that we called the AR.TECH. Auto Ribeiro built a prototype of the final concept ambulance inside a Renault Trafic van, in keeping with French market specifications.(Figure 14)

The life-sized prototype allowed us to test our chosen solutions for usability, functionality, form, and constructive viability. We also used the prototype to perform crash tests (g10) that validate system and equipment compliance with legal requirements.(Figure 15)

Evaluating the AR.TECH

We used the new ambulance(Figure 16) to assess the validity of our research findings. We rated our perceptions and the product's overall value in terms of the functional, structural, and symbolic quality it offered.

The new Type A1 ambulance was presented at the Segurex 2015 trade show. Over the event's four days, the collaborative project team along with a wide range of users and emergency specialists analyzed and evaluated their merits and failures.(Figure 17)

The Type A1 ambulance interior(Figure 18, right) satisfies the fundamental requirements of buyers and users alike. We designed an interior that could fit into existing vehicles, and one that would enable buyers and users to create "flexible" configurations that can incorporate a wide range of medical equipment and consumables, depending on the type of market. The AR.TECH was initially developed for the French market, where it has

Figure 19 1 to 5 scale-model (thermo-forming prototype) of the AR.PRO sanitary compartment work area layout. Copyright © 2015 ARBOX Project.

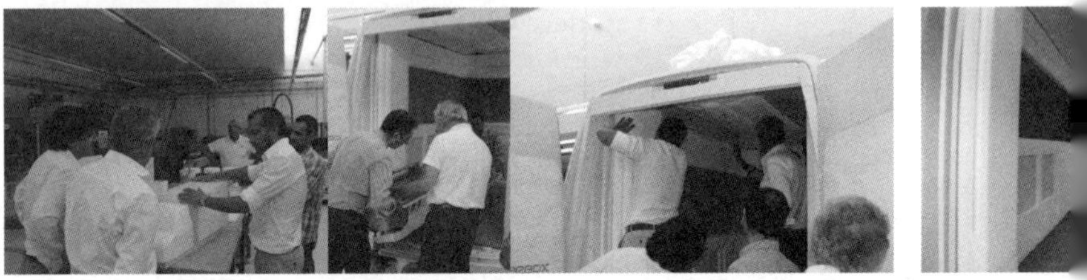

Figure 20 (L) Our design partners evaluating the prototype. Copyright © 2015 ARBOX Project.

Figure 21 (R) 1 to 1 scale prototype of the AR.PRO Emergency Medical Ambulance interior, mounted inside a Mercedes Sprinter van. Copyright © 2015 ARBOX Project.

Figure 22 Construction of a structure to house the vehicle and prototype. Copyright © 2016 Augusto de Sousa Coelho.

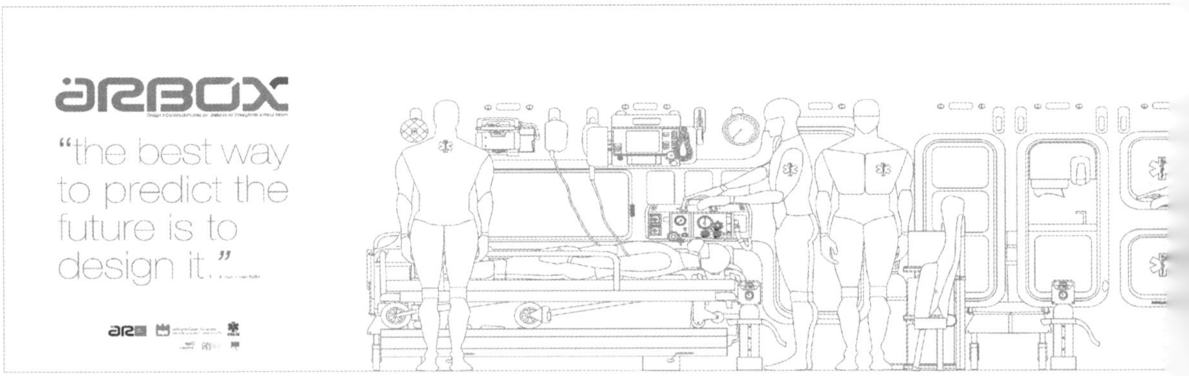

Figure 23 Outside view of the closed space containing the prototype and the evaluation area. Copyright © 2016 ARBOX Project.

been sold since 2016. We treated the AR.TECH outcome as a "beta test" of our design research, especially the CRF, whose findings we could use to narrow down our design choices for a medical emergency ambulance.

The AR.PRO Emergency Medical Ambulance

To generate general product architecture solutions for a Emergency Medical Type B and C Ambulance, called the AR.PRO, we analyzed and compared the flexibility, technical geometry, productive solutions, and assembly processes of techno structural solutions and materials used in other vehicle types. From this, we developed concept drawings of the AR.PRO sanitary compartment to explore its potential spatial organization and assembly process. We synchronized these findings with the syntactic and symbolic requirements that the users had identified previously. To test our conclusions, we built and mounted a 1 to 5 (thermoforming) scale-model inside a Mercedes Sprinter van.(Figure 19) Our concept development process enabled us to systematize the conclusions we drew from our study of existing norms, product architecture proposals, and the 1 to 5 scale tests.

We used CAD to model the solutions we had chosen during the development phase in greater detail. This was not only an important step toward refining the proposal at scale, but also contributed to modifications in the final AR.PRO proposal. We built and mounted a life-sized mock prototype inside a Mercedes Sprinter van,(Figure 20) which gave our project partners the chance to evaluate various elements and equipment. **Figure 21** shows the final AR.PRO sanitary compartment redesign proposal.

Project Research and Design Evaluation

AR.PRO Design Evaluation

Together with our industry partners, we then prepared a "clean" prototype evaluation structure to house the vehicle. We wanted the structure to reduce ambient noise and emphasize the look and feel of the prototype. The structure would enable participants to evaluate the overall solution more freely, and learn about its materials, shape, and future technical specifications gradually, and in detail.(Figures 22, 23)

We carried out our evaluation of the AR.PRO Type B ambulance at the first European Medical Transport Congress, in June of 2016 in Portugal. It was organized by the Portuguese Ambulance League (LPA) and by the Spanish National Association of Ambulance Manufacturers (ANEA; *Federación Nacional de Empresarios de Ambulancias*). We based our survey on the AtrackDiff[14] evaluation tool, which enabled us to gather both hedonic and usability feedback. We also asked participants to evaluate the quality of the ambulance in terms of its function, its technological and architectural structure, and the meaning they ascribe to new proposal.

Medical staff members, emergency technicians, ambulance

14 Marc Hassenzahl, Michael Burmester, and Franz Koller, "AttrakDiff: Ein Fragebogen zur Messung wahrgenommener hedonischer und pragmatischer Qualität," *Mensch & Computer* (2003): 187–96. For more information on AttrakDiff, see http://attrakdiff.de/index-en.html.

Figure 24 Results of the prototype evaluation survey based on an adaptation of AtrackDiff. Copyright © 2016 Augusto de Sousa Coelho.

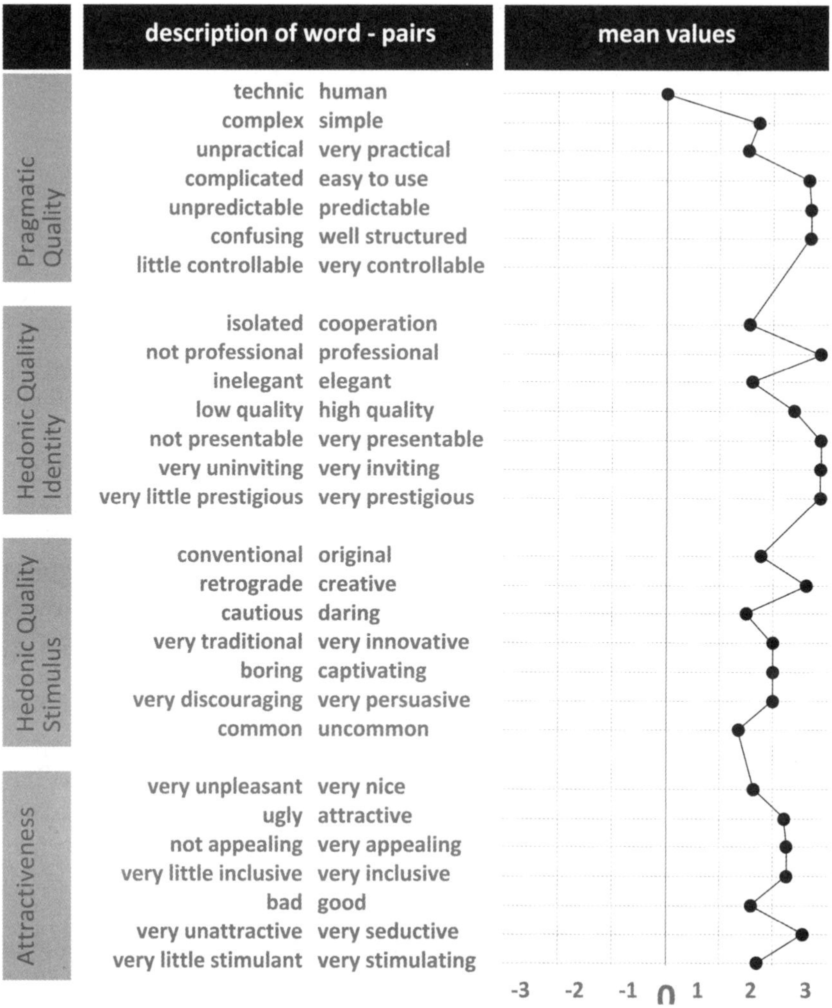

Figure 25 Results of the prototype evaluation survey based on an adaptation of AtrackDiff. Copyright © 2016 Augusto de Sousa Coelho.

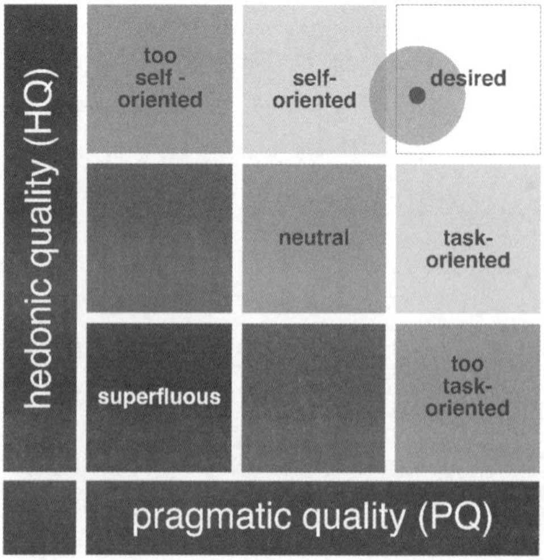

manufacturers, the competition, and one vehicle manufacturing company all evaluated the prototype.

Before assessing the prototype, participants walked down a short corridor where printed panels provided information about our design research, and described how the ARBOX project had evolved. We also posted images of our final designs.

At the end of the corridor was the area housing the scale model prototype. In this area, people completed their evaluations either in small groups of two to three, or individually. A design researcher was present merely to provide participants with a brief analytical description of the prototype and its initial framework, and some complementary information about the materials, finishes, colors, functions, and ways that the design might be reconfigured.

Thanks to the description, participants had an opportunity to complete their own mental image of the product. Our intention was to reinforce participants' impressions of the prototype's utility.

The user evaluations provided qualitatively and quantitatively different pictures of the prototype. These users know the business first hand, and this gave richness to the data, as they were authentically motivated to contribute to the design of a new emergency ambulance. They used their everyday knowledge to inform their responses, and suggested some smaller, more specific prototype improvements. Figure 24 contains the results of their evaluations.

Evaluation survey results showed that the participants saw the design from an entirely new perspective. In a second survey, whose participants were INEM professionals, results classified general equipment satisfaction using a scale that included the terms "enough" or "good." These evaluation results show that enough and good have become "desirable."(Figure 25)

This confirmed the perceptions we had in the first evaluation results obtained through the survey (Figure 25) and, after the four days of the 2015 Segurex trade show.

When we compare user evaluations of existing equipment with evaluations of the new prototypes, it becomes clear that significant changes in the functional and symbolic dimensions were widely recognized and valued by the users.

A Summary of the ARBOX Project and Its Challenges

Our perception, based on informal contacts during our design research, made it clear that ambulance manufacturers tended to take into account only two main directives: the rules and laws governing the sector or product and the technical and technological requirements that, when combined and executed, would create the impression that it was a "good product"—a good ambulance. Also, we noticed that buyers tended to order new ambulances according to very generic sets of specifications–often requesting the standard equipment associated with each type of ambulance, and then selecting certain accessories or mobile equipment that suits their circumstances.

Design choices related to sanitary compartment layout, workspace design, and interior materials, colors, and textures have largely been at the discretion of ambulance manufacturers up to now, perhaps because ambulance buyers frequently order their new model "as is," or with specific, service-related modifications only. These two tendencies have contributed to ambulance designs that are not aligned with users' real needs. This generic approach—common in many European countries—has also given rise to a multitude of factory-driven "evolutions." In most cases, such changes are only variations of pre-existing ambulance models and interiors, and as such are largely defined by existing business and (public) service models.

As we sought to redesign a touchpoint of the public healthcare system, we first set out to observe the current landscape of pre-hospital emergency medical care (PREM) in Portugal. We discovered that we needed more than a literature review—without partners from the pre-hospital healthcare sector and ambulance industry, we could not adequately plan and set the parameters of our solution, and achieve our design goal.

During the *DRE* (Discovery + Research + Engage) phase, the INEM provided us with input that was crucial to the future of our research, and to the tasks we used to understand Portugal's PREM sector.

Our participatory observations shed light on ambulance interactions between thing-to-thing, person-to-person, and person-to-environment, and helped us to map out an ambulance crew's roster of responsibilities—for example, the emergency medical procedures and practices they used and the ways they handled support equipment such as stretchers and transport chairs. We also watched them restock consumables, observed the cleaning procedures that were part of their daily and weekly routines, and noticed how and when they did a deep clean of the equipment. This portion of our research also helped us prepare a well-informed user questionnaire. Our ethnographic research revealed the incredible creativity, flexibility, and ingenuity of INEM employees seeking to resolve problems that hindered their performance.

The user questionnaire was an important means for us to collect suggestions from INEM staff. We compiled and systematized their responses and used this data to fuel the working group discussions and evaluations. The working group articulated a fine-grained Conceptual Reference Framework (CRF) that we used to determine the functional and semantic needs of a future ambulance, and configure layout proposals for a new EMA sanitary compartment. The CRF would also help us decide which visual design choices we should integrate into our concepts.

We were able to provide the INEM with a very valuable piece of research for its future policies. Understanding how its ambulance acquisition specifications impacted performance had an unexpected benefit—it could send a very strong signal to employees that it is constantly looking for new and improved solutions to increase performance and ease the constraints experienced by its technical staff.

The DREAM (Discovery + Research + Engage + Approve + Make) approach established the conditions for the design and implementation of a new ambulance. But first we had to identify stakeholders' key constraints and interests and map out their relationships, before we could establish the collaborative conditions that would support our design efforts. Managing different attitudes and behaviors, different systems, and different technical languages and meanings, and then leveraging their combinations to create a project solution was a major challenge for the research. We had to strike a balance between these factors during each phase of the project, especially the design development and implementation stages.

Our main challenges occurred at two distinct times: during partner engagement in the process and during the concept approval stage that would lead to project implementation. Each of these moments required the complete confidence and total commitment (and approval) of all our partners. These moments form the pillars that support this research. At the foundation of these pillars stands a set of strategic decisions—of a political, economic, technical, practical, technological, organizational, and logistical character—which led to further cycles of research and action.

The users wanted an ambulance that would convey the message that the INEM was a forward-thinking organization whose services and skills were at the cutting edge of medical care practice. We would have to reconcile this desire with the very real need to adhere to CEN standards, national legislation, and vehicle maintenance requirements, and all of this within the available budget.

Because our industry partner Auto Ribeiro operates in several countries—each with a different set of needs for services, equipment, procedures, and vehicles—the new sanitary compartment design needed to be versatile, so it could be adapted to suit each market.

The experience we gained throughout the ARBOX project demonstrated to us that the "design process never ends"[15]—it is always negotiated and renegotiated. Satisfying the needs of Auto Ribeiro's various clients means the design will have to go through re-scaling and resizing so it can be used in different vehicle types and models. We also had to begin the process of reconfiguring Auto Ribeiro's existing products line homogenize its offering With this kind of never-ending cycle, the best product is always just around the corner.

15 Donald A. Norman and Pieter Jan Stappers, "DesignX: Complex Socio-technical Systems," *She Ji: The Journal of Design, Economics, and Innovation* 1, no. 2, (2015): 83–106.

Outcomes and Impact

This project produced a holistic participatory design approach that includes user needs. It created a new and innovative interior ambulance that improves functionality, safety, hygiene, and comfort, and the experiences of patients and medical staff.

The design process had to solve a complex equation that had to resolve desirable and possible concerns, and eventually configure a product whose industrialization represented a viable business opportunity that respected technical and financial constraints.

Users see the final product as a facilitator of multimodal interaction between people, equipment, and context. It can be adapted to existing vehicles in the market and allows for a "flexible" interior configuration that can incorporate of a wide range of medical equipment and consumables required by different markets.

The designers were able to give the final product a kind of formal and semantic sophistication that reflects health professionals' high levels of expertise and promotes a sense of security, comfort, and technological rigor, an impression that the technicians "silently" demanded. The research results emphasized the pivotal role designers can play in the pre-hospital emergency and patient transport field, and changed our sector and industrial partners' perceptions of the value of good design.

Our industrial partner has changed its attitude toward design—rather than merely a cosmetic tool, design is part of an integrated problem-solving and solution configuration process.

The company understood that designers could make an important contribution to the company's strategic decisions at the product level, but also at the level of business strategy. This led the company to create a new department of design research, trends, and concepts, whose mission is to follow up on the work we developed during the ARBOX project. The design vision that the company currently has is "infecting" its trade partners; a well-known automaker has shown a keen interest in the project's results. In the market, Auto Ribeiro is no longer seen as a vehicle transformation company—it has emerged as an important player in the emergency health solutions market.

Conclusions

The design research intervention revisited a complex component of pre-hospital emergency medical service that required: a great deal of time, negotiation, discernment and a deep knowledge of the business itself. It was driven by objectives common to all partners.

In this project, design practice functioned as the conductor orchestrating the interactions of the actors, using methods and tools that allowed, in an integrated and systematized way, to create interrelationships that permitted project development and consistency that endorsed implementation. For this to happen, it was necessary to constantly adapt the actors involved in the project, so that there could be, at the same time, the use, in whole or in part, of methods and tools common to all, from a strategic and operational design management perspective.

The attitude generated by the partners, was a strong commitment, based throughout the project time, making it indispensable the involvement of design team during its development and industrialization phases, made possible several concessions, conveniently combined the knowledge of the whole team to achieve the goals.

This design research case demonstrates that design can generate new opportunities for business and community value. Understanding the value of design as a strategic asset, and knowing how to deploy it across the organization to drive innovation is the primary task the project still faces. Creating an in-company design growth mindset and culture that utilizes government, academia, industry, and company stakeholder input is the work in progress now.

Acknowledgments

Special thanks to Martinho Oliveira (ESAN) and António Gomes (ESAN), for their unconditional support. Special thanks also to Vitor Ribeiro, Martins Fernandes and César Azevedo (AR) because they are always available to support this research; and to Pedro Coelho dos Santos (INEM), for his initial encouragement and engagement, fundamental for the development of this research.

Executive Editor: Crisie Yuan
Editorial Assistant: Jessie Sun, Huilin Zhou
Copy Editor: Jianne Whelton
Book Design: Jiaying Hu

National Library of China Cataloguing-in-Publication Data. A catalogue record for this book is available from the National Library of China
ISBN 978-7-5608-7875-1

Printed and Bound in the People's Republic of China.